MAOISTS IN ANDHRA PRADESH

MAOISTS
IN
ANDHRA PRADESH

By

Shantha Sinha

GYAN

ISBN : 978-81-212-0252-7

Published, 2018

Published by

Gyan Publishing House
5, Ansari Road
Daryaganj, New Delhi-110002
Phone: 011-47034999, 9811692060
www.gyanbooks.com
E-mail: books@gyanbooks.com

Printed at: G. Print Process, Delhi.

Foreword

Dr. Shantha Sinha's brilliant work is the first detailed study of the concrete maoist movement—also popularly known as the Naxalite movement—in a major region and based on detailed documentation, a firm grasp of the ideological, strategic and tactical issues involved, and a sympathetic though not uncritical approach.

Maoist movement, initiated in Naxalbari in West Bengal in 1967, represented a dramatic development which held centre of the stage for nearly a decade for thousands of left-wing youth and a section of the intelligentsia. The movement caught the imagination of and inspired immense devotion and a sense of sacrifice among lakhs of rural and urban youth in large parts of the country. It carries on in old as well as new forms till this day in Bihar and Andhra Pradesh and in small pockets in all parts of India. It is important from the point of view both of contemporary history and of present day politics to understand it and to critically assimilate its meaning. Dr. Sinha's work is bound to be an important input into this effort.

I

Dr. Sinha relates at length the events which constituted the maoist movement in different parts of Andhra during its different phases and under the leadership of different individuals and groups. She describes the advances and retreats of the movement, its different programmes and policies, the social groups on which it was based, the issues that it took up, the forms of mobilization and struggle it used and the strategy and tactics it employed, the changing government policy towards it and the theoretical and ideological debates which tended to unite or divide different maoist groups. In the process, Dr. Sinha makes us familiar with the leaders of the movement at different levels, especially the little known squad leaders who became the local heroes.

In the initial chapter, Dr. Sinha deals with the development of the maoist trend in Bengal and the rest of India within the ranks of the CPI (M). The breaking point came when in 1967 the Naxalbari peasant uprising broke out under the two CPI(M) leaders, Charu Majumdar and Kanu Sanyal, who declared that they were implementing Mao Ze-Dong's ideas (Maoism) in Indian conditions and who visualized the rapid spread of agrarian revolution based on peasant guerilla struggle leading to the formation of a People's Liberation Army and the overthrow of the Indian State. On the international plane, they declared that the Soviet Union was undergoing capitalist restoration, collaborating with US imperialism, were serving as its agent and intriguing with the USA against revolutionary China. Unwilling to let any local constituent over-step the party's overall strategy, however strong the local feelings and justified its actions, the CPI(M) leadership expelled the Naxalbari leaders from the party and, being in-charge of the Home portfolio, ordered full scale police action against Naxalbari rebels for having taken to violent forms of political action. Charu Majumdar and many other dissident leaders, in turn, declared that the CPI(M) leadership was curbing the revolutionary energies of the masses and the rising crescendo of revolutionary upsurge in the country. They accused it of having become class collaborationist and revisionist and having fallen prey to parliamentarianism. Many of the CPI(M) middle-level leaders and cadres now separated from the party, formed a coordination committee and then founded the CPI (Maoist-Leninist) (ML).

Dr. Sinha goes on to discuss the emergence of the maoist trend in Andhra, leading to nearly 50 per cent of the leaders and cadre leaving the CPI(M) and forming the Andhra Pradesh Revolutionary Communist Committee (APRCC) in 1968.

In the next chapter Dr. Sinha examines the important political, ideological and tactical differences between the CPI (ML) and the Bengal maoists and the APRCC of Andhra maoists. According to the Bengal maoists the situation in the country was "ripe for a revolution, a revolutionary mass upsurge existed and the people were fully politically conscious and even prepared to take part in revolution immediately". What was needed was "courageous and determined leadership." Furthermore, "militant struggle must be carried on not for land, crops, etc., but for seizure of state power." This seizure of state power through armed struggle was on the immediate agenda.

The Andhra maoists agreed with much of the basic thrust of Bengal maoists' analysis and programme. Russia had gone revisionist and was going over to capitalism; Indian independence was formal—India was in reality a neo colony; the Indian bourgeoisie was comprador and was allied to feudalism; India was in the midst of a deep economic and political crisis; Indian revolution was on the agenda and was to be achieved through armed struggle or people's war to be based on guerilla struggle by the peasantry. The Andhra maoists, however, had also a basic difference with the Bengal maoists. Despite the economic and political crisis of the ruling class and the complete disillusionment of the masses, conditions were not yet ready for immediate armed revolt all over the country. In a vast country like India, because of uneven development, different tactics would have to be followed in different parts of the country, and people would have to be carefully prepared for a protracted people's war. Consequently, an immediate call for armed struggle could not be given. "Armed struggle for liberation could only be an end-product of a series of struggles by the peasantry against feudal oppression." There were also, as Dr. Sinha brings out, differences among the Andhra and Bengal maoists over party organization, forms and issues of popular mobilization, and nature of the united front of various classes to be mobilized. One result was that APRCC was after some time denounced by the CPI(ML) as "enemies of liberation" and "last reserves of reaction". This led to some sections leaving the APRCC and accepting the leadership of the CPI(ML) and Charu Majumdar.

In the fourth chapter Dr. Sinha traces with master strokes and telling narrative the progress of the communist led mass movement in the Srikakulam district of Andhra Pradesh during the years from 1957 to 1967. The tribal people of the district were suffering from a constantly deteriorating economic and social position and subjected to increasing exploitation and oppression by money lenders and traders. The communist workers organised sanghams (unions or associations) and over the years led series of agitations and movement against *vetti* (forced labour), for higher wages against forest contractors, against the corruption and high-handedness of revenue, excise and forest officials and finally against landlords for fair rents. They also worked for social reforms and participated in panchayati and assembly elections. They succeeded in a large measure in instilling a sense of self-respect, dignity and self-confidence among the tribal people.

In time, however, the movement in Srikakulam entered a stage of stagnation. It faced intense repression by the police, one evidence of it was the involvement of over 600 sangham members in police cases in 1964 and the killing of some 70 activists from 1952 to 1968 in Srikakulam and Telengana areas. How was the movement to overcome this impasse ? The dominant tendency was to opt for greater militancy. Most of the Srikakulam communist leaders ended up in 1968 in the CPI(ML) and with Charu Majumdar around the line of raising the movement to the higher stage of armed guerilla struggle. Starting out with armed squads, the leaders hoped to create a people's army and a liberated zone. They ended up along with the CPI(ML) leadership with the tactic of individual annihilation of class enemies, i.e., landlords, money-lenders, police informers and policemen. Initially Ryutu sanghams, youth associations, etc., were organised on a significant scale. In many of the initial acts of armed resistance or seizure of crops of the landlords and occupation of temple lands, etc., larger mass of villagers were involved; but later a shift to pure squad actions were made. The movement also remained confined to the tribal people of the Agency areas who constituted slightly more than 8 per cent of the district's population. Finally, during 1969-70 the Government was able to suppress the movement killing most of its leaders. The movement was, however, able to make major economic and social gains.

Dr. Sinha discusses in great detail the organizational structure and the working of maoist armed squads. Her conclusions in this respect relate to the failure of the leaders of the Srikakulam movement to face up to the reality of the movement on the ground, to mobilize the masses in their armed actions, to gauge correctly the lack of people's preparedness for armed struggle, and to assess correctly the capacity of the Indian state to suppress violent protest or struggle. Whenever the movement was curbed by state repression, instead of making a reassessment of their basic assumptions, the leaders responded only by modifying their tactics or took recourse to such simple formulations as "the more there is repression on the people, the greater is their strength", or that vis-a-vis the police "the gureilla having people's support and sympathy and capable of conducting mobile warfare had an upper hand" or that repression would "isolate the Government from the people and also enable us first to identify our real friends since at this moment one is forced to choose one's sides". The consequence was that, as Dr. Sinha points out, they were inexorably drawn towards adopting a more and more extreme stance, leading to "alienation from the masses".

In chapters six and seven, Dr. Sinha takes up the maoist movement in Telengana area of Andhra Pradesh where the maoists followed different policy, tactics and programme based on a different assessment of the situation. She traces the growth of maoist idea, in Andhra CPI(M) partially to the party's failure on the electoral front. The APRCC grew rapidly but then gradually split into several groups especially under the pressure of the popularity and glamour of the Srikakulam movement, the CPI(ML) and Charu Majumdar.

The Andhra maoists under the APRCC leadership followed in the initial years the line of partial struggles leading to graduated and protracted struggle. For historical reasons the movement was not able to take off in Coastal and Rayalaseema districts of Andhra Pradesh but it grew in the forest areas of the Telengana where tribal population was concentrated. Here popular mass movements were built around such issues as occupation of *banjar* (fallow) land and land seized by landlords in recent years, struggle against *vetti* (forced labour), wage struggles of agricultural labourers and corruption of and oppression by forest and other officials.

The perspective, was that of raising the political and revolutionary consciousness of the masses through "a process of economic and political struggles" leading to the exposure of the true character of the state and development of political armed struggle for the overthrow of the rulers. Nor was guerilla struggle the only form of struggle, though it remained the main form of struggle. The objective, of course, remained the development of guerilla zones and then a liberated area.

The movement led by the APRCC faced two major pressures : one was the popularity of the Srikakulam movement and the other was increasing oppression by the police. How was the mass movement to develop further or even maintain itself ? The only answer, it appeared to the leadership, was for the party to form into armed squads to defend themselves and the people from the landlords and the police. The cadres too were pressing for arms and armed defence. The leadership was forced to adopt a more and more militant line though initially for defensive purposes. At the same time there were several splits in the party. The armed struggle programme soon collapsed in all areas except the forest area inhabited by the tribal people. Moreover, under police pressure the revolutionaries were soon isolated from the masses. APRCC reorganized its activities after July 1970 around a programme of popular agitations, political education and land occupation though the programme of creating armed squads and liberated zones remained the long term objective.

The APRCC began to split up around 1971, the lead being now taken by Chandra Pulla Reddy (CP) who advocated the more militant line of the simultaneous launching of militant mass movements for land distribution and armed struggle. CP was able to carry most of the maoists with him. Since then the maoist movement has continued in Andhra Pradesh till this day, though in an attenuated form. The main reason for this, according to Dr. Sinha, was the failure of the maoists to broaden the mass base of their movement. On the other hand, often their tactical line led to the narrowing down of their base. Question, of course, still remains : could mass work and reliance on the masses have been combined with armed squad action in Indian conditions ?

In the last two chapters, Dr. Sinha discusses the break-up of the CPI (ML) after the death of Charu Majumdar in 1972 and the state of the maoist movement during the Emergency and the post Emergency years. In particular she deals with the strategy and policies of the CP group and the CPI (ML), People's War Group led by Kondapalli Seetaramiah (KS) and the activities of the cultural groups, student unions and civil liberty organizations aligned with the maoist groups.

II

There were major areas of 'darkness' in the fierce debates among the maoist group. None of them took note of or examined the development of capitalism in India. The assumption remained that capitalism could not develop in the period of the general crisis of capitalism especially if the class which could develop it was comprador. The comprador character of Indian capitalism, that is, its subordination to imperialist capital, was treated as a self-evident maxim. The entire trend towards the development of independent capitalism both before and after independence was ignored or denied. The only option before Indian capitalism, it was suggested, was to be dominated by British or US capital or by 'Soviet Imperialism'—unless, that is, it joined the people's democratic front led by the working class.

Similarly, the changes in agrarian structure being introduced from above were ignored as was also the existing as well as the growing class differentiation in the countryside. In practice, of course it became impossible for political workers working deep among the people to do so. Consequently, as has been well brought out by Dr. Sinha, in several areas and phases of the movement the interests of the agricultural labourers and poor peasant were defended and promoted against rich peasant, and not only against landlords and money lenders. But all this found no reflection in theory where the struggle was still seen to be between peasantry and feudalism.

The maoists also ignored any detailed discussion of the character of Indian state, critical differences between the Indian state and society and the state and society in pre-liberation China or Vietnam (something which the 1951 CPI policy documents had recognized), the role of democracy and reforms in the functioning of the Indian state, its basic strength, etc. The state as well as the political and economic structure in India were assumed to be in a perpetual crisis—'tottering' as the phrase went. Similarly the only reaction to state suppression of their efforts at revolution through squad activity or individual annihilations was to condemn the suppression of civil liberties or the 'fascist' character of the state rather than examination of their basic paradigms of taking to violence in a basically civil libertarian society marred by class domination and class violence.

Also left severely alone were such questions as the role of hegemony in the political system and forms of its legitimization, role of violence in a democratic society, relative autonomy of the state, relation between a party and a class, nature of the ruling classes in India and the relation of the different social classes and strata to the state, the possibility of a small minority making a revolution under modern conditions and in a modern democratic country though a bourgeois one, and so on. Nor did the maoists ask why were their movements successful only among the tribal people who were not yet fully hegemonised and integrated into the system as was the rest of the population. They did not discuss in any serious manner even the setbacks to their movements or even raise the question: why could the police succeed in suppressing them? It is interesting and important that none of the successive maoist groups questioned the basic CPI (ML) characterization of the state, economy and society in India.

It was particularly important to reexamine the entire Bolshevik and Chinese Maoist's paradigms as applied to democratic and civil libertarian politics. After all the failure to make or even initiate revolutions had occurred not only in India. In nearly 50 years of its existence (in 1967) Bolshevism had not succeeded in even attempting a revolution in any democratic polity. A critical reading and application of the writings of Marx, Lenin, Mao Ze-Dong and Gramsci would have proved extremely fruitful. This would have of course led to a total rethinking of the role of violence and non-violence and of the past strategies of revolution in democratic, semi-democratic or even non-democratic societies. In particular there was need to rethink the equation of violence with the working class, the peasantry and revolution and of non-violence with the bourgeoisie, landlords and the maintenance of the status quo. The Gramscian proposition of war of position or trench-warfare had also to be examined in this context.

There were of course no simple answers. As soon as radical political workers committed to organizing the masses to defend and enforce and extend their legal rights enabled or led the masses to do so, the exploiting classes in the countryside hit back, often through violent means. The police and bureaucracy sided with the latter. Often the judiciary too did so. But even when a case was won in the court, the verdict could uot be enforced in the field. The militant among the rural poor were beaten up (or even killed in rare cases) by the rural rich often with the connivance of the police. The normal reaction was to hit back at the rural rich and their defenders, the police. What other way was there ? This is where a real innovation or theoretical and practical-political-organizational breakthrough was needed. The choice was either to go on to some form of counter-violence through squads, annihilation, etc., leading to armed struggle and revolution; or to mobilize the people in non-violent struggle, learn to take a beating in order to advance in the long run by compelling the ruling classes to pay a heavy price for violent acts in the from of loss of their hegemony (after all armed struggle also makes one learn to take in one's stride losses in life and property and even defeats), to build wide movements in defence of popular rights, form civil liberties unions, newspaper campaigns, *bandhs, hartals*, morchas and demonstration to agitation in the assemblies and the parliament. Both paths were exclusive of each other. It was not possible to combine the two in the name of combining the legal and the illegal. Both required major theoretical and organizational efforts.

All the questions raised above indicate need not as much to apply Marxism or Leninism or Mao Ze-Dong Thought to Indian conditions as to develop Marxism in the context of the new Indian and world conditions. It is a tragedy that the maoists as also other Indian communists were not even aware of the task.

One way of opening up the possibilities of such basic rethinking would have been to make a critical analysis of the past of the Indian communist movement. But none of the Indian communist parties and groups have so far made any effort in that direction. The maoists also did not undertake the task. In view of their commitment to armed struggle, it was necessary to examine why did the CPI, starting with analysis similar to theirs in 1948-49 and then 1951, end up with the Amritsar Thesis of the possibility of peaceful transition to socialism, or why have the united CPI and its offshoots the CPI and the CPI (M) not taken even once to any form of armed struggle since 1951 even though they particularly the CPI(M), are committed to armed struggle in the final phase for the capture of state power. The only reason assigned for this by the maoists was reformism of the leaders of the CPI and their betrayal. It was assumed that the communist leaders of the 1950s—A.K. Ghosh, P. Sundarayya, E.M.S. Namboodaripad, S.A. Dange, C. Rajeshwara Rao, Harkishan Singh Surjeet, Basavapunniah and others were made of inferior stuff than Charu Majumdar, Kanu Sanyal, D.V. Rao, T. Nagi Reddy, Chandra Pulla Reddy, and others. Except juvenile romanticism there was no historical or theoretical 'truth' or usefulness in this ascription. This need to analyse the past and the road leading from armed struggle in 1948 to Amritsar in 1957 was not realized even by those who were giving up immediate and permanent armed struggle in favour of mass organizations, mass movements, partial struggle, raising of the revolutionary consciousness of the masses and making preparations for future armed struggle. After all, they were doing exactly what the CPI leaders had done in 1951 and after. Some leaders like the CPI(M) People's War Group, led by Kondapalli Seetharamiah (KS) did see the similarity; but not wanting to travel down the old road, they stuck to modified armed struggle strategy. Similarly, those who have criticized the maoists have not asked whether the rise and growth of maoism was not the result of the type of Marxism and political militancy which they themselves—and the communist movement—have practised and represented as the quintessence of revolutionariness.

In fact, the rich experience of the maoist movement should enable the forces of socialism to draw important theoretical and strategic conclusions: otherwise, I have a bitter feeling that the adage that those who refuse to analyse the past are condemned to reliving it would continue to apply to them. All those who want to make a basic analysis of the past of the communist movement in India or who want to learn from the past will find in Dr. Sinha's work an indispensable tool.

Centre for Historical Studies
Jawaharlal Nehru University
New Delhi 110067

Bipan Chandra

Acknowledgements

A work of this size and spread over, as it was, for so many years would not have been possible, but for the generous help of a large number of friends and well-wishers. First of all I would like to mention Prof. K. Seshadri under whose affectionate guidance this study was originally made.

My debt to the Late Sri Ravi-Subba Rao is also enormous. Without his sustained help and interest it would not have been possible for me to have had access to most of the material on which this work is based.

I am also greatly indebted to Prof. Bipan Chandra who has been a constant source of inspiration. But for his guidance and support this book could not have been published. I am particularly grateful to him for having consented to write the Foreword.

As a friend and critic Harinath Polasa has played a major role in the finalisation of this book. I am specially grateful to him for having devoted so much of his time to this work and for his valuable comments on every aspect of this study.

I would also like to express deep gratitude to my colleague and friend Rajen Harshe who took it on himself to persuade me into getting this book published.

And, how does one thank those very special friends, some of whom are no longer alive, who were with me through every page in the book.

Contents

CHAPTER 1

Introduction

Introduction

The first version of this book was completed some ten years ago. At that time emergency had been declared and the political atmosphere of the country was highly charged. There was an added element of uncertainty about the likely course the future political developments in the country would take, as no one knew just how long emergency was going to last. This was more so in the case of the maoist movement in India which after a period of intense activity in the late sixties and early seventies had got completely disorganised following the death of Charu Majumdar in 1972. The declaration of emergency saw most of the prominent leaders and some of the cadre go underground. As the nation prepared itself for what seemed to be an indefinite period of suppression of a civil and political rights, it appeared as though the maoist movement in the form that it had existed for ten years was over and done with. Thus in all respects the year 1976 seemed to be the ideal cut off year to review the maoist movement in the country. The project, however, fell through for various reasons and by the time the work was taken up again several new factors had to be taken into consideration, the main one being that far from being over and done with the movement, at least in Andhra Pradesh, had in fact stabilised and what was more in several parts of Telangana it had widespread support.

Much of what has been written on the maoists in recent years has largely concentrated on West Bengal. Even the

Srikakulam movement which most authors agree was the high point of the maoist activities during that period receives only a cursory treatment. Thus for instance very often the basic fact that the maoist activity in Srikakulam between 1968 and 1971 represented but one phase is glossed over. In fact, the efforts of leaders like Vempatapu Satyanarayana and Adibhatla Kailasam, and the nature of evolution of Srikakulam movement cannot be assessed properly if the pre-maoist phase in the region, which was run with only nominal support from the Communist Party and which stretched over ten years from 1957, is ignored. In this work, therefore, an effort has been made to trace the roots of the maoist phase of the Srikakulam movement as a choice the leadership made which resulted from to attain their *elusive* goal after ten years of frustration and disappointment. In doing so certain fundamental weaknesses of the movement have been brought to light.

While the movement in Srikakulam as it existed before the advent of CPI (ML) has not been given the importance it deserves, the movement in Telengana, i.e., Khammam and Warangal, even after the active participation of the maoists, has throughout been featured, if at all, as something in the "also ran" class. Nothing could be further from the truth. While it is true that the movement in these areas never quite achieved the high pitch it did in Srikakulam it is nevertheless an undeniable fact that in extent and duration, the movement in Telengana outdid the one in Srikakulam by a wide margin. In fact it is one of the contentions of this work that the roots of the movement in Telengana can be traced to as far back as the 1948 Telengana Armed Struggle and that it continues albeit with certain modifications even today. In contrast the Srikakulam movement despite all its claim to fame has been more or less suppressed and today, after a lapse of 12 years since the last of the movement's leaders was removed from the scene, there are hardly any signs of any revival. Even in respect of the groups mobilised and issues taken up, the Telengana movement has proved to be far more broad based than the one which took place in Srikakulam. Thus it is with the conviction that the true nature of the maoist movement in Andhra

Pradesh is reflected by the happenings not so much in Srikakulam as in Telengana, that considerable space in this work has been devoted to describing what exactly has occurred in Telengana since 1967 when the Andhra Pradesh Revolutionary Communist Committee was formed.

In studying a movement or movements as has been done in this work two aspects have to be dealt with. The first relates to the events that took place during the course of the movement and the second to why the movement progressed the way it did. The two aspects are linked in the sense that unless one knows exactly what happened it would not be possible to deal with the question of why it happened. It is felt that the gaps in the descriptions of the movements hitherto given are so wide that proper understanding cannot be arrived at. To this extent this work is descriptive in nature. In the process it also lays out in detail the theoretical stand adopted by each of the maoist groups in the State, and traces their progress from their origins through to the present day.

A word about the title. Most of the works on this subject have argued in detail about the nature of 'maoism' in India and have tried to relate it to the Chinese experience. To a certain extent this is inevitable, because the Indian maoists themselves did just that. In this work, however, the word maoism has been used in a broad sense without attempting to analyse to what extent the Indian version of 'maoism' is in fact the 'ism' which Mao propounded. With this in view this work deals with the politics of some dominant groups who came to be known as maoists. While it would be quite possible to list out the characteristics which define a maoist group, it is dispensed with here in order to avoid unnecessary discussion on the matter. At present the simplest common denominator among all the parties claiming to follow a maoist line is that all of them can trace their origins back to either the All India Co-ordination Committee for Communist Revolutionaries (AICCCR) or the Andhra Pradesh Revolutionary Communist Committee (APRCC) directly or indirectly.[3] For the purposes of this work this can be taken as the basic characteristic of a maoist group.

Andhra has been chosen as the specific area of study for the obvious reason that it provides an abundance of variety with groups subscribing to almost all the shades of maoism operating here. Even at the outset this region saw two parallel movements developing—one in Srikakulam and another in Telangana. This enables us to compare the progress of movements of this type under differing conditions with relative ease.

While we have by and large restricted the treatment to the developments in Andhra Pradesh on occasions it has become essential to deal with events elsewhere especially in Bengal. This is because these events had direct repurcussions on the course of the movement in Andhra Pradesh. Thus a large section has been devoted to developments leading to the formation of AICCCR in the first chapter and also those resulting in the breaking up of the CPI(ML) an issue which we take up later in chapter 7.

One of the facts that emerges from this study is that even within Andhra the movement has had regional peculiarities. This implies that while at a very broad level there exist several points of similarities between maoist activities, at the micro level there are wide variations. The issues raised, the groups mobilised and even the tactics employed differ considerably from region to region. Thus though on several occasions a single process called the maoist movement has been referred to, by and large the activities in the various regions have been treated as being components of different movements. For instance, we have referred to the 'Telengana movement', the 'Srikakulam movement' and so on. Such a loose use of the word 'movement' it is felt, does not lead to any loss in rigour.

To a large extent we have relied on party writings and official party publications as source material for this work. Propaganda forms such an essential part of their working that each group spends a lot of time and even money writing and publishing articles explaining their point of view. While some of these writings serve as the main force for the movements others are mere rationalisations and justifications for actions already taken. Very often debates on purely tactical questions relating to practical issues of a very specific nature are blown out of proportion and discussions are raised to incongruous levels. For instance the debate between CP and TN group originally started on the question of the nature and scope of squad actions. But ultimately each group carried the discussion to an exotic plane where questions like whether the Arab-Israeli conflict represented the breaking out of U.S. Soviet contradictions at world level, or whether the 1967 split in the Congress represented the breaking up of Pro-Soviet and Pro-US groups within the bourgeoisie.

Given the amount of research undertaken and the thought given to these matters, the felicity with which generalisations are made in regard to these issues leads one to strongly suspect that these statements are mere rationalisations made in support of certain steps taken out of sheer compulsion. All this, however, is not to suggest that all theoretical formulations are mere rationalisations. Usually the first time a line is announced it is based on the group's understanding of the situation. Rationalisation comes in the next stage when the line is put into practice and certain alterations are found necessary.

The other characteristic of maoist groups' writings is that they are given to gross exaggerations. Statements like "hundreds of militant struggles are taking place all over the country after declaration of Emergency" and "India is a land of perpetual famine and millions are dying of starvation each year" are very common. One can only presume that the purpose of such exaggerations is to heighten the effect of the statements and thus have a greater impact on the reader. To what extent they serve this purpose, however, is a moot point.

In the process of utilisation of all this written material a lot of care has been taken not to draw too many conclusions from the party pronouncements, especially while assessing the scale of an operation or the success of a move. All the incidents referred to in the party publications have been cross checked with the police records in order to ascertain if there is an official acknowledgement of the fact that the incidents had actually occurred. At all stages the success or otherwise of a move has been gauged more from the police reaction to it than by the exultations in the party documents. A successful move usually brings as a reaction a large number of special armed policemen into the area, whereas a minor move does not.

In this context, it may also be pointed out that the police reports are no less exaggerated than the party's. More often than not they are couched in a language meant to attract the provisions of the Indian Penal Code and Criminal Procedure Code rather than to set out the facts of the incidents. Sometimes they border on the fantastic as for instance in one incident in which an attack on an individual is alleged to have taken place and the attackers are said to have made off with a pair of trousers and some change, the police claim that the leading role was played by Vempatapu Satyanarayana.[3] It is hardly likely that such an important leader as Vempatapu would stoop to conducting a raid of this trivial nature and at the same time expose himself to the danger of being arrested and indeed even shot for making pecuniary and tactical gains of such negligible proportions. Under the circumstances what is required for a balanced approach is to restrict oneself to only those incidents for which corroboration is forthcoming. This is what has been done in this work. If partiality has been shown to the maoist sources and documents it is only because of the exhaustive manner in which these sources deal with the theoretical aspects of the movement. Sometimes however, the high degree of "exhaustiveness" itself creates a problem because there is so much matter to be sifted. Also there is the additional complication brought about by the fact that a number of writers and indeed the documents themselves are underground. Because of this in the first place, the documents are not freely available and in the second, views expressed at one point of time by a leader take a long time to get published and by the time they are actually published these views have lost their relevance as other events have taken place which have drastically altered the situation. This is more so in the period between 1968 and 1970 when publications could not cope with the hectic pace at which events were rapidly overtaking one another. Lack of communication between various leaders only serves to complicate the issue further. The most cogent writings appear during the party congresses which are held every now and then. By and large the writings are in Telugu. Some of the more important documents are sometimes translated into English for the purpose of ensuring wider publicity. A number of leaders however are as proficient in vernacular as in English.

In this book an effort has been made to refer to various persons by the names they are popularly known by. Thus continuous reference to Chandra Pulla Reddy as CP, T. Nagireddy as TN and so on has been made. This has been done deliberately because it appears very incongruous to refer, to CP or TN or DV by their full names in the book when no one refers to them in this fashion. The book also contains several small details which don't appear necessary. Thus for instance the names of a number of landlords killed in Srikakulam, the names of some minor activists who played but a passing role and in some cases the names of places where small incidents not of much importance occurred have been mentioned. This has been done because while in the larger context of the logic of the development of the maoist movement it does not appear to make any difference whether a particular landlord or a 'class enemy' was killed, as far as the politics of the area where the killing took place is concerned, the consequences are enormous. More than altering the equation between the maoists and the landlords these attacks changed the equilibrium existing in the relationship between one landlord and another in the area. Even some 10-15 years later a visitor to these places will feels the reverberations of the old event though the movement itself may have died down. In the remote villages which formed the setting for much of the maoist activities between 1968 and 1971 changes, if and when they come take place at a leisurely pace and old incidents like these are not easily forgotten. At the same time many of the villagers in these areas remember the movement not because it brought about any drastic change in their living conditions but because of the characters it threw up and the incidents that occurred. For these people more than the top leaders like CP, TN or Charu who actually formulated the policies it was the smaller area or squad leader who caught the imagination and because of this the names of a number of smaller leaders whose contribution, if anything, was only minimal are included.

Broadly this work deals with the movement in three stages. The first concerns the movement in Srikakulam, the second relates to the movement in the forest areas of Telangana in the period 1968 to 1975 and the third deals with the post emergency situation. The treatment given at each stage, however, has not been uniform and has depended on the detail in which earlier writers have covered the topic. In other words a start has been made from where the others have left off. Thus in the case of Srikakulam the broad details of which have already been described by several writers the treatment has been micro level. On the other hand, the post emergency developments have attracted little attention so far and hence as a first step rather than going in for a detailed description of events, a broader treatment has been given.

In the first chapter the origins of the maoist groups are traced and the broad pattern of difference which emerged right at the start leading to the formation of the two major co-ordination committees the APCCCR and the AICCCR is discussed. The basic ideological differences, between the two are discussed in the second chapter which provides the background to the rest of the work. The next two chapters concentrate on Srikakulam. In the third chapter the course of movement prior to the commencement of the maoist phase is dealt with in detail. The period that is covered are the years 1957 to 1967. The primary aim of this chapter is to impress the fact that the Srikakulam movement had progressed considerably even before the maoist phase started, and that it was only later that the leader of the movement unable to make further progress, took a conscious and deliberate decision to join the maoists in the AICCCR rather than the APCCCR. The next chapter discusses the maoist phase of the Srikakulam movement. It shows how despite maoists' claims the movement remained strong only in the Agency areas and how the tribals continued to be its staunchest supporters. It also describes the manner in which the movement proceeded from one phase of militancy to another, because of the maoists' refusal to make a reassessment of the situation in terms of the people's preparedness for an armed struggle. The chapter also seeks to highlight the limitations of the movement in terms of the support it received from the people both because of its earlier history of being a tribal movement and because of the lack of emphasis on mass contact by the maoists.

The next two chapters, i.e., the fifth and the sixth discuss the progress of the movement led by the other maoist groups active in Andhra Pradesh. In the first of two chapters the position of this group via-a-vis the CPI(ML) is restated and some of the earlier struggles they supported is described. The next chapter shows how even the APCCCR was not a single unified group and how the pressures of the popularity of the movement in Srikakulam as well as of the repressive measures of the State forced certain elements in this group to form a separate, more militant, party. Both these chapters deal with an area not hitherto covered by other writers. While in terms of State reaction or press coverage the movement heie never achieved the status which the Srikakulam movement did it nevertheless set the background for developments to take place later on in the late 1970s and early 1980s.

The arrest of Charu and his death in jail removed the unifying force which had kept the CPI(ML) together for so long. While dissensions always existed within the party the charisma of Charu and the obvious admiration which a number of other leaders from both within and outside Bengal had for him had always prevented a major split. Once he was gone, however, the cracks began to show. In the seventh chapter some of the groups that emerged consequent on the breaking up of the CPI(ML) led by Charu which ultimately influenced maoist politics in Andhra Pradesh is discussed. The series of alliances and splits which occurred between 1972 and 1975 when emergency was declared are discussed in the chapter. Also put forth in this chapter are the views of the major maoist groups on the implications of the proclamation of Emergency.

The eighth chapter describes the post emergency scene in Andhra Pradesh with the Srikakulam movement coming to a close and showing no significant signs of revival. The scene shifts entirely to Telangana where the CPI(ML) People's War Group (PWG) led by Kondapalli Seetharamiah (KS) emerged as the dominant group and which rapidly gained popularity. The policies and programme of this group and its relationship with the existing CPI(ML) are the subjects discussed in this chapter. In presenting the above, those policies of the People's War Group which have contributed to its growing popularity are highlighted.

The ninth chapter forms the concluding chapter. In the summing up, the changing approach of the government towards tackling the maoists is also discussed in order to complete the survey of all aspects of maoist activity within the State.

In short then, this work aims at describing in detail the major activities of the maoist groups in Andhra Pradesh in the last seventeen years, analysing their policies and programmes and finally predicting what the future has in store.

NOTES & REFERENCES

1. Sumanta Banerjee, *India's Simmering Revolution, The Naxalite Uprising*. New Delhi, 1984.

   Biplab Dasgupta, *Naxalite Movement*, Bombay, 1975. Sachchidanand Pandey, *Naxal Violence, a Socio-political Study*. Delhi, 1985.

   Khawaja Ahmad Abbas, *Naxalites*. Delhi, 1979.

   Sohail Jawaid, *Naxalite Movement in India—Orgin and Failure of the Maoist Revolutionary Strategy in West Bengal*, 1967-1971. New Delhi, 1979.

   Asish Kumar Roy, *Communism in Asia. A Study in Strategy and Tactics*. Calcutta, 1976.

   Sankar Ghosh, *Naxalite Movement, A Maoist Experiment*. Calcutta, 1974.

Partha N. Mukherji, *From Left Extremism to Electoral Politics—Naxalite Participation in Elections.* New Delhi, 1983.

Mohan Ram, *Maoism in India.* New Delhi, 1971.

J.C. Johari, *Naxalite Politics in India.* Delhi, 1972.

2. It must be noted that these groups themselves have laid emphasis and derived their analytical logic within the framework of maoism, no matter how they understood and assessed it.
3. See for example, Crime Numbers (Cr. Nos.) 397 of P.S. Kurupam and also Cr. No. 25/68 of P.S. Elwinpet of the Naxalite Conspiracy Case (NCC), 1975.

CHAPTER 2

Initial Developments

Initial Developments

By the end of the 1950s it was clear that the Communist Party had been upstaged by the Congress. In most parts of the country this process had begun soon after independence when in the euphoria of that great event the elections of 1952 saw the Congress Party practically smothering all others under the weight of its reputation. In a few parts the process took a longer time, but even here the Communist Party could survive not because they had a programme that was radically different from that of the Congress, but because they claimed to be in a better position to implement them. All the same when elections were held once again in 1957 the Communists were reduced to a nonentity even in the two states of Andhra Pradesh and West Bengal where they had always had considerable support. To the Communist Party in Andhra Pradesh this was particularly mortifying after the tremendous public sympathy and support which they had received in the wake of the Telengana Armed Struggle of 1948-51. Further, while all that the Congress had done was to echo the policies of the Communists in this area, it made off with a majority of the seats in the Legislative Assembly with little credit accruing to the latter. The situation was not much different in West Bengal, and many party members began to feel that a change in the party's outlook was required.

Performance in the elections was only one of the issues which provoked rethinking among the party members. In the early sixties a new factor was introduced when the more militant members began to demand greater commitment, on the part of the party towards the revolutionary principles. In raising this demand these members were guided not, as had been the case in the past, by the Russian experience but by what had taken place more recently in China under the leadership of Mao. The issue itself was provoked by the somewhat indifferent attitude which the Communist Party had been adopting towards the agrarian struggles taking place in various parts of the country. To some communists these struggles represented the foundation on which a movement on maoist lines could be based and they were impatient to seize the opportunity. To others, for whom maoism had not the same significance the whole issue smacked of adventurism. It was thus a situation of confrontation and there was no way in which both groups could survive in the same party.

Maoism with its emphasis on the leadership of the rural proletariat was not something which was entirely unknown to the Indian Communists. Its implications in the Indian context had been discussed extensively during the final phase of the Telengana Armed Struggle by the Andhra Communists but subsequent events had overwhelmed this issue and the matter did not come up again until the sixties. How it re-emerged on the Indian scene, what were the immediate causes of its revival and what were the implications to the Communist Party in general are some of the issues that we shall deal with in this chapter.

The Nature of the CPI-CPI (M) Split

A number of factors played a role in the 're-emergence', as it were, of maoist politics on the Indian scene, but by far the most important one was the organisational crisis which enveloped the Communist Party in the early and mid sixties. The first major outcome of this crisis was the CPI-CPI(M) split that occurred in 1964. Trouble had been brewing within the Communist Party for quite some time over several issues especially in regard to the attitude that the party was to adopt towards the Congress Government. After having initially followed a radical and militant line between 1948 and 1951 the Communist Party of India (CPI) slowly shifted its stand "to support constitutionalism and parliamentary action coupled with support given to specific policies of Indian National Congress...The Amritsar Thesis signifies acceptance of parliamentary democracy as principal avenue through which party would secure power in India.".[1] Briefly stated, the CPI's understanding of the Indian situation and the method by which power is to be captured is based on its assessment that the state in India is the organ of the class rule of the national bourgeoisie which ucholds and develops capitalism in the national economy in India. In the changed international conditions wherein imperialism has weakened in comparison to the socialist camp it is possible for the Indian capitalists to independently industrialise the country. However, they are obstructed by various reactionary forces like the monopoly groups, landlords and wholesale dealers. On its own the national bourgeoisie cannot overcome these obstructions and build an independent and strong India. Therefore the role of communists in this context is to ally with the progressive sections of the bourgeoisie and build an alliance of all patriotic classes to defeat the reactionaries. The leadership of this alliance will be shared between the national bourgeoisie and the working class, in other words, the Congress Party representing the former and the CPI representing the latter. In this process the constitution of India with its reliance on universal franchise and fundamental rights would provide a good platform and instrument for the people to defeat the reactionaries.

Not all within the party supported this trend. They felt that in aligning with the Congress government, the party principles were being diluted. Around this time the difference which had developed within the party on the issue of Sino-Soviet split also surfaced with one section supporting the Communist Party of Soviet Union (CPSU)'s stand and the other the Communist Party of China (CPC). This issue would perhaps not have achieved any significance had not the CPC's foreign policy vis-a-vis India changed after 1958 on account of differences on the issues of Tibet and the alignment of the international border. With this development the polarisation between the pro-Soviet, pro-Congress sections and the pro-China, anti-Congress sections was complete and when hostilities actually broke out between China and India the latter came out openly against the "chauvinistic" policies of the party. When the split came ultimately in 1964 and the Communist Party of India (Marxist), CPI (M) formed, it was a development which did not surprise any one.

While broadly this was the course of events which ultimately brought about the split it is not the complete story for at every step a combination of local factors played a very important role. We shall now attempt to trace some of these factors and indicate the part they played in bringing about this split in Andhra Pradesh.

The popularity of the Communists in Andhra Pradesh was based on the powerful peasant struggle in the Telengana area which they had launched in the forties and the other broad people's movement it led in the Andhra part of the erstwhile Madras province. In fact, so high was the prestige accorded to the party in the immediate post-Telengana Armed Struggle period that in the 1952 elections it gained significant electoral victories both in the Andhra as well as Telengana areas. This euphoric state, however did not last very long and following their election successes in 1952 there was a continuous and steady erosion of their support base. A series of factors were responsible for this downfall, the most crucial one being the 'neutralisation' by the Congress of the independent cultivating class of rich peasants which had been the party's backbone thus far. By abolishing the *jagirdari* system and by various tenancy and land ceiling laws the Congress Government, created a situation wherein it was no longer possible for the big absentee landlords, the *jagirdars* and the *deshmukhs* to continue in the manner they had done earlier. At the same time these radical legislations still left enough room for the rich peasants to manoeuvre and retain their interests. All this coupled with the fact that the *Visalandhra*[2] question on which the Communists had rallied much support was rendered superfluous with the creation of a separate Andhra state reduced the Communist Party to a situation wherein they could no longer maintain an aggressive stance against the Congress. By a series of moves the Congress had managed to pull the rug from under their feet.

In the elections that followed after 1952 the performance of the party was dismal and at the time of the split it had been reduced to a non-entity incapable of influencing any government decision.

The more radical elements within the party were fully conscious of the developments and felt that the only way to revive the declining fortunes of the party was to adopt a more militant and aggressive line. When the split, therefore, came in 1964 these elements were quick to identify themselves with the CPI (M's) pro-Chinese policy which was in tune with the maoist line they had espoused during the Telangana Armed Struggle. Apart from these factors there was one other which was peculiar to the Andhra Pradesh State unit of the CPI. As mentioned earlier the Telangana Armed Struggle was the starting point of all the ideological debates which took place among the Andhra Communists. When the armed struggle was called off in 1951 following police action there were a number of ideological issues still to be settled. In fact even as the decision to end the struggle was being taken a serious debate was raging within the party on the question of armed struggle and other allied issues. These unresolved disputes continued to play a part in the initial politics of the CPI in the early 1950s so that even long prior to the CPI-CPI(M) split, the party, at least as far as Andhra Pradesh was concerned, did not present a completely unified picture. When the split finally took place the attitudes which each member had adopted towards the Telangana Armed Struggle leadership also played a role in deciding which group the member should join. Thus for instance in a broad way one can generalise, though there certainly were exceptions, that all those who had supported the continuation of the armed struggle shifted to the CPI (M) while those who had argued for its termination stuck to CPI. We thus find that local factors played a very important role and such issues as the CPSU-CPC split were by no means the only cause for the split that took place.

The Maoists Before 1967

Between 1964, when the split occurred, and 1967 when fresh elections were ordered the situation within the CPI (M) remained in a state of flux. While the split had placated certain sections it had by no means resulted in an equilibrium and perturbations in the form of strongly pro-maoist tendencies still existed. The fluidity was further increased by the fact that the Central Committee of CPI (M) did not come out with a definite stand on the ideological issues till 1967. Throughout this period the pro-maoists in the CPI (M) continued to persist with their propaganda for an alternative line. In Andhra Pradesh publicity was given to Peking's views on all important issues through artices published in *Janasakti*, while in Kerala *Sengadi* was the forum for Peking's views[3]. In Bengal groups such as the "The Revolutionary Council" led by Parimal Das Gupta, the "Chinta Group" of Amulya Sen and the "Marx-Engels Group" by Sushital Roy Choudhary were actively carrying out maoist propaganda.[4] However, by far the most active proponent of the maoist cause was Charu Majumdar (Charu). Between 1965 and 1967 he wrote eight letters to the party members analysing the Indian situation and laying down a strategy for carrying out revolution in the country[5]. He also formed the "Siliguri Council" along with Sanyal, Jangal Santhal and several other maoists from Bengal and published cyclostyled leaflets through this council calling for instant armed peasant revolution.

The difference within the CPI (M) surfaced as early as 1965 when the maoist elements in the party came out with a document entitled, *The Differences Among Jail Leaders*, severely criticising Sundarayya's letter from Moscow for attempting to support the CPSU's stand on various issues[6]. However, matters came to a head only in 1967 when two events having separate repurcussions occurred. The first was the starting of the Naxalbari peasant revolt and the second the holding of general elections in which the communists, for the first time, contended as two separate parties the CPI and the CPI (M).

Naxalbari—A Brief Review

Naxalbari is a village in the Siliguri sub-division of Darjeeling District with a tradition of supporting militant peasant struggles. It was a maoist stronghold and the leadership of the CPI(M) in this area was in the hands of two devoted maoists, Charu and Kanu Sanyal. As early as in May 1966 they had formed a parallel party centre in Darjeeling and were intent on establishing Naxalbari as the "first testing ground of the theory of area wise seizure of power" a programme which was first attempted in the Spring of 1967 when they launched what they described as a "struggle not for land or crops but for political power."[8] Whatever intentions the CPI(M) as a party had for supporting the struggle vanished with the announcement of the election results. The CPI(M) had done well enough both in West Bengal and Kerala to be able to participate in the governments. To the party this meant, in these two states if not everywhere that the fortunes of the entire party were "closely linked with the successful running of these ministries..." With this perspective in view they tried to persuade the local leadership at Naxalbari to withdraw their plans for a struggle but failed miserably. When the struggle began in Naxalbari in May 1967, the CPI (M) reacted initially with caution and moderation. The police were ordered not to enter the maoist strongholds until the party had settled the issues at a political level. Efforts in this direction did not bring about any settlement because the maoists refused to have any truck with the party emissaries.[10] It thus became clear to the CPI (M) leadership that the maoists in Siliguri backed by Chinese moral support were determined to set up the Naxalbari struggle as an example of the implementaion of their political line. Once this realisation dawned their attitude hardened and on July 5, 1967 the West Bengal cabinet ordered full scale police action. Within a month more than a thousand persons were arrested. Jangal

Santhal was arrested in 1967 itself and what little resistance there was to the police after this was effectively snuffed out with the arrest of Kanu Sanyal and Khokan Majumdar on November 11, 1968.[11]

Naxalbari's importance in the history of Indian maoist movement is based not on the intensity of the movement or its success (both of these were quite limited) but on its symbolic significance and theoretical value. It had a symbolic value in the sense that it came to represent idealism and revolutionary ardour for many young people. It raised the hopes of many and goaded them into action. To the Indian communist movement it posed the question of seizing political power and of directing all struggles towards that direction. Also, theoretically it aimed at the implementation of an agrarian, peasant based guerilla struggle in rural areas with the specific intention of destroying existing power structure. It was also the first recent example of the practice of maoist path in India. According to the Andhra Pradesh Revolutionary Communist Committee (APRCC) "Naxalbari peasant armed struggle brought forward the issue of people's war path ; led to ideological discussions in the party ; played a historical role by exposing neo-revisionist ideas ; it brought out the internal struggle in party ; it encouraged revolutionary struggle in other states to intensify ideological struggles".[12] To an extent it became an exercise in translating maoism from theory to practice in Indian conditions.

Developments in Andhra Pradesh

The relationship between the maoists and the Communist Party in Andhra had its own logic. Whereas the events following the Naxalbari movement served to crystallise the differences between the maoists and CPI (M) in Bengal the situation remained fluid in Andhra Pradesh in the absence of any such confrontation. At the same time continued lack of success in the electoral front only strengthened the arguments of the Andhra maoists that without bringing armed struggle on to the party agenda the party would not be able to make much headway. Moreover, in Andhra Pradesh the CPI(M) could not even maintain the position which it did in Bengal. The maoists, attitude was also influenced by the then ongoing peasant movements, one in Telangana, and the other in Srikakulam which the CPI (M) was spearheading. Both these movements were facing severe repression from the police as well as the local landlords. Between 1952 and 1968 some 70 activists had been killed[13]. Sympathisers were subjected to a lot of harassment making it very difficult for the party to operate. False cases were reported to have been foisted against them and in Khammam alone as many as 1300 cases involving party sympathisers are alleged to have been instituted[14]. In these circumstances the maoists line that armed struggle was essential for the progress of the movement found enthusiastic support from among the cadre.

The Naxalbari incidents however, served to bring the issues into a sharper focus even in Andhra Pradesh. In 1967 when the Bengal Government ordered a crackdown on the maoists, the State Committee of the CPI (M) in Andhra Pradesh, in which the maoists were a majority passed a resolution condemning the Central Committee's attitude and calling for a withdrawal of the party from the Ministry. This was followed by further propaganda by party functionaries like Kolla Venkaiah, a member of the Central Committee of CPI(M) and Chandra Pulla Reddy, a member of the State Secretariat of the CPI (M)[16]. Following this the Andhra maoists continued their propagation of "epoples' war path" by translating and circulating Chinese documents. In June 1967, they even went to the extent of conducting a political school to educate the cadre on these matters. It is significant that the CPI (M) leadership had nothing to do with this venture. Refering to the suppression of the CPI (M) led peasant movements in Telangana and Srikakulam the maoists argued that the only way to raise the level of the movement to a higher stage was to engage in "armed resistance".

The CPI (M) Stand

The situation created by the maoists in Bengal and Andhra Pradesh forced the CPI (M) to clarify their stand on various ideological issues. While they could afford to ignore the maoists in Andhra Pradesh and deal with them firmly, they could no longer do so with Bengal maoists. In the first place unless they cleared the organisation of the maoist elements and dissociated themselves from their activities it would become impossible for them to continue in the United Front Government. Again, unless they clarified their stand on ideological as well as programmatic issues it would become difficult for them to maintain their position within the party. At the same time they would be denying an opportunity to the maoists to spread their ideas among those party members who did not have any definite ideas in the matter.

The first step taken in this direction was to expel these members from the party. They dissolved the party's Darjeeling District Committee and the Siliguri sub-divisional committee which spearheaded the maoist alternative and replaced them with *adhoc* committees. Prominent members of these committees like Charu Majumdar and Souren Bose were expelled from the party. This was followed by state-wise expulsions of maoist leaders like Sushital Roy Choudary, Ashim Chatterjee, Parimal Das Gupta, Asit Sen, Suniti Ghosh, Saroj Dutt and Mahadeb Mukherjee. According to Sankar Ghosh "the purge continued for quite sometime and at the end about thousand extremists had been expelled from the party".[18] The CPI(M) followed up the expulsion by physically capturing the party *Deshahitaishi* office which was at that time being edited by Sushital Roy Choudary[19].

The second step was to clarify their position on various issues by endorsing a series of articles and documents. The first set of articles came from M. Basavapunnaiah, a Politbureau member of CPI(M). He accused the maoists as being agents of vested interests and ruling classes and felt that the political objectives and policies set by maoists "have absolutely no relationship to the reality of class alignments obtaining either in the State of West Bengal or in the country as a whole and the slogan of boycott of the parliamentary institutions that they the Naxalites are raising is nothing but left sectarian and adventurist".[20] Basavapunnaiah's writings were followed by B.T. Ranadive's articles after which the *Madurai Draft* was submitted in August 1967.

In his articles Ranadive clearly differentiated the CPI(M)'s position from that of the maoists on questions of strategy, tactics and the assessment of the situation in India. He maintained that according to the CPI(M) while India was in the midst of an economic crisis, the political crisis had still not fully matured, and in this situation they should all work carefully using all forms and instruments of struggle.[21]

The Madurai Draft laid forth CPI(M)'s position on international issues like the character of the new epoch and the question of its main contradiction, the possibility of avoiding war and the chances of peaceful transition to socialism. Though in general they followed the Chinese views on these matters there were significant differences. The document characterised the new epoch as that in which imperialism had been weakened on a world scale and in which there had been a strengthening of the forces of revolution. As such it was an era in which socialism and communism would triumph on a world scale. However, imperialism though weakened was seen as being strong enough to require the unity of all revolutionary forces to defeat it. The armed might and the diplomacy of the socialist camp, the forces of national liberation movements in colonial and neo-colonial countries, the proletarian revolutionary movements, in the advanced capitalist countries and the peace movements, would be able to defeat imperialism provided they united and exploited the contradictions within imperialist countries.[22]

On the question of contradiction it was held that the contradiction between the world socialist camp and the imperialist camp was the main one. But it was also held that at the present stage of development the antagonism between imperialists and oppressed nations had become "the focus of all other contradictions in our time"[23] and as such the revolutionary struggles in Asia, Africa and Latin America now take on an importance for the success of socialism not only in these countries but on a world wide scale.

On the questions of war and peace they generally followed the Chinese view that wars could be eliminated only after the destruction of imperialism and for the time being they could be avoided by unity, determination and by increasing the armed strength of the socialist camp. In this context disarmament and peace movement are tactical slogans because, strategically only the victory of revolutionary forces could stop war.[24] On the question of peaceful co-existence they held that it was a concept of respite necessary for the consolidation of the socialist State, economically, politically and militarily.[25] But they added that it was "a fighting and revolutionary concept which permits no breeding of pacifist and utopian illusions about imperialism",[26] and on this ground they denied the possibility of peaceful transition to socialism in advanced countries.

The Madurai Draft also criticised the Soviet Union for transforming the dictatorship of proletariat to the dictatorship of the party; for offering material incentives to workers and for differentiating between physical and mental labour. However, it was felt that the unity of socialist countries was essential for success of revolution in any place and to this extent advised China to "unite in action" with the Soviet Union in giving aid to Vietnam.

The CPI (M) also dissociated itself from the Chinese view that the sharpening social contradictions in India had forced Indian Government to become a "puppet", "stooge" and a "lackey" of imperialism. In their view the Chinese were exaggerating the degree, depth and maturity of the contradictions in India because though the crisis in Indian economy was in fact deepening, there still existed "an excessively marked lack of correspondence between the objective revolutionary situation and the weakness of subjective factors".[30] In other words they held that the Congress Party continued to hold considerable political influence among the people despite the worsening economic situation. On the other hand, the revolutionary party was far from being properly organised and as such to talk about immediate revolution at this stage amounted to neglecting to take into consideration, the realities of the situation.[31]

Reaction of Maoists

The reaction of Bengal maoists to the Madurai documents was to give a call to overthrow the leadership of CPI (M). These views were presented in an article written by Charu Majumdar called *It is time to build up a revolutionary party*. He held that the Central Committee of CPI(M) had become class collaborationist and revisionist in ideology and that it had rejected the entire doctrine of Marxism-Leninism, because it had opposed the Chinese party regarding Soviet Union as still being a member of the socialist camp; it had favoured peaceful transition and progress through parliamentary democracy ; it had refused to lead the countrywide mass upsurge and the mass movements by its policy of continuing in the United Front ; it had beautified the reactionary Indian Government by pointing out that the Congress Party still holds considerable political influence among the people and finally, that it had rejected the entire doctrine of Marxism-Leninism.[32] In conclusion he held that "the duty of every Marxist-Leninist is to oust the Central Committee from the revolutionary front."[33]

The document also held that economic crisis in India was ripening into a political crisis through mass upheavals and that "agrarian revolution was the only path for liberating the country".[34] Simultaneously, it saw the need to have a strong revolutionary party to realise the potentialities of the situation. It was felt that the defeat in Naxalbari was due to lack of such a party. At the same time the document did not advocate the formation of a separate party but expressed the view that while still remaining within the CPI (M) and conducting sustained ideological campaigns in favour of maoist lines without paying any heed to party disciplines or Central Committee's commands a revolutionary party could be built up.[35] According to Sankar Ghosh "at this stage Mazumdar was thinking more in terms of transforming the CPI (M) into a revolutionary party than of forming a new party...For him the party was still the CPI (M). He repudiated only the leadership".[36]

Within a month after publishing the article Charu Majumdar and the other Bengal maoists formed a provisional committee of revolutionaries within the CPI (M). This was in November 1967. The main idea expressed at this meeting was that though a revolutionary party was necessary for the success of the revolution it could neither be willed from above by a few people nor brought about by ideological struggle however intense it might be. Therefore revolutionary struggles must be unleashed wherever possible and out of these struggles would emerge a revolutionary party. In other words "the birth and growth of the genuine revolutionary party is possible only through the storm and stress of sharp revolutionary class struggle."[37]

The Madurai document also faced severe criticism from the Andhra unit of CPI (M). This was not very surprising because the unit was dominated by maoists. The maoists criticised it "for supporting Soviet neo-revisionist policies and opposing the revolutionary line brought forward by the CPC."[38] They also introduced four resolutions in the State Committee of CPI (M). One proposed discussion of *Madurai Draft* at all levels of the party, another sought permission for presentation of an alternative draft, the third condemned the release of the document before it had reached party members and the fourth suggested that in view of the importance of the document it should be finalised in a party Congress and not by the Central Plenum of the party. All except the last of these resolutions received majority support.[39]

After the State Committee meeting the Andhra maoists sent a draft containing alternate proposals on ideological issues written by Devulapalli Venkateshwara Rao (hereafter DV) a member of the State Secretariat of the Central Committee and requested that it be circulated among party members throughout the country as an alternative to the Madurai proposal. This request was turned down. The Andhra maoists followed this up by a propaganda campaign touring various districts, distributing Chinese documents and holding discussions with the party cadre.

Finally on 19th January, 1968 the Andhra Pradesh State Committee of CPI (M) held its Plenum meeting at Palakollu.

This meeting provided the Andhra maoists with an opportunity to bring out their ideological and programmatic stand and place it before the entire State party cadre as well as to manoeuvre for capturing the State organisation of CPI (M). Two hundred and thirty one delegates from various districts and taluq levels participated in this meeting. It was also attended by P. Sundarayya and M. Basavapunnaiah, (both members of CPI (M) Politbureau) who tried to persuade the maoists to reconcile themselves to the Centre's views but they did not meet with much success.

The plenum elected to the Presidium two maoists Tarimela Nagi Reddy (hereafter T.N.) and DV as well as one follower of the Central leadership Gunturu Bapanayya. The entire meeting was dominated by the maoist faction and it passed by an overwhelming majority a resolution demanding that the Central Committee of CPI(M) should prepare a new draft on the basis of the general line proposed by CPC. The meeting also approved two resolutions each of which put forth a set of formulations on the basis of which the Central Committee was requested to reconsider its ideological draft. One of these resolutions was written by TN and C. Pulla Reddy (hereafter CP) the other by Kolla Venkaiah.[40]

The resolutions criticised the *Madurai Draft* for presenting a wrong understanding of the international situation. Specifically they alleged that the *Madurai Draft* did not expose the Soviet leadership's anti-revolutionary activities, and that it did not point out the class roots of Soviet revisionism. Moreover, it was felt that it neither realised that the Soviet Union was trying to destory the socialist ideale and restore capitalism, nor did it realise that Soviet Union was implementing class collaborationist line with U.S. imperialism.[41]

The resolutions held that the new epoch 'is characterised by final collapse of imperialism and the final victory of world wide socialism".[42] It was an era in which "the national liberation struggles are becoming the decisive force for the final destruction of imperialism."[43] At the same time they were undermining the imperialist system by weakening the foundations of the system in the metropolitan country itself, and by doing so were also contributing to the cause of peace and strengthening the socialist countries by thwarting the plans of U.S. imperialism for world domination. Because of this "the U.S. imperialism with its 300 military bases throughout the world is concentrating its main military strength in the continents of Asia, Africa and Latin America to drown the national liberation movement in blood".[44] Thus it was the task of the international working class movement and the socialist countries of the world to extend all possible support to the national liberation movement.

The resolutions further held that the CPSU leadership was collaborating with U.S. imperialism in their plans to gain world hegemony. For this purpose they had come "to an agreement to maintain the monopoly of nuclear weapons so as to blackmail weaker nations".[45] They were also trying to isolate China which was the centre of world revolution. Thus in different ways both U.S. and U.S.S.R. were obstructing world revolution. While the U.S. was trying to physically suppress the revolutionary movements the Soviet Union was "sapping the fighting will of the proletariat" and "demoralising, disrupting and sabotaging the national liberation movement, by its concepts of peaceful transition to socialism and of peaceful co-existence."[46]

The resolutions also described the CPSU leadership as representing the bourgeoisie "who have usurped the leadership of the party and the State".[47] This privileged strata in Soviet Union have transformed the dictatorship of the proletariat into a capitalist State and were trying to cover up the fact with talk about the Soviet Union being the "State of the whole people". They had also subverted the Communist Party and turned it into an instrument of bourgeois rule and by introducing material incentives, allowing competitive economy and free market, investing all authority in the hands of bureaucrats managing industries and by entering into collaboration agreements with international imperialists e.g. with the Japanese capitalists for joint exploitation of Siberian mineral wealth, they had restored capitalism in Soviet Union.[48] In this situation it was felt that it was not possible for the world revolutionary forces to join hands with the Soviet Union "for forming a United Front against U.S. imperialism. The Soviet Union "sees possibilities of peaceful co-existence and visualises broad areas of co-operation with the United States" and is in fact "planning collaboration with U.S. imperialism for world domination."[49] Therefore the Soviet Union's call for unity of action in Vietnam "is a clever camouflage for greater disunity and greater disruption within the socialist camp and within the working class movement."[50] The resolutions agree with the CPC's position on relations with the Soviet Union which is that "there can be no unity of action regarding Vietnam for while the Vietnam war aims at a decisive defeat of U.S. imperialism the sole aim of CPSU leadership is to bring the Vietnam issue into U.S. Soviet collaboration."[51]

In the alternate draft that was proposed maoism was described as the Marxism-Leninism of the modern times. Maoism was defined as "Peoples Democracy, Peoples war, completion of the socialist revolution through the cultural revolution, an irreconcilable ideological battle against modern revisionism".[52]

The resolutions followed up their formulations on international issues with their analysis of the Indian situation. It was asserted that the big bourgeoisie in India was becoming more and more comprador in its nature. The dependence of Indian industries on imported machinery, technical knowhow and foreign capital were making the Indian bourgeoisie agents of foreign imperialism. The growing number of foreign collabotion agreements was seen as a clear evidence of this.

Devaluation of the rupee as well as liberalisation of import and export policy were the concessions Indian bourgeoisie was offering to the foreign imperalists. India was regarded as being completely dependent upon U.S. imperialism not only for military hardware and food supplies but also for funds to implement the five year plans. They did not think that the Soviet aid made any difference to the situation but that it was only serving the monopoly interests and helping foreign imperialist enetration.[53]

The most important feature of the document however was its views on strategy and tactics of the Indian revolution which set the Andhra maoists apart from both the CPI(M) and the Bengal maoists". "In the first place", according to this document, "prolonged agrarian armed revolution is the only path left open to all backward countries for social emancipation."[54] Further the Andhra maoists did not object to the CPI(M)'s formulation that legal and illegal work must be combined and so must be parliamentary work with mass struggles. At the same time they maintained that unless a perspective of armed resistance was added to these, the revolution would not become a reality and the revolutionaries would "endlessly remain waiting for an insurrection to take place".[55] This line varies from the Bengal maoists' complete rejection of legal and mass work and insistence on immediate armed struggle. In doing this the Andhra maoists rejected the view that armed struggle was the beginning of the revolution, as well as the view that the armed struggle came only towards the end of the revolution. In their perspective armed struggle was a product of a certain stage of revolutionary development and was necessary for taking the revolutionary process to higher stages.

This document did not take a clear cut stand either for or against the participation in elections and ministries. What it did was to criticise the understanding and the aims with which CPI(M) entered the elections and the parliament. In their opinion representative institutions were just a facade, since they were "part and parcel of the bourgeois landlord constitution which is pledged to the preservation of bourgeois landlord system of exploitation."[56] So the CPI(M)'s tactical slogan of participating in the provincial ministries "to bring into existence Government's pledge to carry out a modest programme of giving relief to the people" was wrong. The CPI(M) leadership's understanding of the role of ministries, they felt was leading to "the subordination of mass agitations to the need of existence and continuation of the ministries"[57]. Citing an example they said that on the question of food shortages the attitude of United Front Governments was to explain to the people that they were not responsible for the situation, while the revolutionary attitude to take was to mobilise the masses against the Central Government on this issue and unleash militant mass movements. But this was not being done since it might come in the way of continued existence of the ministries. Thus the Andhra maoists while criticising CPI(M)'s participation in elections and the ministries limited their criticism to the tactical plane and did not oppose it as a strategy. There was no total rejection of the parliamentary institutions but only of the manner in which the CPI(M) was participating in them.

In March 1968 the maoists leaders in Andhra formed the Andhra Pradesh Revolutionary Communist Committee (APRCC) with the intention of organising ideological propaganda and co-ordinating the activities of maoists within the CPI(M). This gave some sort of organisational shape to the Andhra maoists. At the same time it also implied that they would not as yet leave the CPI(M) but try to convert the whole of CPI (M) to its point of view.

In May 1968 the All India Co-ordination Committee of the Communist Revolutionaries (AICCCR) was formed with Sushital Roy Choudary as its convenor. It called upon all the revolutionaries who believed in the maoist path to join it. At that time it did not specify any detailed programme on which AICCCR was to be based. This was because though all the maoists of India at that time were agreed on certain general issues like the Soviet Union having become revisionist and the necessity of armed struggle in India, many differences of opinion existed among them. In such a situation the founders of AICCCR did not think it wise to risk splits in the movements by imposing uniform views on ideological issues.

The Andhra maoists did not join AICCCR immediately because they felt that in spite of its all India pretensions, AICCCR was essentially an organisation of the Bengal maoists. The Bengal maoists were also maintaining direct contacts with certain sections of the Andhra maoists and this was not liked by the dominant TN, CP faction of the Andhra maoists. The pro-Bengal faction of Andhra maoists was at this time centred around the Naxalbari Solidarity Committee whose activists consisted mainly of students and the erstwhile Students Federation of India (SFI) cadre. The leading lights of this organisation were Murlapudi Venkataratnam, a student of Guntur Medical College, and Chauganti Bhaskara Rao an eminent surgeon with a thriving practice at Ongole. They acted as catalysts for the split within the Andhra maoists which took place subsequently and in which the Srikakulam maoist leaders and many other senior members of Telangana area broke away from the T.N., D.V, leadership.[58] Several other maoist groups e.g. Kerala and Maharashtra also kept away from the AICCCR at this time.

The Burdwan Plenum and the Split

The Burdwan Plenum of CPI(M)'s Central Committee met in June 1968. During the Plenum the maoists from Andhra Pradesh carried out a relentless struggle over ideological issues. Ultimately, though the alternative drafts presented by T.N., C.P. and Kolla Venkaiah were defeated by big margins (22 for and 159 against) they were successful to the extent of forcing the leadership to accept amendments to the official draft. These amendments made the draft more critical towards Russia and changed some original formulations like the one calling for unity in action between CPSU and CPC.[59] However, the acceptance of these amendments did not in any way conciliate the Andhra maoists who did not see any fundamental change in the leadership's views. Only D.V. seems to have been temporarily placated by the sharp criticism of CPSU, which was incorporated in the ideological resolution. He voted for it, but soon under pressure from fellow maoists he wrote a letter to the party leadership withdrawing his support.

Burdwan made it clear to the Andhra maoists that there was going to be a change in leadership's attitude and that their days in the CPI(M) were numbered. They decided to make the best of the situation and convert as many as possible to their line of thinking so that when the split came about they could take the largest number of party cadre with them.

At the same time the CPI(M) leadership took various steps to meet the situation. The party politbureau nominated two members to the Provincial Committee Secretariat and four members to the Provincial Executive Committee. thus creating a majority for the anti-maoist faction.[60] The Politbureau also prohibited T.N., D.V., C P. and Kolla Venkaiah from addressing any meeting and from touring the state to explain to the District Committees the decisions of the Burdwan Plenum. It also authorised the CPI(M)'s local committee in which the pro-leadership faction was in a majority to take all steps required to discipline the members. Though T.N. and C.P. were spared, notices of expulsion were served on many lower level maoists, especially in Khammam district. The cultural troupe of Subbarao Panigrahi which was propagating peoples war path was also disciplined.[61]

The Central Committee of CPI(M) followed up these organisational steps with a *Letter to Andhra Comrades* in which they held that the Andhra maoists' positions were in "fundamental opposition" to the CPI(M)'s stand on various issues concerning the Indian revolutionary movement and the international communist movement. They criticised the Andhra maoists for holding that the Soviet Union had joined the U.S. in order to destroy China which was the only base of world revolution and liberation. They also disagreed with the view that the national liberation movements play the decisive role in the destruction of Imperialism.[62]

This was followed by a detailed criticism of the Andhra maoists' stand on various issues. These were mere repetitions of the *Madurai Draft* and they did not even take cognizance of the fact that there were several issues on which the Andhra maoists disagreed with the Bengal maoists. Thus for instance in criticising the Andhra maoists for underestimating the efficacy of the parliamentary path and the role of mass struggles they seem to have assumed that the Andhra maoists like the Bengal maoists had disallowed both these forms of struggles when in fact the situation was quite different.

The Andhra maoists issued a strongly worded reply to this letter in their Open letter to party members. The overall effect of this was a hardening of attitudes both organisationally and theoretically towards the CPI(M). While the previous discussions and criticisms of the CPI(M) leadership were conducted at an inter-committee level now the criticism of party leadership was made publicly and aimed directly at the party members. It signified that the Andhra maoists could no longer see the party leadership voluntarily reforming and as such had decided to abandon them and take as many of the party members on the "correct line" as possible. The *Open Letter* symbolises a clear polarisation on ideological issues and on organisational operation. In the letter the CPI(M) leadership and its political line was clearly characterised as "nothing but a neo-revisionist line covered with deceptive revolutionary phraseology".[63] The CPI(M) arguments were seen as being aimed at weakening revolutionary struggles[64] and it was accused of supporting repressive measures against the Naxalbari peasant movement, and of attempting to disrupt the movements in Srikakulam and Telangana areas. The letter rejected CPI(M)'s middle path (one which is different from both Chinese and Soviet positions) as a "myth" and said that they were destroying the revolutionary content of concepts like peoples democracy and agrarian revolution and replacing them in practice with reformist ideals like "non-Congress democracy".

The *Open Letter* expressed the view that the Socialist Camp came into existence only after the Chinese Revolution.[65] China was seen as the centre of world revolution which was struggling to complete socialist revolution, internally through the cultural revolution, and externally through help to national liberation movements.[66] On the other hand the CPSU leadership was acting as an agent and friend of imperialism. Its policy was one of preservation of capitalism in capitalist countries and restoration of capitalism in socialist countries. It had joined hands with the imperialists and reactionaries to suppress revolutionary movements and conspired to encircle and isolate China, economically, politically and militarily.[67]

In spite of this counter revolutionary collusion an "excellent revolutionary situation existed in the world"[68] it went on "Imperialism was fighting its last-ditch battles and its complete destruction was on the agenda. This task was to be fulfilled by the national liberation movements, on whose victory the fate of world humanity depends"[69]. It was the duty of all socialist countries to help these movements. But they felt it was wrong to hold, as the CPI(M) did that their victory depends on the "revolutionary combination of socialist diplomacy and the armed help of the socialist countries". On the other hand the national liberation movements could stand upon their own legs and play a decisive role in destroying imperialism in colonial and semi-colonial countries as well as at a world level.[70]

The *Open Letter* resolutely declared that "Peoples War" was the "Universal method for national liberation movements". It observed that "in all backward countries the mass movements after reaching a particular stage have to face severe repression of the, Government. After this stage has been reached the peoples movements could make further advance only by beating back the repressive measures, only by combining the mass movements with armed struggle".[71] But the letter sounded a note of caution and stated that it was by no means calling for an immediate armed revolt. "Ours is a vast country with uneven development. Peoples, movements are also developing unevenly. In these conditions, in today's economic and political crisis, militant struggles are bound to break out in various parts of the country. The Communist Party must boldly lead these struggles... resist the repressive measures... develop the anti-landlord struggles... co-ordinate all these struggles and according to a plan develop these struggles towards a people war".[72]

The *Open Letter* took a tougher stand on United Front with non-Congress parties and formation of ministries. It was felt that such alliances and ministries were only leading to increasing illusions among the masses. It dubbed such alliances as "nothing but renunciation of the theory of class struggle and adoption of a class collaborationist policy".[73] An interesting aspect of the *Open Letter* was that it contained no specific and clear cut condemnation of participation in elections.

Significantly the *Open Letter* characterised India as a neo-colony of American imperialism.[74] Thus the Andhra maoists moved away from their previous stand in which they seemed to have allowed some independence for Indian bourgeoisie. This shift must have been due to the realisation that acceptance of even a little independence for the Indian bourgeoisie would imply acceptance of a contradiction between Indian bourgeoisie and imperialism and thus, possibility for progressive role of the Indian bourgeoisie a line which the CPI(M) supported.[75]

The *Open Letter* ended by giving a call to "build a strong and disciplined communist party through struggles based on Marxism-Leninism".[76]

In June 1968 the expelled State Committee members held a meeting in Vijayawada which was attended by representatives from various districts. Here it was decided to completely break with the CPI(M) and the Andhra Pradesh Co-ordination Committee for Communist Revolutionaries (APCCCR) was formed.

Organisational Implications of the Split

Various accounts exist of the strength of the maoists when they broke away from CPI(M). Sundarayya stated to the press in June 1968 that of the 16,000 party members in Andhra, a quarter would go to the maoists, another quarter to the CPI(M) while fifty per cent of them would remain inactive.[77] The CPI(M) *Political and Organisational Report* submitted to the Cochin Congress (1968) noted a fall from 16,456 to 9,248 in the membership figures of Andhra Pradesh. The CPI(M) figures submitted for their Ninth Congress at Madurai show the membership of CPI(M) in Andhra, as only 5870. The maoists themselves claimed about 10,000 defections from CPI(M). However, the defections from CPI(M) cannot be taken as an accurate indicator of the actual strength of the maoists at that time. For estimating this we must deduct those who became inactive to various degrees and add all those new members who started their political career not in CPI(M) but directly in APCCCR.

Not many details are available as to the exact break-up of the defections from the CPI(M). However, an attempt at analysis can be made. At the top leadership level the split seems to have been even. People more closely connected with the central leadership like Sundarayya, Basavapunnaiah, Moturi Hanumantha Rao and Nanduri Prasada Rao, who were either members of the Politbureau or organisationally linked to running party organs at Central level remained with the CPI(M), while those leaders whose political fortunes and interests were more deeply rooted with the state of movement in Andhra Pradesh went over to the maoists. At the district and taluq levels of the leadership also, the split seems to havebeen even. Among the rank and file, with the older cadre which was in the Telangana peasant movement opted for the maoists. In the trade union frontmost of the units appeared to have stayed with the CPI(M) while a fewunits like the railway workers in Warangal area, the jute unions in West Godavari and some units in Singareni Collieries went over to the APCCCR. The Kisan Sabha in Andhra Pradesh was almost defunct, but whatever little organisation was there, was under the influence of Nanduri Prasada Rao and Uddamaraju Ramam and it stayed with the CPI(M). The reason for this was that after years of a united front line in village areas, the Kisan Sabha was firmly in the hands of the rich peasantry who were sceptical about the radical intentions of he maoists. The Students Federation of India, Andhra Unit went into the maoists' hands. A majority of CPI(M) sympathisers in the Teachers Organisation also threw in their lot with the maoists. All the maoist leaders in Telangana and Srikakulam areas like K.G. Satyamurthy, Kondapalli Seetharamaiah, and Vempatapu Satyanarayana were teachers. Many of CPI(M) cultural organisations after some initial vacillation, went over to the maoist side led by their President Sri Sri. The party leadership as well as the workers in areas where there was a militant peasant movement going on, went over to the side of maoists. This was the case both in Srikakulam and Mulug, Yellandu, Bayyaram etc. taluqs in Telangana. Significantly, there was no rural-urban dichotomy in the split and the maoists had as much following in the urban party committees as in the rural.[78]

Conclusion

Two factors emerge clearly from the foregoing. The first is that the process of the split between the maoists and the CPI(M), took place differently in different areas. While in Bengal it occurred decisively and abruptly in Andhra the process was more drawn out. More specifically the maoists in Bengal were in a minority in the state committee of the CPI(M) and hence the CPI(M) had no hesitation in expelling them as soon as matters came to a head over the Naxalbari issue. In fact it would have been detrimental to the interests of the CPI(M) to tolerate the maoists any further because it would only have resulted in providing the latter an opportunity to increase their influence within the party. That Charu initially made an effort to operate within the CPI(M) is an indication of the fact that even the maoists were not unaware of the advantages of remaining with the parent group under the existing circumstances. On the other hand the state committee in Andhra Pradesh was dominated by the maoists and as a consequence until it became fully evident that there was no meeting ground between the CPI(M) and the maoists the former was not keen on expelling them for they were fully aware that by doing so they would be left with a shrunken base in the State.

Again, while the entire process of emergence of the maoists as a distinct group proceeded in two stages in Bengal, the first consisting of the separation of the CPI(M) from CPI and the second of the maoists from the CPI(M)— this pattern was not strictly followed in A.P. In Bengal the fact that the CPI(M) was able to muster a sizeable number of seats in Assembly following the General Election in 1967 gave it a status of its own. To those in the CPI(M), who were vacillating between supporting the maoist line and the CPI(M) line the CPI(M) had something tangible to offer and as a consequence many chose to remain with the parent party. In Andhra Pradesh on the other hand the CPI(M) having fared miserably in the elections never really emerged as a force and from the day it was created it was the maoists who dominated the proceedings. Thus when finally the APCCCR was created in 1968 it took away with it a very large section of the District Committee as well as a large chunk of fence sitters. Mention must also be made of the fact that the Telangana Armed Struggle loyalties played a part even during this split and a number of the old cadre moved in with the maoists more as a result of these loyalties than due to similarities in ideology. Several of these reverted to CPI(M) or even CPI when they founu that they were not really in tune with the maoists.

The second factor that emerges is that right from the start difference of opinion existed between the Bengal and the Andhra maoists. In fact we notice that within the Andhra group itself there were dissenting voices which called for greater support for the Bengal maoists line. How this trend emerged and what it resulted in are some of the questions we shall discuss in the next chapter.

NOTES & REFERENCES

1. Ralph Retzlaff,. "Revisionist and Sectarians" in Scalpino (ed), *The Communist Revolution in Asia* (Prentice Hall, 1969) p. 336 and also Victor Fic, *Peaceful Transition to Communism in India* (Nichiketa, 1963).
2. The movement soon after independence for carving out a State on linguistic basis, in the Telugu speaking areas of the Madras Presidency was populary called the Visalandhra Movement.
3. *Anti-National Activities of Pro-Peking Communists*, Statement of the Minister of Home Affairs laid on the Table of Parliament in February 1965, pp 38-39.
4. See Document *On Left Deviation*, CPI(M), pp 20-21.
5. Sankar Ghosh, *The Naxalite Movement*, *op. cit.*, p. 55, For original version of these letters see *Mass Line* (Kerala), May-June 1975.
6. Document C-28 of Hyderabad Conspiracy Case (HCC), p.4.

7. Sankar Ghosh, *op. cit.* p. 27.
8. Charu Majumdar, "One Year of Naxalbari", *Liberation*, June 1968.
9. *The New Situation and the New Tasks Confronting our Party*, (CPICM) 1967, p. 67.
10. Charu Majumdar did not even grant an interview to Hare Krishna Konar, the then Revenue Minister who had been sent to discuss the issue with him.
11. Manoranjan Mohanty, *Revolutionary Violence: A Study of the Maoist Movement in India*, New Delhi, Sterling Publications, 1977.
12. Document C-28, *op. cit.* p. 7.
13. *Raise your voice against Landlord Terrorism in Andhra Pradesh CPI(M)*, 1968, p. 34.
14. *Ibid* pp. 23-24, All these facts cannot be dismissed as being exaggerated or false because these allegations were made in a letter addressed to the Prime Minister.
15. Document C-28 *op. cit.*
16. *Ibid.*
17. *Ibid.*
18. Sankar Ghosh, *op. cit.* p. 34.
19. *Hindustan Standard*, June 22, 1967.
20. Basavapunniah, "Our Party's stand on Naxalbari", *Peoples' Democracy*, July 23, 1967.
21. See B.T. Ranadiva, "Anti-Party Tendencies", *Peoples' Democracy*, July16 to August 20, 1967.
22. See *The Draft on the Ideological Question*, CPI(M), 1967.
23. *Ibid*, p. 11
24. See *Ibid*, pp.15-16
25. *Ibid*, p. 21
26. *Ibid*, p. 23

27. *Ibid*, See pp.37-38
28. *Ibid* p. 51
29. *Stand on Ideological Issues*, CPI(M), November 4, 1969, pp 52-5.
30. *Ibid*, p. 57
31. *Ibid*
32. West Bengal State Committee of CPI(M), *Collected writings of our respected leader comrade Charu Majumdar*, Volume 2 (CPI(ML), 1972, pp. 1-3.
33. *Ibid*, p. 5
34. *Ibid*
35. See *Ibid*, p. 6
36. Sankar Ghosh, *op. cit.* p. 40
37. *Liberation*, May 1968
38. Document C-28, *op. cit.* p. 6
39. *Ibid*
40. Both these resolutions are published together with an introduction in book, *Andhra Plenum Rejects The Neo-Revisionist Ideological Draft* (*Janasakti*, 1968).
41. *Ibid*, See the Introduction.
42. *Ibid*, p. 8
43. *Ibid*
44. *Ibid*, p. 20
45. *Ibid*, 19
46. *Ibid*
47. *Ibid* p. 23
48. See *Ibid* p. 23
49. *Ibid* p. 35
50. *Ibid*

51. *Ibid* p. 38

52. *Ibid*

53. *Ibid*, pp 48-50

54. *Ibid*, p. 57

55. *Ibid*, p. 60

56. *Ibid*, p. 32

57. *Ibid*, p. 57

58. The details of the difference and the organisational results of these differences between T.N.- D.V. group and Charu Majumdar group is traced in the next chapter.

59. See Ashish Kumar Roy *Spring Thunder and after* Minerva Associates, Calcutta, (1975) p. 138.

60. *Resolutions of APCCCR*, 15.6.1968, (printed) p. 1.

61. *Ibid* p. 2

62. "Letter to Andhra Comrades", in *Stand on Ideological Issues*, (CPI(M) 1969), p. 6.

63. *Open Letter, op. cit.* p. 5

34. *Ibid* p. 7

65. *Ibid* p. 5

66. *Ibia*, p. 19

67. See *Ibid* pp. 16-18.

68. *Ibid* p. 5

69. *Ibid* p. 8

70. *Ibid* pp. 8-10

71. *Ibid* p. 14

72. Emphasis added. *Ibid* p.13. In the *Rajakiya Nirmana Sammeksha* (December, C-28) published in 1969, the APRCC maintained that their denial in the *Open Letter* of giving a call for Immediate armed struggle, was only meant to escape immediate arrest of their cadre. This self-criticism does not seem to be sincere. The *Open Letter* had

clearly taken into account (a) the necessity of struggles to develop to a certain extent before they can take an armed form and (b) uneven development of struggles in the various areas of India. It looks much more probable that APRCC's self-criticism of 1969 was a result of their efforts to appease the radicals and to assure their revolutionary bonafides to the cadre who were questioning their intentions because of the influence of Srikakulam Struggle which was being conducted under the guidance of Charu Majumdar faction. Thus this self-criticism was more a part of the 1969 "Left-Line" taken by APRCC rather than intrinsic part of their theoretical formulations.

73. *Ibid* p. 15

74. *Ibid* p. 23

75. For example, see p. 24, *Ibid*, for the ridicule they pour on CPI(M) for saying that the "Congress Government may be able to achieve to *some extent* industrial development" (emphasis added).

76. *Ibid* p. 32

77. *Statesman*. June 26, 1968.

78. For details see Document C-28, *op. cit.*

CHAPTER 3

Two Shades of Maoism

Two Shades of Maoism

The years 1964-68 saw the birth of a large number of maoist groups as in state after state breakaway units from the CPI (M) began to be formed.[1] To begin with, there were certain issues that all the groups agreed upon. For instance they had a common assessment of the international situation whereby Russia was branded revisionist while it was China that was to be looked up to as the centre of the world revolution. There was also unanimity in the assessment of the broad nature of the Indian situation. Indian independence they all agreed, was only formal and it was ruled by the comparado bureaucratic bourgeoisie which was allied to feudalism and was subservient to imperialism. The path to India's liberation they concluded lay in guerilla struggles based on peasantry. Beyond these basic agreements, however, lay a vast grey area of conflicting assessments by the various groups in regard to the state of preparedness of the people, the strategy to be employed and the organisational set up to be created in furtherance of a revolution. There was heated discussion on all these issues and in the process two distinct and clearly discernible shades of maoism began to emerge based on the assessment of the West Bengal group and that of the Andhra group. With the passage of time all the other groups rallied around either one or the other of these two major groups.

The Bengal group was led by the leaders of the Naxalbari peasant struggle and included such charismatic personalities as Charu Majumdar and Kanu Sanyal. Much of this group's popularity among the maoists stemmed from the large role which its members, especially Charu Majumdar had in the formulation of a maoist line even as early as in 1964. In fact Charu Majumdar was the first to translate and circulate the Chinese documents among the members of the Communist party. Further, this group had been the first to set up a parallel committee within the CPI(M) to propagate maoism and also the first to form an all India body within the CPI(M) in November 1967. Ultimately in May 1968 it even became the first group to severe links with the CPI(M) and form an independent organisation for maoists. But an even more important reason for the popularity of the Bengal group lay in the fact that it was the only group which had the recognition and open support of the Communist Party of China (CPC). The high prestige that accrued to it due to all these factors was further enhanced by the active support that it received from the people outside the regular communisticadre. In fact it was the only maoist group which could even boast of such a following at that time. Among its supporters there were young men inspired by Naxalbari, Land student members of the pro-maoist Progressive Students Co-ordination Committee (PSCC)[3] which in the 1967-68 students' union elections emerged as the dominant student group. Quite a few of the well known figures from the cultural and intellectual scene had rallied around this group. In the event, as the situation developed further the Bengal maoist faction was able to carry behind it the Bihar, U.P. maoist groups as well as certain significant chunks of the Punjab and Andhra group.

The Andhra group on the other hand was led by men like T.N., D.V. and C.P. who had achieved certain status within the communist movement at a national level. Its strength lay in the comparatitive soundness of its organisational structure and as a group was supported by the Maharashtra maoists along with K.P.R. Gopalan and Ramdas factions from Kerala.

Between the two, the Andhra and the Bengal groups along-with their supporters accounted for nearly 80% of the maoists.

Apart from them, there were few smaller groups such as the one led by Parimal Das Gupta of West Bengal and certain others in Punjab and Tamil Nadu. By and large such of those groups which could attract only a minority of the members of the parent CPI(M) aligned themselves with the Bengal group whereas those which separated out enbloc supported the Andhra group.

This fact itself affected the stand which each of the groups took towards certain issues especially in regard to their attitude towards the parent CPI(M). The Andhra group with its relatively large breakaway unit felt that there was no need to precipitate the impending split within the CPI(M). Their view was that one should stay in the organisation as long as possible, conduct ideological struggles and win over as many members as possible to their side before actually splitting. A hurried split they felt would only isolate them and be detrimental to their interests.

The Bengal group, however, dependent as it was on the support from non-party elements, thought otherwise. For all practical purposes by 1967 they were no longer a part of the CPI(M) and as such they saw no reason to have any more truck with the CPI(M) which they felt had fallen into "economist" ways of functions as a result of the "rut of revisionism and bourgeois pattern of activity"[4] which it had adopted. They were strongly convinced that if they relied on the 'revolutionary forces' within the party they would never be able to build a revolutionary party. "We must", they said "lay our stress on the hundreds of thousands of young people outside the party".[5] Thus according to them, "those who think our main task is to attract the great majority of the members of the so-called marxist parties towards us and that a revolutionary party can be built up this way, are consciously or unconsciously thinking of forming only another party for fighting elections."[6]

The sharply contrasting backgrounds of which the two groups were products influenced their respective assessments of the revolutionary possibilities of the existing situation. The context of the Bengal group was provided by the terrorist tradition of Bengal, the growing self-activity of the working class in terms of its *gheraos*, *dharnas*, sit-in strikes, the miserable state of its industries, the enormous problems of the metropolitan city of Calcutta, the enthusiastic support to the maoists by students and unemployed youth of Calcutta, the hunger riots of 1966 and above all the experiences of Naxalbari. On the other hand, the Andhra maoist group was more of an outcome of an organisational crisis within the communist movement and it was situated in the relative socio-political calm of Andhra Pradesh. Concretely, the Bengal faction saw mass upsurge and a revolutionary situation all around. It was very optimistic about its prospects and was in a great hurry to utilise what it saw as a favourable situation. The Andhra faction on the other hand was much more cautious and felt that the people were not yet fully conscious of the necessity of revolution. They thus thought in terms of a long drawn out struggle and were unwilling to agree with the Bengal faction which felt that a "*single spark*" was enough to set off a *prairie fire*. In other words while the Bengal faction saw the situation as ripe for revolution and as only needing courageous and determined leadership, the Andhra maoists felt the need for educating the people and for carrying out revolution in a phased manner and at a much slower pace.

The Bengal faction based its philosophy basically on two conclusions which they arrived at on the basis of their experiences. The first was that, within the country a 'revolutionary mass upsurge' existed and the people were fully conscious and even prepared to take part in revolution immediately. The second, which they drew as a lesson from their Naxalbari experience, was that "militant struggles must be carried on not for land, crops, etc. but for seizure of state power".[7] Through these two observations the perspective of the Bengal group evolved into that of seizure of power through armed struggle. This perspective proved to be all pervading and was evident in all their views whether it be on organisation on strategy or on tactics.

The Bengal group held that the "sole criterion of whether a party is revolutionary or not is whether the party is directing armed struggle or not".[8] The party which was to be the chief instrument of the seizure of power, itself was viewed as being not only a revolutionary party but also the people's armed force as well as the people's State power.

In other words they equated the party and the peoples' army thus implying that there was no distinction between the tasks to be performed by either of them. According to Charu Majumdar "the primary condition for building up of a revolutionary party is to organise armed struggle in the country side"[9]. Thus the party was to be built not by recruitment of members, through propaganda and so on but by organising armed struggles in the countryside and converting the participants into a party. With this, armed struggle becomes a precondition for the existence of the party which would consist only of those who were termed as "revolutionaries in deeds" and others who had proven themselves in an armed struggle.[10] Participation in elections, propaganda, meetings, demonstrations, education of people through papers and pamphlets all were viewed as being totally unnecessary. People were to learn through participation and participation alone.[11] And since the willingness of the masses to participate in revolution was, to the faction, a foregone conclusion the question of convincing the people to participate was not even considered as worth debating. As a consequence even economic struggles which most other parties viewed as one method of concientising the masses were seen as being nothing more than calls for armed struggle and only those struggles were to be taken up which led to physical confrontation with the landlords as for instance seizure of crops and lands. Issues like raising of wages or reduction in rents found no place at all in the Bengal group's agenda.

The deep commitment of the Bengal group towards armed struggle, which is so evident in the foregoing description also influenced their views on the United Front. Like the party, the United Front was also viewed as something that "can be built up only in the course of an armed struggle led by a revolutionary party".[12] In other words the "United Front followed rather than preceded the armed struggle and United Front can be successfully built only by directing an armed struggle...the party that is not engaged in directing an armed struggle has no business to talk about a United Front"[13].

The United Front was to be based essentially on the peasants. As a consequence, even though the group in the traditional Marxist fashion called for a working class leadership the peasants were to be the main force of revolution for "the victory in the revolution depends on arousing and arming the peasant masses".[14] The party workers therefore "must be sent to the rural areas actively in organising the agrarian revolution. In this way the leadership of the proletariat over the agrarian revolution will be realised in an effective form".[15] No attention was to be paid to the demands of the working class themselves, for example, for higher wages and so on. To the students and intellectuals too the Bengal group gave the same advice—they were to go to the villages, integrate themselves with the peasants and participate in the armed struggle.[16]

Not surprisingly, the Bengal maoists ruled out the possibility of any kind of unity with existing political parties for "today all the political parties of India have turned into accomplices of U.S. imperialism...and become enemies of the revolution."[17]

The views that have been represented so far as that of Bengal group are basically those of Charu Majumdar who in no small measure dominated the maoists. But it was not as if these views were accepted by all the Bengal maoists without hesitation. In fact, one finds considerable evidence to support the contention that a difference of opinion did exist, in regard to issues like participation in elections, need for mass organisation and efficacy of trade unions.[18] For instance, the February 1968 issue of *Liberation*, the official organ of the Bengal maoists, carried a lead article which maintained that the communists would continue to participate in elections if allowed to. "We are not aware of any marxist in this country who claims that the role of bourgeois Parliamentarianism as a political weapon has outlived its usefulness".[19] Again Kanu Sanyal's Terai assessment unequivocally commended the role played by mass organisation in the Naxalbari struggle while, as late as in May 1968 the AICCCR unanimously approved a draft proposed by Satyanarayana Singh and Parimal Das Gupta which proposed participation in Trade Unions—even in those which were led by the Congress Party.[20]

The Bengal groups' or in other words Charu Majumdar's stand, on various issues hardened and a certain unanimity was achieved only subsequently towards the end of 1968. Even then, it appears, the unanimity was only superficial. As long as the movement was kept alive dissensions were muted but once the movement began falling apart at the seams one by one the Bengal maoists voiced their criticisms.

The Andhra group totally disagreed with the premises on which the Bengal faction evolved its perspective of immediate revolution. It accepted neither the Bengal faction, assessment of the people's level of preparedness for an armed struggle nor in their strategy of immediate seizure of power. On the other hand its own perspective was one of protracted war wherein the achievement of revolution was seen as the outcome of a long and arduous struggle. Thus while the group was at one with the Bengal maoists on the necessity of an armed struggle it differed considerably on the issue of the *modus operandi*. In their *Open Letter* they emphasised the fact that it was not their desire to call for an immediate armed struggle. In fact, considerable stress was to b laid on the process of party building and as far as possible mass organisations were to be encouraged. Ideological struggles, out of which a revolutionary party would emerge, occupied a very important place and was even viewed as a precondition to revolutionary struggles. To the Andhra group thus an armed struggle was in no way a pre-requisite for building up either the party or a movement. Again, though the Andhra group agreed that the party organisation was to be secret in nature, they did not concur with the Bengal groups' view that the party activities must be limited to armed struggles and illegal activities alone. In their view every form of activity potentially capable of raising the level of peoples consciousness and this included mass movement, activities of civil rights associations and trade unions, was to be harnessed.[21]

The group also felt that neither in regard to the issues involved nor in the stage of preparedness of the people to participate in an armed struggle was there any uniformity. Both these factors, they felt varied from region to region and had to be taken into account while devising an appropriate strategy. Under the circumstances they felt that issues on which, struggles should be conducted would depend on the level of people's consciousness and the nature of problems faced by them. During the initial stages struggles could be started on such issues as higher wages, distribution of waste land and even on exemption of taxes.[22] The form of struggle was not restricted by the Andhra group to armed struggle alone as the Bengal group did. Use of pamphlets, rallies, meetings, demonstrations, and so on all were recognised as legitimate party activities as long as they were conducted with a view to raising the people's consciousness.[23]

The Andhra group recognised the unevenness of the development of movement in different areas of the country and therefore prescribed different types of tactics for different types of areas. They categorised the areas into three types-a) areas where there was active struggle, b) areas in which party organisation existed but there was a general lull in the people's movement, and c) new areas.[24] In the areas of struggle the party felt that the main task was to consolidate their gains and to defend them from the attacks of police and landlords. For this purpose, it was thought necessary to mobilise masses, form volunteer squads and give a secret form to the party organisation. Solidarity campaigns were to be conducted in adjoining areas, so as to propagate revolutionary politics as well as to lighten the burden of police concentration in the struggle areas.

In the second type of areas where there was a party organisation but where no struggle had developed the first step to take was to hold meetings of party cadre and convince them of the necessity to organise people. Once the party cadre was prepared demands were to be formulated on various issues and extensive propaganda conducted about these among the people. Subsequently, the people were to be organised to struggle on the more pressing problems of their areas. Pamphlets were to be distributed and meetings held. In general if the landlords were prepared to concede the demands, a temporary compromise might then be arranged, but if the people were enthusiastic and prepared to struggle the movement could be taken to a higher pitch. As soon as people started a movement, volunteer squads, peoples defence squads, *village sanghams*, *ryotu sanghams* and so on were to be formed. These would be "embryonic forms" of the future governmental organisations. For the present they would be responsible not only for conducting peoples struggles and defending them, against repression but also for looking after the general welfare of the people.

In the third category of areas where there was neither an organisation nor a movement work was to begin by sending cadre from areas where the movement was strong.

The above elaborate exercise which the Andhra group conducted stands out in strong contrast to the one track method of armed struggle followed by the Bengal group. By making just one assumption, that the people were prepared to launch an immediate revolution the Bengal group rendered unnecessary the task of raising the level of people's consciousness. Again the fact that unlike the Andhra group they totally disregarded the "organisation" automatically simplified the task they set for themselves.

By mid 1968 matters reached a climax in West Bengal. In May that year the maoists formed the AICCCR, within the CPI(M) which was a first step towards the formation of a new party, which event ultimately took place in May 1969. At around the same time, viz. June 1968, the Andhra group, no doubt influenced by these events 'formed the APCCCR. This event occurred at a meeting in Vijayawada and already the differences between the Bengal group and Andhra group had reached such a pitch that several Andhra leaders including Panchadri Krishnamurthy, Vempatapu Satyanarayana, K.G. Satyamurthy and Kondapalli Seetharamaiah who supported the AICCCR stayed away from the meeting.

Because of the inherent differences in their approach to various issues the relationship between the APCCCR and the AICCCR was from the beginning antagonistic. The latter was highly critical of the APCCCR and in the June 1968 issue of *Liberation*, charged the APCCCR of not having clear conceptions about the nature of Soviet revisionism, and of vacillating in its commitment to about the path of armed revolution in India. It also maintained that the Andhra maoists were unnecessarily delaying their break with the CPI(M). It accused the Andhra maoists of having illusions about elections and the efficacy of Parliamentary a path.[25] Subsequently when the dissidents in the Andhra group formed the Naxalbari Solidarity Committee (NSC) the AICCCR had no hesitation in recognising it as its units in Andhra Pradesh the act which in effect amounted to setting up a maoist organisation as an alternative to, if not in direct opposition to the APCCCR. Further, harassment of the APCCCR followed when in October 196. the Srikakulam District Committee of maoists abandoned it and joined the AICCCR.[26]

All this while the APCCCR was calling for the unification of all maoist groups in the country and for extensive debates on various issues. They strongly contested the AICCCR's claim of being the top maoist organisation in the country. In as much as many groups from Kerala, Maharashtra, Tamil Nadu had not joined the AICCCR, it felt that the AICCCR was only a "self-proclaimed all India body". Despite these criticisms and in an effort to claim back those Andhra elements who were aligning themselves with the AICCCR, the APCCCR joined the AICCCR in November 1968. The high prestige of the Bengal group as well as the fear of losing its credentials as a revolutionary party no doubt weighed heavily on the minds of the leaders of the APCCCR. Whatever the reasons, the primary differences continued and in the end the unity proved ephemeral and was more organisational than programmatic.

As could only be expected the entrance of the APCCCR did not make much difference to the AICCCR. It continued with its old formulations and activities. The APCCCR was not even treated by it as a State Committee which had joined an all-India body. It was seen merely as a small faction which h.d joined a national organisation. The AICCCR continued to maintain direct links with Srikakulam District Committee and the Naxalbari Solidarity committee neither of which submitted to the organisational superiority of the State Committee. The APCCCR leaders, at least four of whom were erstwhile members of the CPI(M) Central Committee, were not given any position in the organisation's decision making bodies. They were not even taken into the editorial board of the party's magazines and the Andhra Committee's official paper *Janasakti* was not even mentioned in their list of revolutionary newspapers in India.[27]

The immediate issues on which the differences between the two groups crystallised included the assessment of the Srikakulam struggle, the issue of participation in election and T.N.'s stand on the attacks of police stations in Kerala. Ultimately when the brief honeymoon between the two groups came to an end the AICCCR resolution expelling the APCCCR cited differences of opinion on these three issues as the main cause for its action.

The AICCCR and the majority of the Srikakulam district committee regarded the Srikakulam struggle as a liberation struggle. This had two implications. The first was that it was the immediate aim of the struggle to seize political power. The confrontation thus was physical and direct between the people and the ruling class. It was simply a matter of the armed forces of the people destroying the armed forces of the ruling class. The second implication was that the liberation struggle had a priority over and in fact was an essential prerequisite to, the completion of the agrarian revolution and for the solution of the other problems of the people. In other words, it meant the acceptance of the line that the people's problems could not really be solved before they were liberated. For example land could not be redistributed or the people's standards of living raised until and after the successful completion of the liberation struggle. As long as the present State power existed any attempt at agrarian revolution would be meaningless. So the first task was to destroy this power and liberate the people.

The whole idea of liberation struggle was based on the assumption of people's preparedness for participation. The APCCCR which was sceptical about the level of people's preparedness, put forward the concept of an agrarian revolution which was intertwined with the struggle for liberation. In their view armed struggle for liberation could only be an end product of a series of struggles by the peasantry against feudal oppression. In this process the peasant was to learn of the need to sieze power through armed struggle. The people's movement could be taken to higher stages only by such acts as seizing landlords' crops and lands and cancelling all debts. To the peasant liberation meant freedom from the feudal system and satisfaction of his hunger for land. A liberation struggle which is not preceded by and combined with actions relating to these issues according to the APCCCR becomes abstract and unintelligible to the peasantry. The APCCCR therefore advocated an immediate struggle which would have as its first step, not total liberation but mobilisation of the people for the completion of the agrarian revolution. This mobilisation and the resultant struggles would ultimately lead to a liberation struggle. The only concession which the APCCCR was willing to make to the AICCCR's faction was to hold out the optimistic prediction, that because of the overall revolutionary situation this process would not take a long time and they could very soon lead a liberation struggle.[28]

These differences led naturally to a difference of views, on the conditions under which a guerilla struggle could be launched. In concrete terms this was a question about when exactly guerilla struggle could be started in the Srikakulam area. The APCCCR's viewpoint was that following the intensive police attacks in March 1967, the morale of the people of Srikakulam was destroyed and the movement was in a state of lull. It felt that the way to get out of this lull was to re-establish contacts with the people, conduct political propaganda and mobilise them to struggle for various demands. If there were attacks by the police during this period they were to be resisted by the people and militants with whatever weapons that were locally available. Thus the APCCCR stressed on people's mobilisation and defensive actions in the face of repression. On the other hand, the AICCCR group did not accept demoralisation of the people as a fact. They felt that the inaction of the people was the result of the absence of a proper leadership and organisation, which alone could give them confidence and show a means of defeating the enemy's forces. For this purpose they advocated the immediate starting of offensive struggles against landlords and police.[29]

Against the background of these ideological differences events occurred which ultimately led to the expulsion of the APCCCR. During November 1968, about 300 people led by Kunnikal Narayanan carried out attacks on the police stations of Tellichery and Pulpally in the Wynad forests in Kerala. Several conflicting reports about these incidents came out in the papers.[30] T.N. in a statement to the press described this incident as an act of *agent provocateurs* financed by the CIA and the Central Government of India. The first reaction from Charu Majumdar was a cryptic comment that attacking police stations was not in his programme.[31] However, when Radio Peking broadcast its support to the Kerala events Charu Majumdar changed his original and stand in December 1968 in an article *We salute the Peasant Revolutionaries of Kerala*, he commended "the heroism and courage displayed by the impoverished masses of Kerala" and maintained that every revolt against Government is just.[32] The differences of opinion on this incident continued to dog the APCCCR even after it was expelled and ultimately T.N. had to recant when APCCCR formulated its Immediate Programme in April 1969.

Participation in elections was another issue on which there were differences of opinion between the APCCCR and the AICCCR. In view of impending mid-term elections in Bengal in June 1968, the AICCCR passed a resolution which maintained that "Naxalbari has proved to be the burial ground of parliamentary path in India. The people of India so far wallowing in the mud of parliamentary path have now seen the light. They are now realising that the Naxalbari path is the only path for liberation... So down with elections...(and) total boycott of elections".[33] This was followed by attacks on candidates and polling booths in West Bengal. The APCCCR meanwhile was still maintaining that boycott or otherwise of elections was purely a tactical issue to be decided on merits (they were to be boycotted in areas where parallel people's institutions have been set up) depending on how useful it would be for mass mobilisation and for increasing people's consciousness.[34] But the AICCCR resolution maintained that "the question of participation in elections was not a question of tactics but that of the strategy i.e. whether to take a parliamentary path or a revolutionary path".[35] The APCCCR was hesitant about accepting this and postponed the issue by saying that it would have to discuss the whole issue before making a final decision. Around this time T.N. was still a member of the Andhra Pradesh Legislative Assembly and he received a directive from the AICCCR to resign following its resolution on elections. T.N. accepted but with the reservation that it would be a personal decision. On this issue too the APCCCR leadership was to succumb to the AICCCR line ultimately when they formulated the *Immediate Programme* in April 1969.

While the above three issues were cited by the AICCCR itself as the main reasons for expelling APCCCR a closer look reveals that on the whole the AICCCR had a lot to gain by the expulsion and would have gone ahead with it in any case. Given the basic differences of opinion on tactical issues, continued unity would be of use only to the Andhra Committee-by giving the latter the high prestige and credibility which AICCCR was enjoying at that time among the young maoist cadre. By expelling them, AICCCR would destroy their revolutionary credibility and pave way for the formation and strengthening of a maoist organisation in Andhra Pradesh which would sincerely implement the AICCCR's line. Thus expulsions were carried out without consulting even their followers in Srikakulam and other regions so much so that when Kolla Venkaiah (whose stand on ideological issues was between AICCCR's and APCCCR's) went to the AICCCR to mediate, he was not even given a hearing.

The expulsions paved the way for the crystallisation of the two maoist lines in different organisational frameworks. The AICCCR soon transformed itself into a party—the Communist Party of India-Marxist-Leninist CPI(ML) and determinedly went forward to implement its line based on the perspective of immediate revolution.[36] The Andhra Committee also came out with an explicit programme of its own and went on to build a movement on that basis.

Delivering the keynote address Kanu Sanyal (who was released from the jail by CPI(M)) said that for the first time in India a revolutionary party was being formed, and "I firmly believe that the great Indian people will warmly welcome this event, will realise that the formation of this party is an historic step forward for the Indian revolution, and will come forward to raise the struggle to a higher stage under the leadership of the party".[37] Several reasons have subsequently been given as to why the party was formed. According to Biblab Das Gupta "the kind of tactical line which was going to be followed from February 1969 onwards could not be implemented without a strong centralised leadership... A more important reason was the fact that the Chinese wanted such a party".[38] Sankar Ghosh is also of the opinion that the Chinese wishes had a role to play. Both of them depend on the somewhat flimsy evidence of Charu Majumdar's writings to the effect that the international leadership had been reminding them time and again of the importance of building the party. It would be incorrect to draw any conclusions from this. The reminders referred to were most probably nothing more than general exhortations of CPC to form revolutionary parties all over the world. It is more probable that because of their increased confidence due to the successes in Srikakulam at that time and the general feeling amongst them of the imminence of revolution the Bengal faction abandoned all efforts to reconcile the maoist groups in India and instead formed a centralised party.

The inaugural meeting of the CPI(ML) on May 1, 1969 passed a political resolution which gave their assessment of the national and international situation. This was later supplemented by the programme of the CPI(ML) which was adopted at the Party Congress in May 1970.

The news of the formation of the CPI(ML) was broadcast from Peking Radio and other signs of approval came by way of articles in the Chinese press.

However, this did not prevent many maoist groups from leaving or staying outside the newly formed CPI(ML). The Maharashtra unit of AICCCR refused to convert itself into the state unit of CPI(ML) and protested at "the opportunistic bureaucratic phrase mongering" and "adventurist" activities of the AICCCR.[39] The resolution blamed AICCCR for treating other maoists groups in an antagonistic manner and even giving calls to "annihilate" them.[40] In these circumstances "the Maharashtra State Committee of Communist Revolutionaries calls upon the Andhra Pradesh Committee which possess the necessary experience and resources to take upon the great responsibility for uniting all the revolutionary groups in the country into a revolutionary organisation".[41] In Kerala except for Kunnikal Narayanan, all the other groups for example those led by Kosala Ramdas, K.P.R. Gopalan etc, were in favour of the Andhra Committee. Even Kunnikal did not explicitly accept CPI(ML). The cadre in Punjab and Tamil Nadu split evenly between the Andhra Committee and the CPI(ML). Parimal Das Gupta formed a rival co-ordination committee at Bengal level and criticised CPI(ML) foı neglecting work in cities trade unions and other mass organisations. Asit Sen, another senior maoist leader who had presided over the May Day meeting of CPI(ML) when it was inaugurated, also left within a couple of weeks to form the Maoist Communist Centre. In his view the CPI(ML) had failed to recognise the importance of struggles based on economic demands. He felt that Naxalbari was the struggle of the peasants for land and it would be an over estimation of people's consciousness to regard it as a struggle for State power. He felt that the first task ahead of the maoists was to build a party, whose cadre would be predominantly drawn from the working class. Such a task could be carried out only in cities. Only after such a party was built should the guerilla struggles in the rural areas begin, otherwise the party would be dominated by the petty-bourgeois cadre and petty-bourgeois ideas and lead to all kinds of deviations.[42] Pramod Sen Gupta was another person to form a maoist group in West Bengal outside the CPI(ML).[43]

These desertions and criticisms did not have any effect on the line followed by CPI(ML). If anything, it made them more determined to carry it out immediately by unleashing Naxalbari type of struggles everywhere. The June 1969 issue of Liberation branded the Andhra Committee as "enemies of liberation" and the "last reserve of reaction". The relations were no longer to be non-antagonistic. This was followed by a couple of nrticles by Satyanarayana Singh[44] which denied the charges of Che'ism (of trying to start armed struggle with a handful of people and without mass participation) and counter accused the "chicken-hearted intellectuals" (referring to Asit Sen and Parimal Das Gupta) of trying to "divert the present armed struggle along the old lines of mass economic struggles.[45] Satyanarayan Singh also denied Asit Sen's contention that the revolutionary party must consist of a working class majority because the compulsions of a semi-colonial and semi-feudal society would necessarily lead to a poor and landless peasant majority in the revolutionary party. As against Asit Sen, Satyanarayana Singh maintained that "the revolutionary party was to be built in rural areas and in the process of armed peasant struggle. To think of building a party of workers in urban areas through theoretical education was crass revisionism"[46].

Charu Majumdar replied to the charges levelled against him and these replies more or less represented crystallisation of his stand. He denied the charges of following Che'ism and said that though there might be some superficial resemblances, they have really nothing in common. Che's guerilla theory he said depended on petty-bourgeois intelligentsia and technically sophisticated weaponry whereas, his own depended on peasant masses and people rather than arms.[47] In Charu's opinion the party becomes the only class organisation of the proletariat in a revolutionary situation. "So, when we say a revolutionary situation now prevails in India it necessarily follows that in India our task today is to build underground party organisations and not mass organisations."[48] Charu felt that a mass organisation represents a United Front of different ideologies and whether it would work in a revolutionary way or not would be determined entirely by the ability, of the party to work independently. This implied that if a mass organisation had to be built, it had to be done only after the party had made some progress in carrying out the armed struggle. He specifically rejected any kind of participation and utilisation of trade unions. He felt that the use of trade unions as a training school for the proletariat to increase and to teach them the tactics of struggle would be possible only when there was no revolutionary situation. According to him, "the politics of agrarian revolution must be brought to the proletariat from without, from outside trade union struggles".[49]

The CPI(ML) implemented its line of unleashing Naxalbari type of struggles in various areas in 1969 with varying degrees of success.[50] The line as it was implemented in early 1968 had extremely limited success, that too only in the areas of Srikakulam, Musahari, and Lakshmipur. Even in these areas the movement was ultimately suppressed by police forces. In those circumstances the choice before the CPI(ML) was either to abandon its basic assessment of the situation (as being favourable to immediate armed activities for capturing State power) or to make certain tactical innovations which might enable them to continue armed struggle. The CPI(ML) chose the latter alternative and as a result fell into a process which can be termed self-accelerating extremism, i.e. by persisting with their original assessment of the situation they had to shift from armed mass uprising of the Naxalbari; and early Srikakulam type to limited guerilla actions and then to individual annihilation and abandonment of peasant struggles and finally to terrorist activities.

We shall examine the working of this process in the State of Andhra Pradesh at Srikakulam in the next two chapters. The policy, tactics and programme and results of the APRCC's actions which were based on a different assessment of the situation will be examined in subsequent chapters.

NOTES & REFERENCES

1. The strength of these groups as against that of the parent CPI(M) varied from region to region. In Andhra Pradesh 10,000 of the 16,000 CPI(M) members sympathised with the Maoists, in Jammu and Kashmir 200 out of 800, in Punjab 100 out of 600, in Delhi 150 out of 400, in Bihar 300 out of 2,600, in Orissa 150 out of 800, in Maharashtra 150

out of 2,300, in Tamil Nadu 1,300 out of 8,500 and 5000 out of 16,300 in West Bengal. But subsequent events were to prove that the members by themselves were not verysignificant as the Bengal faction with a mere 500 out of 16,300 CPI(M) members developed into one of the most dominating groups. See *Spring Thunder and After*, Minerva Associates, Calcutta, 1975, p. 141.

2. *Ibid*, pp. 112-113.
3. A clear illustration of this analysis is the behaviour of Jammu and Kashmir and U.P. groups which in spite of being closer to the West Bengal group in most matters supported the Andhra group.
4. Charu Majumdar, "It is time to build a Revolutionary Party". *Liberation*, June 1968, p. 15.
5. Charu Majumdar, "The Indian Peoples' Democratic Revolution" *Liberation* June 1968, p. 15.
6. *Ibid*, p. 14.
7. Charu Majumdar, "One Year of Naxalbari Struggle" *Liberation*, June 1968, p. 27.
8. Charu Majumdar "Undertake the work of building a Revolutionary Party" *Liberation*, October 1968, p.27.
9. Charu Majumdar, "The Indian Peoples..." *op. cit.*
10. *Ibid.*
11. Charu Majumdar, "Develop Peasant Class Struggle through class Analysis, Investigation and Study", *Liberation*, November 1968, p. 17.
12. Charu Majumdar, "The United Front and Revolutionary Party", *Liberation*, June 1968, p. 6.
13. *Ibid.*
14. Charu Majumdar, "Undertake the work..." *op. cit.* p. 5.
15. *Ibid*, pp. 12-13.
16. *Ibid*

17. See Charu Majumdar "The United Front..." *op. cit.* and "The Indian People..." *op. cit.*

18. Satyanarayana Singh (S.N's) *Self Critical Report of CC of CPI(ML)* (1973) has maintained this stand.

19. Asit Sen, "The Revolutionary Situation—Has it matured", *Liberation*, February 1968, p. 20.

20. S.N. '*Self Critical... op. cit.* p. 8.

21. See "Party Letter No: 1" in *Vyavasaya Viplavamu—Mana Kartavyalu* APCC (Revolutionaries) Printed, April 1974.

22. July 23rd Resolution of APCCCR.

23. *Ibid.*

24. Party Letter No: 1, *op. cit.*

25. See Editorial in *Liberation*, June 1968.

26. *Srikakula Girijanodhyamaniki Sambandhinchina Konni Satyalu* APRCC (Type Script).

27. Which was published in *Liberation*, December 1968.

28. *Vyavasaya Viplavamu... etc. op. cit.* pp. 43-45.

29. *Ibid*, pp. 46-47.

30. For example, Ramji in *Frontier*, November 24, 1968 speculated that these might be the plots of Congress, CPI(M) etc. to discredit the maoists and disorganise them by finding a pretext to arrest them.

31. This comment might have been guided by the fact that Kunnikal Narayanan was refusing to align his group under AICCCR. See Document C-28, of Hyderabad Conspiracy Case.

32. "We Salute to the Revolutionaries of Kerala", *Liberation* December 1968.

33. "Revolution on Elections", *Liberation*, June 1968, p. 30.

34. See Document C-28, *op. cit.*

.35 *Self-critical Report, op. cit*, p. 8, and also see Charu Majumdar, "Boycott elections—International Significance of the slogan", *Liberation*, December 1968.

36. The 11 members were viz: Charu Majumdar, Kanu Sanyal, Sushital Roy Choudary, Saroj Dutta, and Souren Bose, from West Bengal, Panchadri and Choudary Tejeswara Rao from Andhra Pradesh, R.P. Saraf from Kashmir, S.K. Misra from Uttar Pradesh, Satyanarayan Singh from Bihar and Appu from Tamil Nadu.

37. Kanu Sanyal's "Address at the May Day Rally", *Liberation*, May 1969, p. 119.

38. Biblab Das Gupta, *op. cit.* p. 32.

39. *Resolution on the Differences with the AICCCR*, Maharashtra State Co-ordination Committee, May 1, 1969.

40. *Ibid.*

41. *Ibid.*

42. See Asit Sen, "Another Dangerous Line" and also his "Turning the Revolutionary Situation" in John Gerassi (ed.) *Towards Revolution* Vol. 1, Weidenfield and Nicholson, London, 1971.

43. All these groups were more in favour of the Andhra Committee and later in 1970 some organisational link was established and a newspaper called *The Proletarian Path* was published jointly.

44. See Satyanarayan Singh, "Agrarian Revolution and Crisis of the Ruling Class"' *Liberation*, September 1969, and "Building up the Revolutionary Party", *Liberation*, November 1969.

45. "Agrarian Revolution... etc." *op. cit.*

46. "Building... etc.", *op. cit.* p. 53.

47. Charu Majumdar "Our some Current Political and Organisational Problems" (1973).

48. *Ibid*

49. *Ibid.*
50. The Union Minister of State for Home Affairs, V.C. Shukla in a statement to Rajya Sabha on Novembeı 26, 1969, showed the following areas as centres of maoist activity, viz. Srikakulam, Visakhapatnam, Krishna, Guntur, Warangal, and Nalgonda in Andhra Pradesh; Gopalpada, Kamrup, Darrang, Nagaon, Sibsagar, Lakhimpur and Cachar in Assam; Muzzafarpur, Darbhanga, Champaran, Monghyr, Bhagalpur, Purnea, Saharsa, Ranchi and Singhbhum in Bihar; Darjeeling, 24 Parganas, Jalpaiguri, Hooghly, Burdwan, Midnapore, Birbhum, and Calcutta in West Bengal and Koraput and Ganjam in Orissa.

CHAPTER 4

Srikakulam-I

Srikakulam-I

More than any other maoist movement it was the one at Srikakulam which caught the imagination of the people everywhere. In intensity and in effect it far exceeded any other movement and because of this to many, even today the movement represents all that the Andhra maoists stand for. Like in any movement the initial rumblings came long before the final storm. In this chapter we shall first trace the beginnings of the movement and then go on to describe the events which led to the leaders abandoning their strategy in favour of a maoist alternative. The chapter itself is in two parts. In the first, the background of the worsening economic condition of the tribal is highlighted while in the second the initial efforts of the Srikakulam leaders to improve the situation is described. In the next chapter we deal with the maoist phase of the Srikakulam movement.

I

THE TRIBAL'S EXISTENCE

The Government Census in 1961 described Srikakulam district as one "shaped like a revolver with the "butt" situated in the South-West and the "muzzle" lying in the north-east direction".[1] The district may be divided into two broad geographical regions. The hilly agency area in the north-western part of the district, comprising parts of Parvatipuram, Palakonda and Salur Taluqs, along with the non agency portions of Pathapatnam, Tekkali and Sompeta taluqs forms one distinct part while the other comprises the plains portions which is mostly sandy on account of its proximity to the sea and includes the taluqs of Ichchapuram, Narasannapet, Srikakulam, Cheepurapalle and portions of Tekkali and Sompeta taluqs. The Eastern Ghats run roughly parallel to the sea from the north-east to the south-west and therefore this district drains from the Ghats to the sea.

The forest area of the district is 16 per cent of the total land area. Valuable timber forests are restricted to the Kurupam and Seethampeta agencies. The scheduled tribes in this district live mostly in the agency areas of Salur, Parvathipuram and Palakonda Taluqs, and their proportion to the total population of the district works out to 8.21 per cent as against the State average of 3.68 per cent.[2]

The tribal life in this area before the British intervention was characterised by two basic features, one was primitiveness and the other inconsistency of occupation. Because of this even the primary needs of food, clothing and shelter were hard to come by for the tribal. At the same time there was very little settled cultivation of land. Shifting cultivation was the usual practice and while resorting to this method which in itself was very wasteful the agricultural implements used were extremely primitive. Neither ploughs nor even crowbars were used and the seeds themselves were simply broadcast. Often, such shifting cultivation did not give yields commensurate with the effort put in but the tribal continued to adopt this method because it forms "a part of his cultural milieu in which he is brought up".[3] In fact in Bhadragiri tribal block which covers the Parvathipuram agency area as much as 47.16% of the total cultivated area was used for shifting cultivation.[4] The land in the tribal areas belonged to the village community as a whole. Though the cultivator enjoyed the produce of the land, which he cultivated, he enjoyed no absolute ownership of that land. In fact, he ceased to be the owner once he stopped making effective use of it. Once this happened any one else belonging to the same community could take up cultivation on the same plot. If the tribal had planted a tree in the land, his right over the tree and its yield continued[5]. Permanent hereditary ownership of land was enjoyed only by those tribals who practiced settled cultivation, and who had therefore put in a great amount of labour and effort. But even in such an activity the other tribals would give a helping hand[6] and thus settled cultivation too, became a corporate activity.[7]

Apart from indulging in shifting cultivation, the tribal also took up hunting, fishing and collection minor forest produce depending on the season. But no one activity occupied him full time and he kept shifting from one occupation to another.

The water sources if anything were worse than that of food. For most part the tribal had to depend on rivers and streams which had dirty flood waters during the rainy season and stagnant pools in the hot months of summer. Neither source was particularly safe and the tribal as a consequence became victim to all sorts of diseases whose effects were greatly magnified by the absence of even the most rudimentary health facilities.[8]

Perhaps the only constant feature of the tribal way of life was liquor. Not only was drinking the only form of recreation the tribal had access to, but for four months in a year he practically lived on it. Apart from this it formed an integral part of each one of the large number of festivals which he used to perform to propitiate various gods.

Social relationships among the tribals were by and large based on the principles of reciprocity. Although a certain hierarchy did exist, the *Jatapus* for instance considered themselves superior to *Savaras*, often, especially during festivals the tribals forgot all their social distinctions and functioned as a single unit.[9] As already mentioned such occasions were many. There was a festival for hunting, one just before ploughing, one for general welfare and a host of others including one even for laying new thatch to huts. The tribals on their part took these festivals very seriously. For instance, during the hunting festival no man ever returned home without game for fear of being jeered at and there were times when he took as much as a month to do this. This type of extravagance was very much a part of the tribal culture. During the *Agam* festival a tribal invariably sacrificed a he-buffalo as a mark of respect to his dead ancestors whether or not he could afford it. Again even when the tribals went to their medicine man or *Ejjodu* for treatment of an ailment they had to conduct a sacrifice and organise a feast. One very typical tribal ceremony was one relating to solemnisation of a bond of friendship. This took the form of oath taking or *nestam kattuta* in which each participant swore to sacrifice anything for the other. In fact, in later years when plainsmen moved into the areas they took full advantage of this process to enter into agreements with the tribal. While on the one hand these agreements had no legal validity and hence did not bind the plainsmen, the tribal viewed it with much greater seriousness and to him it was as valid an agreement as one drawn on stamped paper.[10]

On the whole tribals' life was imbued with an element of casualness. They did not have a settled occupation and for a large part lived a day-to-day existence. Production of surplus, savings, planning for the future—all these found no place in his list of priorities If possible he raised a crop, if not he depended on minor forest produce and liquor, and, if even that was not available he simply went hungry. In spite of all this it never occurred to him to try and alter the situation, even after his already unenviable conditions of living deteriorated alarmingly once the plainsmen intruded into his area.

External Intervention

The first set of policies which had any impact in the tribal area was made by the British. Extending their policy of consolidation and maximisation of land and forest revenue to this area also the British introduced the system of permanent settlement in this area. After a survey in Srikakulam and Palakonda taluks settlement rates were introduced in 1890. The district continued to have permanently settled estates until they were abolished by the abolition act of 1948 by the Indian Government.[11] The system suffered from all the defects of a permanent settlement. The British wanted an assured revenue over a long period of time and therefore fixed very high rates of assessment initially. The leading landlords in the area or zamindars, were to collect and make over this assessed amount to the government.[12] In the process a class of territorial landlords was created whose sole purpose was to protect the income of the government. As the initial assessment itself was high, the zamindars found it difficult to extract this amount from the ryots.[13] To solve this problem they auctioned the right to collect the rents to others. The successful bidder, who subsequently came to be known as the *mustajar* or *muttadhar* was to make over the bid amount to the estate holder periodically and in return was given the right to collect whatever he could from the ryots. This was the sum and substance of the *mustajar's* responsibility. There was nothing binding on him in regard to the maximum amount to be collected from the tribals. That was left to him to decide and depended on his capacity for extraction.[14] This resulted in rack renting and oppression of the cultivatiors who had to bear the brunt of the revenue payment.

In course of time the *mustajar* became all powerful and could even decide who would cultivate which piece of land. Since he gave no receipts the tribal never had any proof that he had paid his rent. The *muttadhar* therefore had full control over him and often evicted him for alleged non-payment and either assigned the land to someone else or kept it for himself. The tribals were far too simple to understand the intricacies of the situation. After a while the best lands began to get alienated from them either to the *muttadhar* himself or to one of the many plainsmen who began operating in the area.[15] To prevent this the British Government passed the Agency Act of 1917 which prohibited sale of land to non-tribals but this Act was easily bypassed by backdating sale deeds Faced with a bewildering array of situations he had never encountered earlier, the tribal found himself unequal to the task and slowly slipped deeper and deeper into the clutches of the unscrupulous plainsmen.

Adjustment of sale deeds and land records was rendered easier by the fact that the village level revenue officials, the *karnams* were invariably plainsmen. In fact next to the *muttadhar* it was the *karnam* who played havoc with the tribals, right to cultivate. The tribals' right to ownership of a particular piece of land had always been based on custom, social sanction and practice rather than on any *pattas* issued by the government. But since such rights were no longer recognised and since it was the *karnam* who had the final say in regard to village land records, the tribals had to first settle issues with him. Each village had its own way of appeasing the *karnam*. His daily needs were supplied free, feasts were arranged whenever he visited and in some places there was even a tradition that all male goats should be presented to him.

The *karnam* was not the only government official with whom the tribals came in contact. Along with their revenue policy the British also pronounced an excise and forest policy aimed at further buttressing government income. These brought in their wake the *abkari* and the forest officials, whose job it was to collect various taxes from the tribals and who more often than not extracted far more from the tribal than stipulated by the government. In any case, even when the collection was as per rules, the tribal found that he had to pay taxes for indulging in activities which he had always indulged in freely. For procuring liquor he had to pay the *abkari* official and for exercising his traditional right to minor forest produce collection he had to pay the forest officials.[16] *Mamuls* were collected for permitting the tribal to cut 'dabba' grass used for thatching the roof of huts, for felling trees for fuel and for permitting him to graze his sheep and cattle, and also for shifting cultivation. Thus in every sense their activity was restricted. In another sense too the forest became prohibited territory for the tribal. Large areas were marked off as reserved forest and no longer were the tribals allowed to operate in these areas. These were let out to forest contractors who paid the government for acquiring rights to fell trees for wood. The tribals could not even take advantage of the fact that they could work as labourers under the contractors because they were not accustomed to doing hard labour and working for prolonged periods. Even when employed they were always paid low wages because they kept absenting themselves due to a number of religious and social obligations.[18]

Growing Exploitation

One basic feature of the incursion of the British administrative system into the area was the monetisation of the tribal economy. Money had hitherto never played a major role in the economy of the tribal life style. By and large they indulged in barter as a means of trade and money was rarely, if at all used. But once the system of taxation in all spheres of activity was introduced by the British the tribals some Low had to procure money for these payments. At such a time the merchants cum moneylenders who came from the plains areas appeared as godsend to them. There were two types of merchants who came to the agency area in Srikakulam- (1) the liquor merchants (2) the merchants selling daily necessities like salt, kerosene, beedi leaves and so on. In return the tribal gave them tamarind, and other minor forest produce like roots, honey and even food grains. The non-tribals fully exploited the tribals by making unequal exchanges. The tribals on their part were totally unaware of this. They freely exchanged forest produce which was easily available to them for meagre amounts of the daily necessities supplied by the merchants. Unequal trade was only one part of the story. Apart from being unscrupulous traders, these merchants were also ruthless moneylenders. They took full advantage of the poor liquidity position of the tribals who now had to pay numerous taxes in cash, and lent money at exorbitant rates of interest.

The most notorious of these merchants especially in the Parvathipuram and Palakonda agency areas belonged to the Sondi caste, "a wily class who know exactly how to take advantage of the sin which doth so easily beset the hill man and to wheedle from him in exchange for the strong drink which he cannot do without, his ready money, his little possessions, his crops and finally his land itself".[19] On the whole the main target of these merchants was the land owned by the tribal. The high rates of interest of upto 100% compound very often left the borrower in a situation where he could just not clear the loan in any other fashion but give up his land to the moneylender and work as his *goti* or bonded labourer in which position he received a mere subsistence allowance or *batta*. Such a situation prevailed when the tribal was unable to pay taxes to the *zamindars* or *muttadhar* or any of the government officers.[20]

The situation was further exacerbated by the fact that inspite of the critical situation he was in, the tribal did not cut down on even what one would consider 'wasteful' expenditure and unnecessary extravagance. He continued to have his feasts, his festivals and his liquor. With most of his limited income and property already committed to various people he was once again forced to rely on the money-lender to fulfil his social obligations. Just how exploitative money lending was, is illustrated by the mechanics of a short term loan called *Khandagutha*. The *Khandagutha* was the short term loan given to the tribals during lean months just before harvests on the condition that the next crop from a particular plot belonging to the tribal debtor would be given to the money-lender in lieu of the loan. On the other hand it was obligatory on the part of the tribal debtor to look after the crop as "sold" till the crop was harvested and to hand over the entire harvested crop to the money-lender. The value of loan advanced under this system depended upon the extent and fertility of his field, the value of crop and also the crop prospects.[21] The loan thus advanced was usually a quarter of the total value of the crop at the time of harvest. It meant that three quarters of the crop was collected as interest. In case of a crop failure, the entire value of the expected crop was treated as the principal and along with this the next crop from a plot which was usually double the extent of the previous plot was to be given to the creditors.[22]

As a consequence, the economic penetration from outside resulted in eighty per cent of the tribal families having to put up with scarcities for lengthy periods. The old resources of their livelihood dried up due to innumerable restrictions on the use of forests and forest produce. As a result they had no other alternative but to depend on the money-lender, who charged usurious rates of interests, converting the tribal into a forced labourer and alienating his land.

Government Programme after Independence

The immediate post-independence period saw the Indian

Government merely continuing with the policies of the British. It was only in the 1960s that efforts were made to alter the situation by starting a few forest based industries like sheekai grinding plants, honey pasteurisation units, myrobalan crushing units and so on. They were however all run by non-tribals and the tribals at best, worked as labourers. Being small, these industries could not absorb many workers. At the same time traditional tribal crafts were on the decline due to "the lack of raw material, the restrictions of forest laws, the decline in the demand for some of their fine cane and bamboo works in certain nearby urban centres..., lack of patronage and encouragement to market the tribal arts and crafts"[23]. The industrial sector could not provide much relief to the tribals. All the same the government continued to provide incentives to this sector by way of enhancing infrastructural facilities. Roads were built and a beginning was made in developing support systems like transport and communications. In the end, however, it was the non-tribal who benefited. He made full use of these facilities unlike the tribal who was handicapped by his low standard of living, lack of capacity to invest and above all by his traditional outlook of planning only for the immediate future.[24]

The government programmes of afforestation too met with the same fate. The purpose was to provide large areas of deforested land with adequate tree cover to prevent erosion and at the same time to secure for the tribal means for generating income. To this effect an effort was made to promote teak plantation and those of cashew and coffee. But here again the tribal was hampered by certain inherent inadequacies and could not benefit from the programme. In fact, very few of the 25,000 coffee seedlings supplied in 1966-67 were made use of by the tribals.[25]

Attempts at improving the methods of cultivation too made little progress. Poor planning and inadequate supervision reduced many of the irrigation schemes to mere schemes on paper. Even where the schemes were actually put in operation the tribals did not benefit. Projects designed to generate tribal *ayacut* often benefited the non-tribals more because most of the tribal lands had already been alienated. As we shall see later the land records which were the basis for determining that the ryots benefiting from the scheme were tribals did not reflect the true position. All too often they indicated tribals as *pattadars* when in fact it was the non-tribal who was cultivating the land. Thus according to one area study "one irrigation dam constructed during multi-purpose project period fell under disrepair and thus rendered unserviceable. Another anicut was constructed across the hill stream Dongajole during the year 1963-64 under which an area of forty-eight acres was brought under irrigation. Out of forty-eight acres, thirty acres are owned by the *muttadhar* himself. But he is neither cultivating the land nor does he lease it out to anybody."[26]

Shifting cultivation was identified as one of the major causes of erosion and along with soil conservation schemes like bunding,terracing and so on considerable effort was put in to dissuade the tribals from resorting to this form of cultivation. But inspite of this the tribals continued with it mainly because "it requires minimum investment of capital and can be undertaken with simple primitive imlpements which are within his reach .. In the absence of much fertile land in and around his habitat, *podu* patch is the only alternative in which he can grow the much needed food grains".[27]

A second line of attack which the government pursued was to enact welfare legislations. A large number of acts was passed and these included, (1) The A.P. (S.A.) Land Transfer Regulation I of 1959, The A.P. (A.P.S.A.) Money lenders Regulation, 1960, (3) The A.P. Scheduled tribes Debt Relief Regulation, 1970, (4) The A.P. Regulation for the abolition of muttadhari and malguzari (of 1971). The most progressive of these acts was the A.P. (S.A.) Land Transfer Regulation, 1970 in which it was stated that it would be presumed that, any immovable property situated in the Agency area and in possession of a non-tribal had been acquired only by a transfer from a tribal. But this too was hemmed in by certain exceptions. The same Act allowed grant of *Ryotwari patta* to both tribals and non-tribals who were eligible for such a *patta* under the provisions of the A.P.

Estates Abolition (Conversion in Ryotwari) Act, 1948, and who had been in continuous occupation of such lands from the notified date.[28] Thus many holdings which had been registered in favour of non-tribals prior to the notified date fell outside the purview of this Act. Similarly there was the contrasting problem of lands which were nominally with the tribals but which in actual fact were being cultivated by non-tribals. In the Parvathipuram Agency area for instance, out of a total extent of 17,890 hectares of cultivable land as many as 11,480 hectares were shown by the records as being under tribals. If one were to eliminate cultivable government land only 2800 hectares are found to be under non-tribals which meant that only an extent of 2800 hectares had been alienated from the tribal and was capable of being restored to them. This clearly could not be the true position and even government sources agreed that "most of the land supposed to be under the tribals in law, is in actual practice under the occupation of the non-tribals".[29]

Implementation of these acts carried with it another complication. Their progress could be challenged at almost every step in any court of law. In fact, the 1970 Act was fiercely contested by the non-tribals and the High Court even struck it down initially until a belated appeal, by the government restored it to its original position. However, this was only the beginning. The non-tribals being comparatively less inclined to avoid litigation proceeded to obtain stay orders from the High Court each time they faced eviction. The tribals on the other hand were completely ignorant of the legal processes involved and were unable to contest the claims of the non-tribals effectively. Thus a large number of cases came to be covered by stay orders and even the government was forced to admit "...the progress is slow because the affected non-tribals are trying to perpetuate the possession of lands by filling innumerable writ petitions from time to time and obtaining stay orders from the high court... (and) unless they are all won by the government, it would not be possible to enforce this regulation on effective lines".[30] Even if the stay was subsequently vacated the non-tribals went to court again in his wife's name or some other relative's name, claiming an interest in the land and this case had to be entertained by the Court because clear patta rights did not exist in anyone's name in most cases.[31] Improper land records also contributed to the problems. Lands registered as being under a tribal was often actually being cultivated by non-tribals. Thus while the tribal was nominally the owner it was the non-tribal who came to enjoy all the benefits. Again there are a number of cases wherein land is purchased by a non-tribal using the name of one of his tribal servants. In some cases the non-tribal even married a tribal to acquire land. The marriage was only a formality for the woman was reduced to the status of a labourer.

In 1960 the A.P. Government passed the Money Lender Regulation Act to regulate money-lending activities in Scheduled areas. According to this Act all unauthorised and unlicensed money lenders operating in these areas were to be dealt with severely. However, the framers of Act did not seem to have realised the magnitude of the actual problem. Identifying money lenders was not a simple task and even after considerable effort the government was able to identify a ridiculously low number of 16 unregistered money lenders in the entire Srikakulam district.[32] A decade later in 1970 the Andhra Pradesh Scheduled Tribe Debt Relief Regulation was passed which scaled down the "debts incurred by a member of Scheduled Tribe living in Scheduled Area to the amount of the principal as originally advanced and stipulates that no interest need be paid by the Scheduled Tribe borrower irrespective of the fact whether the debt is incurred inside or outside the Scheduled area".[33]

All these regulations had no meaning, however, as long as the tribal continued to go to the private money lenders. According to one study "inspite of multiplicity of government institutions such as the Co-operative Credit Society, Girijan Co-operative Corporation, Tribal Development Block, Taluk Office etc. only 12 per cent of the indebted families borrowed from government sources indicating the poor performance of the government agencies in relieving the tribals from the hold of a private money lender".[34] The study goes on to report that "usual hurdles in having credit transactions with the government agencies are a lack of patta-rights, official red-tapism, complicated official formalities of filling up a number of forms and general apathy of the tribal to approach the government officers in view of the prevailing stereotype of any government functionaries which is based on their bitter experience with the previous revenue, police and forest officials".[35] Further the money lender was a more flexible agency in one sense. He lent and collected not only in cash but also in kind which contrasted sharply with the governmental agencies' tendency to deal in cash only. Again consumption loans, for fulfilling social obligations were not entertained by the government agencies and whenever such need arose the tribal had no other option but to go to the local moneylender. Thus despite the fact that the interest rate for institutional credit was a mere 6½ per cent the money lender's operations continued to flourish and most tribals even viewed him as being totally indispensable. All this made it very difficult for the government to proceed against the money lenders. Very often the tribals "do not come forward declaring the debt owingto the fact that the non-tribal may not advance loans at times of need".[36] In fact, of the three hundred and eighty cases involving a sum of Rs. 20,556/- detected in 1964-1965 as many as three hundred and forty one cases involing Rs. 17,758/- were withdrawn. Owing to the fact that "there was a collusion between the creditor and the debtor who deposed before the Court that the debt was discharged".[37]

To break the hold of the money lenders the Government also formed the Girijan Co-operative Corporation (G.C.C.). Meant exclusively for the tribals this corporation had three main functions: (a) purchase of farm and non-farm produce of the tribals at fair prices; (b) supply of domestic requirements to the tribals at fair price and (c) supply of credit for agricultural development. It was also equipped with complete monopoly rights for procuring minor produce from the tribals. Despite its obviously laudable intention the G.C.C. was not an unqualified success. The tribal produced very little surplus. He was thus unable to benefit by the G.C.C.'s operations with regard to purchase of commodities. Again, lack of proper supervision and guidance resulted in the G.C.C. depots running short of the daily requirements of the tribals like salt, kerosene and food grains. Instead, items like soaps and cosmetics for which the tribals had no use whatsoever were more abundantly available. The small merchant as a consequence continued to be the main supplier of essential goods. Finally, the difficulties which the tribal had to face in taking advantage of the credit facilities, a theme which has already been dealt with, saw to it that even in this sector the G.C.C. was not as useful as it was expected to be. Even in regard to purchase of minor forest produce over which it claimed monopoly rights, the G.C.C. was not very successful. Because of the larger overheads and operation costs the corporation could not pay as much for the minor forest produce as did the private traders. Further, the private trader went to the tribal directly saving him the effort of having to go to the depot.

Corruption of the G.C.C. employees further reduced the corporation's utility and credibility. Many depot managers are reported to have made huge amounts of money while cheating the tribals by using false weights and issuing false receipts for loans granted.[38]

Besides starting the G.C.C. the government created special multipurpose tribal blocks (later on renamed Tribal Development Block) to lay emphasis on development of communications, agriculture, co-operatives and land colonisation and education in the tribal areas. To this effect the entire scheduled area in Andhra Pradesh was grouped into twenty four tribal Development Blocks. To make them financially self-sufficient each Tribal Development Block had two types of revenue. Firstly, it had an independent source of revenue raised by way of levy of surcharge, fees, fines and forfeitures, taking up projects for remunerative enterprises like market plantations, and also income from poultry and endowments. Secondly it had a share of land cess, local cess, duty on transfer of property, ferries rent, fishery rents, lapsed deposits, and Inspite of this, the rent from staff quarters. Tribal Development Blocks ran short of finances. Lack of commitment on the part of the Tribal Development Block staff spelt its doom. In the absence of sufficient incentives employees like Village Level Workers who had to cover thirty to forty square miles in a Tribal Development Block with no means of transport often considered their stay as a punishment and kept trying to get themselves transferred to the plains areas.[39] The post of extension staff was thus generally kept vacant for want of candidates.[40] Inadequate supervision and lack of an integrated approach on the other hand resulted in the stoppage of a number of schemes half way. Land colonisation schemes for instance suffered heavily because the associated irrigation works were not completed. "The Kambagadda anicut was completed... as late as June 1966. long after the Kuddapalli colonisation scheme was established. At Jatapukottapadu colonies of the Bhadragiri agency in Srikakulam district, the lands have not yet been cultivated although land-allotments have been made nearly five years ago".[41] At the same time the animal husbandry programme which was a part of the land colonisation scheme also suffered because in the absence of irrigation during the lean months the tribal who found it difficult to maintain even his family had absolutely no way of feeding the animal given to him. In many cases the tribal sold away the pair of bullocks (taken on loan from the Corporation) out of sheer frustration at a very low price unmindful of his obligation to the loaning agency and with the sale was able to maintain his family for some time.[42] Notwithstanding all this land colonisation schemes could not have resettled all the tribals, considering the fact that as many as 43,000 families were engaged in shifting cultivation. In the words of one report "At the rate of two and a half acres per family it requires at least one lakh acres of land to settle all the families engaged in shifting cultivation on settled cultivation. But the land available in tribal areas is very limited and it is already overburdened with the ever increasing concentration of tribal population. So it is not possible to implement land colonisation schemes on a large scale as the available plains land is too meagre to accommodate all the tribals engaged in *podu* or shifting cultivation".[43]

The welfare measures adopted by the government thus clearly had certain inherent limitations. In the normal course.

if the beneficiaries had been highly motivated, these defects would perhaps not have mattered much. But the tribals were far from being motivated. The schemes were new, the methods alien and above all, the people who were supposed to alter their conditions of living were predominantly non-tribals who could at best get second hand knowledge of the tribal's problems. Unless there was perfect liason between the tribals and the framers of tribal policies no drastic change in the standard of the tribal's living could be expected. This liason was totally lacking. Their representatives in the Legislative Assembly were men like Satrucherla Prataparudhra Raju (Naguru, reserved constituency), Vyricherla Chandra Chaudamani Deo (Parvathipuram) and Sree Rajah Lakshmi Narasimha Sanyasi Raju (Salur),[44] all of whom hailed from princely families and had not the remotest of connections with tribal problems. In fact the Raja of Kurupam a leading Congressman of the area once frankly stated "who will go into the deep interior? We are not so unselfish".[45] The introduction of the three tier Panchayati Raj system had hardly any effect on the situation. If anything it worsened matters because it infringed on the areas of functioning of the traditional tribal councils. Reservation of the posts of Sarpanch, President and Vice-President too did not serve much purpose as the local non-tribals always managed to have one of their henchmen elected so that they could themselves run the whole system if not directly, at least by proxy.[46]

It was thus a truly desperate situation for the tribal. While on the one hand there was nothing he could do to prevent the non-tribals from disturbing his traditional way of life, on the other he was equally helpless when it came to utilising the new system to his advantage. As a consequence welfare legislations, and developmental programmes held little meaning for him. For one reason or the other the money-lender and the private trader continued to rule his life which if anything changed from bad to worse as the years progressed. It was clearly a situation which was receptive to other types of solutions.

II
INITIAL EFFORTS

The Setting Up of Sanghams

The political movement in the agency area was initiated by Palle Ramulu better known as the Kuddapalli Master. He was a teacher who had been posted to the school at Manda in the Palakonda agency area, an area where the revenue officials were particularly oppressive and extracted taxes far in excess of what was legally due. Ramulu mobilised the people on this issue and succeeded in submitting several petitions to the higher revenue officers against the local officials. Encouraged by the response of the tribals he went one step ahead and started organising *sanghams* for taking up collective struggles. In 1957-58 he led the first agitation against the forest contractors and demanded higher wages for the tribal workers. As a consequence the influential forest contractors whose interests were being harmed by his activities got him transferred to the Mondemkhal area[47]. It was here that he met Vempatapu Satyanarayana an elementary school teacher aged about 35 years, and started organising *sanghams* in a systematic way, over a wide area. The general purpose of the *sanghams* was to unite the tribals to conduct struggles for the improvement of the quality of their lives. This task was however rendered difficult by the fact that the tribals' level of political consciousness was very low. They were extremely scared of the landlords, contractors and other oppressors and were not very enthusiastic about incurring their wrath especially at the instance of non-tribals of whom they were particularly suspicious. In this situation both Ramulu and Vempatapu realised that their first task was to dispel the tribals' in built fears and to do this they felt that it must be made clear to the tribals as to who exactly was responsible for their condition. The method adopted by them consisted of organising a mobile cultural troupe which wentfrom village to village giving performances highlighting the woes of the tribals and the need to rise and rebel against those responsible for them.[48] Through these activities several young tribals were recruited into the *sanghams* who were later to play an important role in the Srikakulam movement. They included Pyla Bheemudu, Kurangi Vasunarayana and Arika Somulu.

To begin with the general response of the tribals was ambivalent. This was more so in the case of the older tribals who were still to overcome their fears. In order to allay these fears and expose the vulnerability of the landlords the leaders indulged in open physical confrontation with them.[49] Such incidents had an immense psychological effect on the tribals. The image-building process of Vempatapu as an invincible and even immortal leader was derived from such incidents. Many myths were subsequently built around Vempatapu's personality.[50]

Since the tribals in general were meek, submissive and passive, the *sangham* leaders felt that it was essential to instil a sense of self-respect, dignity and self-identity among tribals. To this end they started going around villages asking tribal women to cover their hitherto half-naked bodies and exhorting men to have short and neatly kept hair. Initially resistance was abundant. The women who for generations had not been wearing anything more than the scantiest of apparel felt irritated at having to wear clothes. Often the alarm would go out even as a *sangham* worker approached the village and all the women would disappear to dress and once he left they would discard the dress and put on their original clothes. Over a period of time however, habits changed and dressing, combing and other habits became a way of life. The men too showed reluctance to having their hair cut and the *sangham* workers went around the villages carrying big scissors in their bags and promptly cut off the hair of any tribal they could catch.[51]

The purpose of the entire operation was to remove to the extent possible the unnecessary inequality brought about by difference in dress and other personal habits between the tribals and the plainsmen[52] and also to demonstrate to the tribals that they were in no way physically different from the others.

Vigorous efforts were also made to promote tribal literacy. Night schools were held in many village centres by the *sangham* workers. Besides giving basic education they taught the tribals their political rights and made them aware of their duties. Superstitions and unscientific beliefs were systematically debunked.[53] Gradually the *sangham* spread its activities to all spheres of the tribal life and so persistent were the workers in their efforts that the tribals began to feel that they had a hand in everything including the distribution of PL 480 wheat which was being given at that time.[54]

The *sangham* organisers also worked as 'barefoot doctors' in these areas. By practicing modern methods of dealing with diseases they were able to achieve two objectives. The patient stood a much better chance of being cured and at the same time the costly ritual advocated by the local medicine man *ejjodu* was avoided. The normal method of the *ejjodu* was to call for a feast, and then having fed himself 'cured' his patient by beating the devil out of him. This procedure more often than not resulted only in raising the level of the tribals' indebtedness. The *sanghams* also waged a battle against excessive spending on festive occasions especially during the *Agam* festival when tribals already deep in debt borrowed money from various sources and conducted sacrifices, and made offerings to their ancestors. Even in areas where they were strong it took the *sangham* nearly four years to put an end to this practice.

Of all the *sangham* activities the most effective was the institution of people's courts. It was decreed that all the members of the *sangham* which by now comprised the people of Parvathipuram, Pathapatnam, and Palakonda agency area should settle all issues in these people's courts only. While the petty issues were to be sorted out by the village committees, the bigger problems were to be left to the agency committee members. The popularity of these courts can be gauged from the fact that between 1962 and 1965, only one case between two tribals was referred to a civil court.

Building a Mass Movement

The first popular struggle in the agency area was launched in 1959 and was directed against *Vetti*. It had limited objectives and was essentially propagandist in form. Pamphlets were distributed and the issue was widely discussed among the tribals. This form of struggle helped establishing contacts identifying prospective members and setting up *sanghams* in a number of villages. The struggle was more or less an exploratory one and was launched to gauge the extent of the *sangham's* popularity.

Encouraged by the success, the leaders went one step ahead and gave a call for forcible resistance of forest officials demanding bribes and *mamuls* and of money lenders who extracted high rates of interest. The members were directed to resort to physical intimidation of these exploiters wherever necessary. Several forest guards and money lenders were beaten up in the process. The popularity of this move is evident from the increase in the *sangham's* membership and taking full advantage of it the *sangham* in 1962 gave a call for the occupation of forest lands. The government had a difficult time dealing with these people because they refused to attend courts voluntarily and the numbers involved was so large that ensuring their attendance using policemen was not feasible.

In the next stage the *sangham* took on the Girijan Corporation whose employees were taking as much advantage of the tribals as was any money lender or landlord. Members were assigned the work of supervising the purchase depots to ensure that the tribals were not cheated in the process of weighment. On the price issue the *sangham* went even further and demanded that the tribal should be allowed to sell to whosoever pays the highest price for his produce. In other words, the monopoly rights of the corporation to procure minor forest produce was itself questioned. The *sangham* established shandies in the villages of (1) Valasaballeru, (2) Jumbhiri, (3) Panasabhadra, (4) Mondemkhal and (5) Kukkidichivada and declared that in these shandies the produce brought by the tribals could be bought by anybody. The *sangham* stated "we will resist any efforts to stop these and give complete protection to buyers and sellers. The goods can be sold to Corporation or to traders—whoever pays the higher price". Thus by mid 1960s the *sangham* was practically running the corporation in and around Mondemkhal area.

Throughout these struggles the *sangham* kept up pressure

against corrupt revenue, excise and forest officials by submitting endless petitions and backed it up by physical intimidation In the process it emerged as a powerful and popular representa tive organisation of the tribals and even police constables were vary of entering tribal villages without its permission, so much so that some communist leaders used to be saluted by policemen.[61]

In taking up the aforesaid issues the *sangham* felt that it was only scratching the surface. Its real problem lay in the question of land because it considered the landlords as the main oppressors. Even when the issue was *vetti* or money lending the person to be tackled was the landlord who was the local money lender and employer of labour. Dealing with the landlords was however a much tougher proposition than dealing with isolated forest and revenue officials. In the first place they held a strangelhold over the local economy and all the tribals were dependent on them in one sense or the other for their livelihood. Secondly, they had the required political support of the government and its machinery to rely on. In fighting them the *sangham* felt that it was fighting the State by proxy. It is no coincidence that the entire Srikakulam movement hinged on this confrontation between the *sangham* and the landlords. The first confrontation took place as early as in 1960 when in November of that year the *sangham* raised a call for higher wages and asked the tribals to harvest the landlords' crop in lieu of the same. The landlords tried to wriggle out of the situation by attempting to bribe Vempatapu Satyanarana. When this failed they called him over to Jhumbiri on the pretext of holding talks and tried to have him killed[63]. This also failed as Vempatapu Satyanarayana properly cautioned in advance, escaped unhurt. This precipitated matters and the very next day the tribals moved in a big way and harvested the crop. The largest of such forced harvesting took place between Panasabhadra and Dandusura, where nearly 200 acres were occupied by the tribals[64]. The local police station was not in a position to deal with a problem of this magnitude but reinforcements arrived soon and a camp was established in the area[65]. Cases were booked against the tribals and it became evident that the police meant business. At this stage the district communist leader Vasantada Ramalingachari came and convinced Vempatapu Satyanarayana that rather than invite severe repression so early in the movement he should try and negotiate with the landlords. A compromise was proposed by which two-thirds of the crop had to go to the landlord while the cultivator would retain the remaining one-third. However, since the harvest was in the final stage and immediate work on it was needed, a temporary agreement was made by which the harvest was to be cut but not to be taken home either by the landlord or by the villagers until final settlement was arrived at[66]. The compromise proved illusory as the landlords under the leadership of Gudla Satyam decided to crush the *sangham* rather than accede to their demands. Vempatapu Satyanarayana Adibhatla Kailasam and twenty five other tribal leaders were rounded up by the police on the complaint of the landlords. General harassment by the police followed and ultimately Palle Ramulu the initial organiser of the movement surrendered to the police and quit the movement to escape repression. He was thus ironically the first "casualty" of the movement. The movement was now in the hands of younger and more militant leadership and in future was to take a still more radical turn.

Towards Confrontation

Once the intentions of the landlords became clear the *sangham* played its trump card by calling a general strike of all *palerus* and *palikala* (farm servants). Each landlord had 10-12 farm servants, some even 20 from whom they extracted *vetti* as repayment of loans given to them. The landlords were banking on these farmhands to do the harvesting for them. In response to the strike call the farmhands not only abstained from work but also put forward their own set of demands. The main demand being the doubling of their wages which was usually paid in kind and an improvement of working conditions.[68]

The strike turned out to be a big success. With the crop ready for harvesting the landlords found no hands to employ. Even their day to day requirements had to be attended to by themselves and any move on their part to employ outside labour was effectively countered by the tribals. Faced with such a situation the landlords had no option but to concede all the demands. Cases against the striking workers were dropped, the police camp was removed and negotiations were started with the *sangham*.[69] The *sangham* won a significant victory when the landlords finally agreed to raise the rates for harvesting 1 acre of land from Rs. 5/- to Rs. 18 - in stages. Between 1960 and 1967 a series of struggles were led in the agency area by the *sangnam* to raise wage rates and to extend the area to be covered by the enhanced wages. In 1967 the rates for harvesting an acre stood at Rs. 30/- in most of the agency area and at Rs. 50/- in the area surrounding Mondemkhal where the *sangham* was the strongest. Similarly the rates for seeding, weeding and transplantations rose to three *putlu* from fifteen *kunchams*.[70]

While the *sangham* continued to engage in these struggles the landlords made moves of their own. They attempted first to ally rich and middle peasantry who were also to some extent affected by the wage rise and made arrangements for some sort of labour exchange. The *sangham* countered this by announcing that they would not charge high rates for middle peasants. With this the middle peasants who were tribals and were benefiting from the *sangham's* other activities deserted their short lived alliance with the landlords.

With a substantial portion of their produce now going off in wages and taxes and the profit margin coming down, the landlords resorted to other methods. While some landlords went to the extent of distributing part of their holding among a large number of tribals to gather support for themselves and start internecine quarrels among the tribals, others tried giving their lands to tribals in return for fifty per cent of the produce, by introducing a system of sharecropping which did not exist. This posed a problem for the *sanghams* because they felt that if they charged high rates of wages for the many tribals cultivating the landlords' land they would have to face a split within their own ranks. They came up with two proposals, (1) the wage rate would not be reduced to Girijan peasants tilling landlords' land and (2) the tiller would get two thirds and not fifty per cent of the produce. Besides this the landlord would have to supply cattle and seeds. With these demands the *sanghams* managed to keep unity of its members. As a result of these decisions the landlords would get no more than previously and the tiller peasant would get just as much as any agricultural labour. Ultimately, as a last resort, the landlords began leaving their lands fallow.[71]

Another issue which the *sangham* took up related to trade. Apart from controlling the local economy by manipulating the wage rates, the landlords also had full control over the local trade. The average tribal was a hopeless trader. On occasions he would barter away a basketful of forest produce, collected over a period of days, for just a few kilos of salt and some tobacco. Even the grain that he managed to raise by shifting cultivation he would sell at a low price to the trader, at the time of harvest and purchase it back from him at a much higher price later on.

Under the circumstances, the *sangham* as a first step demanded that the price of grain be lowered. The landlords were selling grain at the rate of 2 *addas* per rupee. The *sangham's* demand was for 6 *addas* at the same price. The landlords refused to give so much more for the same price and began taking away the grain and selling it in the towns away from the agency area. The *sangham* countered this move by stopping the lorries and preventing them from transporting the grain. On one occasion the entire cargo of a lorry was seized and distributed among the tribals. While the police did take measures to prevent this from happening, the landlords decided to play it safe by arriving at an understanding with the *sangham*. They agreed to sell 30 bags of grain at 6 *addas* per rupee to the *sangham* and for every 100 bags they would be allowed to sell outside without being molested. The *sangham* agreed and with the grain so purchased set up sale depots in twelve villages. Those who were members of the *sangham* were given identification chits and the grain was rationed among them.[72]

The *sangham* had however underestimated the demand and found that the grain collected from the landlords did not serve the needs of all the tribals. On the other hand, the landlords had no intention of selling any more grain to them. The *sanghams* resorted once again to their lorry stopping activities. But this time the landlords resisted and when they found transportation of grain difficult they stopped selling grain altogether and began hoarding. Sensing the deep tension between the tribals and the landlords the government decided to take action and reported that it would procure grains from the landlords and sell through the G.C.C. depots. They too were, however, unwilling to meet the *sangham's* demand that the grain produced and procured locally should be sold only locally and not taken out of the area.[73]

Stalemate

During all this period rather than restrict itself to just one or two struggles the *sangham* actively participated in the 1964 Panchayat election in two samithis in order to develop tribal population in every sphere of activity. In one samiti they bagged sicteen panchayats and in the second forty including the presidency of the samiti. Although Vempatapu lost from the Bhadragiri samiti, Appalaswamy Naidu another *sangham* sympathiser won from the Seethampet Samiti. In the 1967 general elections the *sangham's* candidate contested the Parvathipuram Assembly seat but lost. It is however reported that of the total of 10,350 tribal votes in the area they polled 10,000.[74]

The *sangham* also experimented in running labour contract societies and a forest contract society. In neither case could it make much headway. The purpose of the labour contract society was to break the grip of the money lender cum contractors. Normally the money-lender would employ only those tribals already indebted to him and make them work for nominal wages. The *sangham* formed labour contract societies which bid for works and employed tribals at a fair wage. The crux of the matter was landing a good contract but here again " prosperous ryots of Gummalaxmipuram... even saw to it that the Tribal Labour Cooperatives was not awarded any contract by the Block

Development Officer, although there was a specific government directive to encourage such cooperatives".[75] A similar fate overtook the forest cooperative society which never managed to compete with the regular contractors because it was not in a position to boost profits by paying the labourers less or by cutting beyond the specified area.[76]

By 1967 all the *sangham* activities were proceeding along monotonously predictable lines. Each time an effort was made to redress a grievance a struggle would be started with full enthusiasm but very soon it ran out of steam and the *sangham* founditself faced with an impasse. A detailed review of the *sangham's* activities upto 1967 has been given only to illustrate this fact. It will be noticed that the *sangham* tried its hand at every type of activity. It took up wage struggles and land occupation programmes, which brought it in direct conflict with the landlords; it tried working within the legal framework and set up cooperative societies; in the political sphere, finding itself increasingly bogged down because it had no support from the existing political representatives, it even participated in the elections both at the samiti level and to the Assembly. but the result in all cases was the same and beyond a certain point despite the obvious desire of the people to press for their demands, the *sangham* found itself frustrated. This had been the outcome of all their efforts ever since the beginning of organised action in 1957.

Further, operating as they were with one foot steeped in illegality the *sanghams* were always the target for the police. Even as early as in 1964, some six hundred of their members were involved in police cases.[77] This created problems of maintaining morale and of supporting families of arrested members. The top leaders like Panchadri Krishnamurthy and Vempatapu Satyanarayana were forever on the dodge trying to avoid warrants from being served on them. It thus became evident to the leaders that operating the way they were, halfway house between legality and illegality did not serve any purpose.

Under the circumstances, there was a tendency on the part of Vempatapu Satyanarayana and others to view increased militancy as the only solution and subsequently over the years the Srikakulam leaders jumped successively from CPI(M) in 1964 to T N in 1967 and finally Charu Majumdar in 1968.

The Establishment Reacts

The issues precipitated towards the end of 1967. In July that year when the weeding season began the *sangham* reiterated its demands for better wages, restoration of land and so on. The landlords too by this time decided to take a strong line. They organised themselves into a *Ryotu Sangham* under the leadership of Medida Satyam a rich and influential landlord contractor who was also a prominent member of the Congress party. A few negotiations were held to arrive at some sort of a compromise but these efforts failed.[78] On 31 October the *sangham* organised a meeting of all tribals at Modemkhal to discuss the future course of action. The landlords came to know of this and proceeded to disrupt the meeting by attacking and beating up tribals as they were proceeding towards the meeting. Provoked by this gratuitous attack the *sangham* leaders gathered some tribals and approached the landlords of Levidi village demanding an explanation. When they reached Levidi they were fired upon by "prominent Congress leaders led by Medida Satyam" and in the process two *sangham* workers Arika Koranna and Kondagiri Manganna were killed.[79]

This incident led to a lot of consternation among the tribals moreso because of the attitude of the police who did not take any steps to book Medida Satyam. On the other hand at a high level committee meeting in Hyderabad it was decided to take a hard line against the *sangham* and its members. A special Superintendent of Police, a special Deputy Collector and a special Tahsildar were appointed, specifically to deal with the situation. Although some ameliorative steps by way of distribution of *pattas* and restoration of land were taken, the accent was on increased police presence and police action.[80] Section 144 was promulgated in the two hundredvillages coming under Elwinpet Police Station. This was followed by the arrest of some five hundred tribals.[81] In some areas as for example Peddakharja village there were direct conflicts between the police and the tribals and the police resorted to firing. To a certain extent all this curbed the *sangham's* activity.

Decision to Take to Arms

On the whole it was a time for rethinking for the *sangham* leaders, as with macists elsewhere in the country. The way was prepared for future battles and Levidi was only the beginning. The ten months between December 1967 and September 1968 was a period of lull preceding a storm. Intense discussion on theoretical aspects and ideological issues were being conducted, between Andhra maoist groups and the AICCCR, as the Srikakulam district leaders in a desperate attempt to lift the movement from the stagnation it had got stuck in first vacillated between a moderate stand and a mlitiant one and finally succumbed to the temptations of the latter.

The local leadership had always clamoured for a more militant line. Even in 1964 during the lorry stopping episode Vempatapu had criticised sharply the CPI(M)'s view that moderation must be exercised.[82] After the incidents at Levidi and Peddakharja many of the local cadre began expressing discontent at the "defeatist" line being propagated by the CPI(M)'s leadership.[83] These feelings were forcefully put forth by Subba Rao Panigrahi in his touring play *Jamukula Katha*[84] which led to his expulsion from the CPI(M).

When T. N. C. P. and others formed a coordina tion committee for Maoists within CPI(M) on March 4, 1968, the Srikakulam Committee of the CPI(M) lost no time in joining it. Strictly speaking such shifts in allegiance from one party to another did not involve any drastic alterations.[85] In the last week of March a meeting was held to make a fresh assessment of the Srikakulam movement with D.V. as State Co-ordination Committee representative. In the meeting it was felt that intense police activity had thrown the movement in to disarray and the tribals having lost all their stored food and clothing were in no position to retaliate immediately. Therefore, it was decided that "in these conditions the main problem immediately in front of us was not of organising peoples resistance, but of arranging salt, food, clothes and agricultural implements for the people. On the advice of State Committee representatives the district committee decided to arrange for these (salt... etc.) re-establish contacts with people, collect arms and give guerilla training to all important leaders".[86] They felt that once training was given and guerilla squads formed they would be in a position to start armed struggle. It was felt that training could be completed in April and May, and in June 1968 once the rainy season started they could start a movement for occupation of the landlord's lands and that the resultant clashes between police and people could be developed into a guerilla struggle. In this meeting some members also expressed the opinion that the main problem in front of them was one of resisting repression. They felt that if they started guerilla actions, straightaway instead of waiting for the situation to develop people would be enthused and they would break out of their present apathy and actively participate in the struggles. For the time being, however, this suggestion could not rally the majority behind it.

In April and May 1968 the State leadership of maoists (T. N. etc.) was busy conducting an ideological debate with the Central leadership of CPI(M), and trying to win over the majority of Andhra CPI(M) members to their side. Because of this and various other technical problems the guerilla training camps as envisaged in the March 29 meeting of Srikakulam District Committee, could not be organised. When the Srikakulam committee met again in the first week of June, the situation had not developed as had been foreseen in the March meeting, where they had thought that the people's movement on land issue could be started and developed into an armed struggle by June. However, the situation reported at this meeting was that people were still apathetic and in no position to agitate on any issue, and that any activity of cadres was being countered immediately with raids by the police. The State Committee representative who attended this meeting made three suggestions- (a) they must wait until people moved on issues like land occupation and crop seizure before starting regular guerilla armed struggle: (b) before the stage of regular guerilla armed struggle could be reached, resistance to police raids should be organised by arming the local people and local militants with crude bombs, bows and arrows, spears and other weapons; (c) the movement should spread to areas other than where it was centered now (Seethampet and Parvathipuram agency areas) since, the present areas of the movement were surrounded by a network of roads which enabled the police to encircle the area and restrict the movement of guerilla squads.

The more militant sections of the Srikakulam Committee were quite disappointed with the assessment made at the meeting. They felt that the movement could be taken ahead by immediately launching guerilla actions. However, all those who subscribed to this view were from among the lower levels of leadership, for example Vempatapu Satyanarayana, Adibhatla Kailasam and Tamada Ganapathi who had the support neither of the state level leadership nor even of the older members of Srikakulam Committee like Ramalingachari. At the same time many members of District Committee like Appala Suri, Panchadri Krishnamurthy and Choudhari Tejeshwar Rao were vacillating between the pressures from above and below. Ultimately, at least for the time being the district committee approved the suggestions of the State leadership.[87]

What changed the whole situation at this stage was the intervention of the AICCCR. We have already noted that the June 1968 issue of *Liberation* carried an attack on Andhra leadership's stand on many ideological issues. In the same issue they characterised the struggle being carried on in Srikakulam under the Andhra maoist's guidance as being "democratic" rather than "revolutionary" and accused the Andhra committee of neo-revisionism.[88] There was strong similarity between the views of the younger members of the Srikakulam Committee and that of AICCCR and these like-minded members grouped to form the Naxalbari Solidarity Committee (NSC) which had as members Dr. Mallikarjunudu, Dr. Chaganti Bhaskar Rao, Dr. Murlapudi Venkataratnam and several others.

In the second week of June a representative of the AICCCR (probably Asit Sen) was invited to Andhra Pradesh by the leaders of the NSC. He explained to them the exact nature of the differences between the AICCCR and the APCCCR. By the time his visit concluded the NSC. leaders became fully convinced of the need of adopting a more militant line.[89] Ultimately in August a meeting was held, at Boddapadu, of all the Srikakulam leaders who were in favour of launching an armed struggle immediately. This meeting was attended among others by Panchadri Krishnamurthy, Tamada Ganapati and Subba Rao Panigrahi. The resistance offered to the police by the people of Peddakharja was seen as an unequivocal sign of their preparedness to fight and it was unanimously resolved to proceed straightaway with armed guerilla struggle.

By September 1968 when the Srikakulam District Committee met the situation was clearly heading towards a climax. Two resolutions were passed in this meeting. In the first the Srikakulam District Committee while condemning the APCCCR for not joining the AICCCR merged itself with the latter in a motion which was carried through by a majority of four to three In the second it was unanimously resolved to launch an armed struggle.

The actual resolution read as follows: "Between June and August second week, when the state armed police was withdrawn, our cadre went to people and exposed to them the real nature of government's promises and actions. People expressed the opinion that the next time they will fight (the police) but the leadership must stay amidst them. The attacks of police have started again (August second week). We had told the people that we are preparing for higher levels of struggle and will soon resist the police attacks. The attacks have started, but as yet we could not start resistance. With this people and cadre are losing their faith in us. If we delay some more there is the danger of our being totally isolated from the people. So, the district committee requests that armed struggle be started immediately."[90]

Armed with these resolutions Choudhary Tejeshwar Rao, Panchadri Krishnamurthy and Murlapudi Venkataratnam went to Calcutta. They apprised Charu Majumdar of the situation in Srikakuam and were advised to "start armed action immediately against the landlords as well as the government which was the defender of the landlords".[91] Subsequently, a meeting of Srikakulam leaders was held at Boddapadu between 23rd—25th of October 1968, where wide ranging discussions about the future course of action, were conducted and a twelve member district co-ordination committee elected to give a decisive majority to the pro-AICCCR group.[92]

Meanwhile the APCCCR made a last attempt at winning over the Srikakulam Committee, back into its fold. To this effect it aligned itself with the AICCCR in November 1968 and even agreed to the decision of starting armed struggle immediately. But this last minute concession was not of much consequence. Ultimately although the district committee in their meeting on November 20, 1968 did not press Vempatapu Satyanarayana and Adibatla Kailasam's resolution to cut off all relations with APCCCR, for all practical purposes the Srikakulam Committee no longer followed the advice of APCCCR.[93]

NOTES & REFERENCES

1. *District Census Handbook— Srikakulam District— 1961*, Government of Andhra Pradesh (1966), p. 1.
2. *Ibid*. p. XXXIX.
3. Shifting cultivation in Andhra Pradesh (cyclostyled) Tribal Cultural Research Training Institute (TCRTI), 1969, p. 16.
4. *Statistical Handbook* (cyclostyled) TCRTI, (1970) Table 614, p. 50, Shifting Cultivation involves felling trees with axes, knives etc. setting fire to it and spreading the ash all over the potash and phosphate present in the ashes enrich the fertility of the soil which lasts only for two to three years. This takes the whole of the month of April, and just before the onset of rains during the last week of May.

5. *Transfer and Alienation of Tribal land in Andhra Pradesh* (unpublished) TCRTI. (1969)
6. *Ibid.*
7. *Madagada* (TCRTI) p. 151.
8. *Statistical Handbook* (cyclostyled) TCRTI Medical facilities, Table 11.1, 1966-67, p. 105.
9. *Madagada*— op. cit., p.87.
10. D.R. Pratap, "Social and Economic Factors in the Development of Tribals in Andhra Pradesh", in *Tribal*, 1969.
11. *Srikakulam*, District Gazeteers (cyclostyled)— Government of Andhra Pradesh, pp. 6-7.
12. *Ibid* pp. 6-7. Among the zamindars those of Vizianagaram, Bobbili, Andhra, Salur, Pachipenta, Chemudu, Sangamavalasa, Belagam, Merangi, Kurupam and Palakonda were important.
13. *Ibid.* pp. 24-26.
14. T.J. Maltby, *The Ganjam District Manual*, Lawrence Asylum Press, Madras, 1882, pp. 245-246 and also *Srikakulam District Gazeteers op. cit.* p. 30.
15. *Madagada op. cit* p. 18 and also see W. Francis, *Madras District Gazeteers* (1907) p. 186.
16. W. Francis, *Madras District Gazeteers* (1907) p. 186.
17. *The Working Paper* in the Seminar arranged by the Girijan Development Agency, February 1975.
18. See *Ibid* and also *Notes for Study Team on Tribal Development Project*, Committee on Plan Project, Government of Andhra Pradesh, p. 19.
19. W. Francis, *op. cit.* p. 19.
20. *Ibid*, p. 109.
21. *Transfer and Alienation of Tribal in A.P. op. cit.* TCRTI, p. 11.

22. *Ibid*

23. *Socio-Economic Change in Tribals of Andhra* (cyclostyled) Reprint from "Trends of Socio-Economic Change in India, 1871-1961", Indian Institute of Advanced Study, Volume 7, Simla, 1969.

24. *Ibid* p. 25.

25. *Notes for Study, op. cit.* p. 56. By 1966 there were 1,26,316 labourers employed in coffee plantation.

26. *Madagada op. cit.* p. 166.

27. *Shifting Cultivation... etc. op. cit.* p. 16.

28. *Note on Protective Legislation—Srikakulam District* (cyclostyled) Government of Andhra Pradesh.

29. *Ibid.*

30. *Ibid.*

31. *Some Problems of Land Alienation etc. op. cit.* and also *Transfer and Alienation, op. cit.*

32. *Statistical Handbook, op. cit.*

33. *Notes on Protective Legislation, op. cit.* p, 4.

34. *Notes for Study .. etc. op. cit.* p. 47.

35, *Ibid*

36. *Notes on Protective Legislation op. cit.*

37. *Ibid* pp.4-5.

38. Based on intreviews and observation. Also in a letter addresed to President of India, V.V. Giri, from the Sarpanch of Gummalaxmipuram in a printed pamphlet. See also *Working Paper op. cit.* (Problems relating to Cattle development ploughs, Bullocks and Dairy Development) p.2.

39. *Notes for Study... etc. op. cit.* p. 92.

40- *Ibid.*

41. *Socio-Economic Changes op. cit.* p. 23.

42. "*Cattle Development*..." *etc. op. cit.*

43. *Shifting Cultivation etc. op. cit.* p. 37.

44. *See Srikakulam District Gazeteers op. cit.* Annexures 90 and 91.

45. V.M. Nair, "Girijan Revolt", *The Statesman* (New Delhi) April 12, 1968.

46. *Institutional Framework, op. cit.*

47. About Palle Ramulu and the origin of the Tribal Movement in the agency area, V. Ramalingachari *Court Statement* (Printed) p. 28 and Vempatapu Satyam, *Srikakulam Zilla Girijanodhyama Sankshiptha Charitra* Socialist Publications, Vijayawada p. 31.

48. *Ibid.* p. 16.

49. Ryothu Karyakata, *Amara Veerula Jeevita Charitralu,* Pilipu Publications, Hyderabad 1973, p. 147. A small incident can be quoted as an example here. Pegadala Naidu, a landlord of Nilakantapuram area, was considered a terror to the tribals and was notorious for his ruthlessness and vast resources to enforce his power. In a dramatic personal confrontation Vempatapu humiliated him in front of the tribals by physically assaulting him.

50- Document E-1 of Naxalite Conspiracy Case (NCC). See also *Amara... etc. op. cit.* p. 167.

51. Document U-24 of NCC. In one instance it is stated that such a concerted effort was made that the process achieved the propositions of a movement and some 30,000 haircuts were made.

52. *Ibid.*

53. V. Ramalingachari *Court Statament op. cit.*

54. V.M. Nair, *Girijan Revolt op. cit.*

55. V. Ramalingachari *op. cit.*

56. *Ibid.*

57. The case was between two peasants, Ariki Potanna of Vuridi village v/s Nimmalasuri of Gunjavoda village; V. Ramalingachari, *Court Statement op. cit.*

58. *Amara... etc. op. cit.* p. 148.

59. Vempatapu Satyam, *Srikakulam Zilla... etc. op. cit.* p. 20.

60. *Ibid* pp. 36-38.

61. V.M. Nair, *Girijan Revolt, op. cit.*

62. Document 24, *op. cit.*

63. See Vempatapu Satyam, *Srikakulam Zilla... etc. op. cit.* p. 21, V. Ramalingachari, *Court Statement op. cit.* p. 30 and *Amara... etc. op. cit.* p. 148.

64. Vempatapu Satyam, *Srikakulam Zilla... etc. op. cit.* p. 21.

65. *Ibid* p. 22.

66. *Ibid.*

67. *Ibid.* p. 23.

68. Document U-24, *op. cit.*

69. V. Ramalingachari, *Court Statement, op. cit.* p. 40.

70. *One Kuncham* is equal to 3 Kgs. and one *Pallu* is equal to 60 Kgs.

71. Document U-24, *op. cit.*

72. V. Ramalingachari, *Court Statement op. cit.*

73. Document U-24, *op. cit.*

74. V. Ramalingachari, *op. cit. Court Statement op. cit.*

75. V.M. Nair, *Girijan Revolt, op. cit.*

76. Document 1-1, Zilla Committee meeting, dated 15-11-1964.

77. *Ibid.*

78. V.M. Nair, *Girijan Revolt op. cit.*

79. *The Deccan Chronicle*, November 6,1967 reported that while Congressmen were running away the tribals shot at them and by mistake killed their own fellows. This version of the incident is fallacious. Even the Chargesheet of N.C.C. *op. cit.* says "a party of tribals was intercepted at Levidi by landlords headed by Medida Satyam who opened fire resulting in the death of two tribals". C. Subba Rao in "Revolt in Srikakulam" *Times of India*, January 4,1970 further stated that though "practically everyone in the area knew who fired in the procession... because of the money and influence the police were tardy in arresting them".

80. *Andhra Patrika*, March 3, 1968.

81. V.M. Nair, *Girijan Revolt*, *op. cit.*

82. Document 1-1, *op. cit.*

83. Document U-62 of N.C.C. Minutes of Agency Area Plenary Meeting.

84. *Jamukula Katha* is a form of folk art.

85. The control, which any, of the communist parties had over the Srikakulam Movement had always been very little. Thus despite the fact that the Girijan Sangham which was the main organisational force behind the movement was a CPI mass organisation, it was only after the movement had gained momentum that it was considered important enough to be discussed at the District level. The association with the party never went beyond this level and until the maoists arrived on the scene and took active part in the movement in 1968 most of the directives concerning the movement continued to be issued by the *sangham* which consisted of activists most of whom were not even party members. For a brief while in 1964 after the C.P.I. had split the CPI(M) leaders showed some interest in Srikakulam and the party leader Sundarayya even visited Srikakulam a couple of times. But this was more to ensure the support of the District

Committee and of the party members in the *Sanghams* for the CPI(M) than anything else.

86. *Vyavasay a Viplavamu... etc. op. cit.* p. 32.

87. See minutes of March and June meetings of Srikakulam Committee in Document U-62 of N.C.C.

88. *Vyavasaya Viplavamu... etc. op. cit.*

89. *Ibid*, p. 33.

90. For both the resolutions see *Ibid* pp. 34-37.

91. Charge Sheet of Cr. No. 13/74 Hyderabad, p. 2.

92. *Ibid* p. 13.

93. *Vyavasaya Viplavamu... etc.* pp. 39-40.

CHAPTER 5

Srikakulam-II

Srikakulam-II

With the taking of the decision in November, '68 to proceed with armed struggle, a fresh phase in the Srikakulam movement hah begun and from this point onward the movement took a highly militant turn. At the sametime State repression also grew. Time and again the movement got bogged down because the cadre were unable to deal with the superior fire power and organisation of the police machinery. Theoretically such a situation was not envisaged since it was always assumed by the maoists that a revolutionary situation was widely prevalent and that the people themselves would counter State repression and carry the movement. At a more practical level, each time the momentum of the movement was curbed the leaders had to decide whether to modify the tactics being employed or make a reassessment of their acceptance of the existence of a country wide revolutionary upsurge. This chapter describes in detail how the leaders chose the former alternative throughout the turbulent period of two years, and, with what consequences.

The mass phase

Once the decision was taken on 20 November 1968 to proceed with armed struggle the Srikakulam District Committee worked out a scheme of simultaneous attacks on various oppressors. The main effort was to involve as many persons as possible in these attacks.[1] Further, these attacks were to be led by the District Committee members who were to provide guidance.

Acting in consonance with this Vempatapu Satyanarayana personally led an attack on Theegala Narasimhulu, a landlord of Pedagothili village along with 400 tribals armed with guns, bows and arrows, on the night of 24 November, 1968, a mere four days after the committee's decision on armed struggle. This was followed by an attack, the very next day on Ramamurthi, a moneylender of Doddukallu village by the same group. Property worth a sum of Rs. 27,000/- was collected during these raids.[2] These two raids only marked the beginning of this kind of action and they were soon followed by attacks on Dandusura and many other villages. Throughout the period November 1968 to February 1969 attacks on landlords and moneylenders continued to take place in the areas of Parvatipuram and Pathapatnam.

With the situation developing in this fashion the police began to take retaliatory steps. There were nine platoons of Special Armed Police (SAP) operating in the district and functioning in close co-operation with the Orissa Government.[3] Continuous raids were conducted on most tribal villages and hamlets in an effort to flush out 'offenders'. The raids were also utilised for teaching all tribals a lesson especially those suspected of harbouring the activists. Very often these raids met with stiff resistance from the villagers. In the Althi hills of Pathapatnam taluk, for instance the tribals were raided by a police party led by a District Superintendent of Police (DSP) and two Circle Inspectors for having beaten up some prohibition officers. As the police party approached they were confronted by nearly 500 tribal men, women and children variously armed with bows, arrows and spears. The policemen were heavily stoned by the tribals who were all the time chanting slogans in praise of Mao and armed struggle. As a result of this counter attack the DSP and nine other police personnel were injured. In the end the tribals could be overcome only after firing was resorted to and two of them were killed.[4]

Again, in another incident, this time in the Pulipathi hills a strong party of SAP consisting of several platoons, 25 trackers and a large number of supply carriers were prevented from reaching their destination for four days by armed tribals. The police party was heading for Eguvaballerugudem village near Pulipathi to apprehend Vempatapu Satyanarayana about whose presence there they had earlier received information. However, as they entered the Egu valley they found themselves totally surrounded by the tribals who were waiting in ambush. Boulders were rolled down on the police from the mountain tops by the tribals and in a fight which lasted more than two hours before the police withdrew the latter were treated to a continuous barrage of arrows. This was on the 19th of December 1968[5]. Two days later, fortified by fresh reinforcement the police made a renewed assault. This time after a five hour battle the tribals were forced to retreat towards the villages of Sivada and Valagamanaguda villages. Beyond that the police could not proceed because the tribals, now numbering one hundred set fire to the forest bushes.[6] Ultimately it was only on 23rd that the police could finally reach Eguvaballerugudem and even on this day they had to disperse a 800 strong group of tribals before setting camp.[7] Vempatapu Satyanarayana and most other leaders had by that time left the place. The main purpose of the police was to chalk out a route linking the interior with the more accessible parts of the district. Ultimately a jeepable road was laid in this area to make patrolling more effective. Ironically enough, this came to be known as the Ho Chi Minh Trail. Similar incidents of tribal resistance took place in Domada village of Santoshpuram hills, and Gangannadoravalasa of Kuttam hills.[8]

In the plains areas the strongholds of the movement were in the Boddapadu area in Sompeta and in the Bobbili Taluk. Unlike in the tribal areas where a spontaneous movement had already been built up by Vempatapu in the plains areas the movement had to be nurtured carefully. Already efforts in this direction had been made by various activists. In Boddapadu, Tamadi Ganapati a self educated poor peasant with a considerable diplomatic and oratorial skills had been organising peasants. In this he was aided by Janaki Rao the headmaster of the high school in the area. The school had become a breeding ground for communist revolutionaries and a number of persons who were later to take active part in the movement were products of this school. They included Urlam Malleswara Rao, Putsa Appalaswamy, Pyla Vasudeva Rao, Juttu Umapati and Dummu Appalaswamy. Over the years Boddapadu became an important centre for communist activities not only in the Sompeta taluk, but in the entire district. Top leaders like Panchadi Krishnamurti, his wife Nirmala and the famous poet revolutionary Subba Rao Panigrahi came and settled down in this village. They organised a number of organisations and activities in the area. For instance they started a youth association, one for the peasants, a sports organisation, an adult school and even a hospital of native medicine. All these were utilised to propagate revolutionary politics, develop contacts among the people and to increase the peoples' political consciousness.

In Bobbili taluq too the initial activity ran along similar lines. In this area the key figure Adibhatla Kailasam who was a close associate of Vempatapu and who had led the peasants in the area to agitate for land ownership against his own father. In subsequent years he was aided in his activities by M.V. Ramamurti who was the president of the Bobbili teachers, union. Adibhatla Kailasam organised *Ryotu Sanghams* in about fifty villages in his area and followed it up by organising a more militant group called *Tegmpu Sanghami*.

After the district committee took the decision to start an armed struggle the activities in both the taluqs took a more militant line. In the Boddapadu area a number of meetings were held to explain to the people the new tactics. Usually these meetings culminated in raids on the local landlords by groups of as many as 500 people. One favourite target was Maddi Kamesam of Garubhadra village. He was a big landlord cum moneylender besides being a Congressman with considerable political influence. On several occasions in the past he had been the motivating force for attacks against the *sanghams*. The activities in Bobbili taluq too consisted mainly of seizure of crops of landlords by groups led by armed squads, occupation of temple lands and seizure of hoarded grains. Landlords in Reddivalasa, Ramayannapeta, Kammandavalasa and Lakshmipuram were attacked in quick succession.

The plains areas however suffered from two major disadvantages in comparison to the agency areas. In the first place the terrain was not conducive to the guerilla type of hit and run methods and secondly the ranks here did not present the same cohesion and unity as the tribals did in the agency areas. Further, they had to face the retaliation from the landlords in the form of announcement of rewards for the capture of Adhibhatla Kailasam, M.V. Ramamurti. This was in addition to the repression from the police who had warrants issued against most party workers and their family members as well.

With the setting up of an additional police camp at Narayanapuram most of the activists had to leave the area for the Parvathipuram forest. In this situation, Adibhatla Kailasam, M.V. Ramamurti and others expressed the opinion that unless they eliminated the local landlords and other police informers it would be impossible for them to continue. However, at that time Appalasuri who came to meet them as a representative of the State Committee did not concur and instead issued a circular *Spread the struggles to non-struggles areas.* Despite the general exhortations in the circular to spread to the new areas the activities in the plain areas floundered in the face of severe repression and almost came to a stand-still by the end of December.

Change of Tactics

Despite this when Charu visited Srikakulam and met Vempatapu and Tejeswara Rao at Gangannadoravalasa on January 21, 1969, he was presented with a very optimistic picture.[10] This was perhaps based on the undeniable spontaneous response which the movement had received in the tribal areas. In any case it only buttressed the viewpoint which Charu was already harbouring and he went back to Calcutta firmly convinced that the moderate line being advocated by T.N. was more of a hindrance than anything else. As a consequence on February 6, 1969 the All India Co-ordination Committee for Communist Revolutionaries disaffiliated the Andhra

Pradesh Revolutionary Communist Committee and decided to go it alone.

Subsequently, some time in the second week of February Charu visited Andhra once again. A secret meeting of all top revolutionaries in Andhra who owed allegiance to the AICCCR was held at Guttikondabilam of Narasaraopet taluq in Guntur district. In this meeting a State Co-ordination Committee was elected with Tejeswara Rao as the Convenor. It had ten other members. They were Panchadi Krishnamurti and Mamidi Appalasuri for Srikakulam and Nagabhushan Patnaik, M. Venkatratnam for Visakhapatnam, Mancha Venkata Narasiah for Guntur, G. Koteswara Rao for Koraput and Ganjam area, Dama Chenchiah for Nellore, K.S. Mahadevan for Chittoor and and K.G. Satyamurti and Kondapalli Seetharamaiah for the Telangana area. To these members was given the task of organising activity at the district and taluka levels.[11] In this meeting a decision was also taken to extend and intensify the armed struggle both in the agency and plains areas not only of Srikakulam but also in other districts. To this extent the meeting also laid down certain guidelines on the methods to be adopted.

Guerilla squads were to be organised each with seven to eight members and the members of the squads were to be given training in the use of fire arms and local weapons. These squads were assigned the twin tasks of being in the forefront of resistance moves and to take active part in the mass mobilisation programme. The mass base was to be built up around *Ryotanga Sangrama Samities* which were to be formed in every village.[12]

The meeting of the Srikakulam District Committee was convened near Sobha of Parvathipuram taluk on the 11th February 1969 to discuss the ways in which Guttikondabilam decisions were to be implemented. The main decisions of this meeting were to extend the movement in the plains areas, to send cadre from agency areas to organise party cadres and activities in the plains, and to procure weapons by snatching arms and ammunition from the police.[13]

The meeting divided Srikakulam district into four areas for operation of guerilla squads. These areas were to be looked after by area committees which were to supervise the operations of the squads. There were to be separate taluq committees to look after political and organisational work. Consequent on these decisions efforts were made to organise *Ryotanga Sangrama Samiti* in the villages. Leaders like Panchadi Krishnamurti went around the villages meeting local sympathisers and militants in order to form *Ryotanga Sangrama Samiti* which were to identify the 'class enemies' and decide on suitable action. These *samities* were also to co-ordinate their activities under the guidance of District Co-ordination Committee.[14] In the plains areas of Boddapadu and Bobbili, squads had already been formed and the above decisions only served to give them official sanction.

The call given to 'extend' the movement in the plains area served the purpose of rejuvenating the floundering mood there. On 15.2.1969 almost immediately after the meeting one of the Boddapadu squads led by Hemachandra Panigrahi carried out an attack on Tangadu Dharmaraju who was a local merchant and a 'police informer'.[15] This was followed by some more attacks on police informers in the nearby villages.[16] In Padmapuram village of Sompeta taluq a squad led by Panchadi Krishnamurti, Tamada Ganapati and 40 others attacked Varanasi Nityanandam, a rich landlord, killed him and seized Rs. 40,000 worth of property.[17] This incident, subsequently referred to as the "Bathapuram incident" was often quoted by Charu as an example of the initiative and enthusiasm which the people were prepared to exercise in order to eliminate an oppressor. He even compared it with Father Gapon's peasant march on the Tsar's palace in 1905 and the peasant rebellion of Hunan. An incident which did much to boost the morale of the cadre took place at around this time near Pathakota village and involved a much hated local Circle Inspector Patro. A police party led by him was ambushed while it was combing the Kappalasaroj hills and Patro himself was severely wounded.[19] A number of such incidents continued to occur in the Boddapadu area especially under the guidance of Panchadi Krishnamurti and his squad.

The manner in which they treated the object of their attack varied and in this they did not follow any fixed policy. For instance when they raided Varanasi Nityanandam's house, they went to the extent of killing him. However, when they attacked Marripatruni Suryanarayana Patnaik, a rich landlord of Padmapuram village who was equally if not more notorious for his oppressive treatment of the villagers, they did not resort to killing.[19] By and large police informers were dealt with more harshly than any one else, as for instance one Bathina Bhima Rao who was attacked and killed on 19.4.1969 by Panchadi Krishnamurti' squad.[20]

The call to extend the movement in the plains areas affected the activity in Bobbili Taluq as well. The party cadre which had gone into hiding in the agency area after the December events now came back again to take up the struggle with renewed vigour. The presence of Vempatapu helped to reinforce their confidence and activity began afresh with the symbolic forcible fishing in the Gowripuram village ponds, in which as many as four hundred people participated.[21] This situation however did not last very long. Adibhatla Kailasam and M.V. Ramamurti felt that it would only be a matter of time before the police came down heavily on them and therefore they should quickly seize the advantage, conduct some more actions and then seek shelter in the agency area forests. The District Committee however did not agree with this view. The reasons appear to be two-fold. In the first place the belief, as propounded by Charu and others in the AICCCR, that there was a nation-wide revolutionary upsurge was very strong and, secondly, the activities of Panchadi Krishnamurti's squad in and around Boddapadu had been quite successful. With these factors in view the Committee suggested that activists in Bobbili split themselves into two groups, one group was to proceed to conduct actions in the Badevalasa area the other was to lay an ambush for the police who they felt were sure to come. The scheme ran into trouble from the outset. At Gowripuram their attempts to attack a landlord failed because the local contact betrayed them. However, at Badevalasa itself they looted the houses of three local landlords and burnt promissory notes worth

Rs. 70,000/-[22]. The second part of their scheme ended in total fiasco. When the police arrived the local citizens instead of co-operating with the group, as used to happen in the agency areas, failed to assist in the ambush. Not only this, they even informed the police of their whereabouts.[23] As a consequence the squad had to beat a disorganised retreat. The situation became even more grim thereafter when Kailasam who was nursing a swollen leg at the Kalamrajpet hospital being run by Dr. Siva Ram Reddi and Dr. Mallikarjunudu were nabbed by the police along with the two doctors on the basis of information passed on to the police. With this the activity in the Bobbili area once again ground to a halt.

Throughout this period the activity in the Agency area continued. Raids were carried out against petty shopkeepers and moneylenders as also on big landlords.[24] There seems to have been a general tendency not to resort to annihilation in these cases. It was only when a particular person, by virtue of his being a police informer, was considered dangerous to the activists that he was killed. Thus while landlords like Thimmakka Aisarayya were let off others like Pattika Jammayya and Simhadri Naidu were killed.[25] The latter two had actively campaigned for the setting up of police outposts in their respective villages. The activitists organised resistance against the activities of the police and even direct attacks on them in offence Police combing parties were almost invariably attacked when they came near villages. There were at the same time several attacks albeit unsuccessful on the police camps at Vobbangi and Bollivada.[36] In one instance the Andhra Pradesh Special Police platoon from the Polla camp was ambushed.[27]

Annihilation: The Highest Stage of Class Struggle

With activities being carried out on such wide scale State repression was inevitable and the party now had to face the question of operating under these testing circumstances. It was around this time that the AICCCR met in a plenary session and decided to form a new party, the CPI(ML). Choudary Tejeswara Rao and Panchadi Krishnamurti represented the Andhra group. On their return from Calcutta they toured the whole State to conduct a general review of the situation and to convey to the local leaders a meeting was held at Visakhapatnam from 14.5.1969 to 16.5.1969. In this meeting the old State Co-ordination Committee was converted into an organising Committee for the newly formed CPI(ML).[28] At the same time a four-point immediate programme of seizure of landlords' property, organising *Ryotanga Sangrama Samities* and other governing bodies in the villages, organising guerilla squads and of annihilation of landlords, police personnel and informers was worked out.

While the previous meeting had called for an extension of the movement this meeting called for its intensification by resorting to new forms of struggle in the same area. In a sense this meeting can be regarded as a turning point of the Srikakulam movement. Organisationally it called for a shift of emphasis from mass activity to guerilla squads while programmatically it adopted annihilation as the only method for achieving the objectives of the revolution. The theoretical backing to the programme of annihilation was subsequently given in the *Political and Organisational Report of 1970.* This report directed the maoists to "realise and apply methodically the correct thesis that the annihilation of class enemy is the higher form of class struggle and the beginning of the guerilla war and people's war... realise that the class struggle i.e. battle of annihilation can solve all problems facing us and lead to a higher stage, create conditions for the emergence of a new type of man... who fears neither hardship, nor death, develops the peoples army and thus can ensure formation of a permanent base areas. Thus battle of annhilation liberates the people not only from the oppression of landlords class and its state apparatus but also liberates them from the shackles of backward ideas and removes from their minds the poisonous seeds of self-interest, clan interest, localism, religious casteism and superstition". The two most important aspects of their theory of annihilation were the equating of class struggle with annihilation of individuals and the acceptance that the tactic of annihilation was a necessary pre-requisite for starting the guerilla struggles.[29]

A necessary concomitant to this theory was their concept of class hatred as a motivating force of revolutionaries.

Thus, "success in a guerilla action depends on the class hatred and class consciousness of the guerillas. This is what boosts up their morale and releases their boundless creative power".[30] The importance of this concept of class hatred was that it replaced the idea of class consciousness as an object of the movement. Since the peoples' revolutionary consciousness was already assumed the need for efforts to rouse people's consciousness was denied and since guerilla struggle coupled with annihilation was argued to be the only form of struggle, all that was seen to be missing was class hatred. The lull in the movement caused by police activities was thus viewed as something that could be broken by fanning hatred against the police activities.

Detailed instructions as to how the annihilations were to be carried out and guerilla struggles was to be conducted were given by Charu Majumdar in *A Few words about Guerilla Actions*.[31] This article instructed the cadre on the actions necessary before and after an annihilation. In the first stage the member of the party possibly a "petty bourgeoise intellectual comrade" was to go to the village, approach a few poor peasants, who in his opinion had the most revolutionary potentiality and whisper in his ear "Don't you think it is a good thing to finish off such and such a *Jotedar*". Depending on the response the next stage, that of recruitment of guerillas was to be taken up. This recruitment was to be done in "complete secrecy" and in a "wholly conspiratorial" manner. Nobody outside the guerilla unit-not even other members of the Party were to know either the names of the guerillas or the identity of the class enemy to be annihilated or even the time and place of action. Political propaganda prior to the operation though not strictly banned was to be avoided to minimise security problems. It would be allright to conduct some political propaganda before the guerilla action but it was thought to be neither absolutely necessary nor very advisable from the point of view of security. After forming the unit some investigations were to be conducted among people for choosing the target. The most hated landlord in the area was to be chosen. After the target had been chosen careful planning was to be done about the time and place of action and of the paths of retreat and places of hiding for the participants. Only local weapons were to be used in order to signify and heighten peoples' hatred. However, "petty bourgeoise intellectual cadres and those who have to travel far and wide may carry small pistols for personal defence". All available guns and weapons were to be stored for use in future when pitched battles with police would become part of the programme. For the present the idea was only to kill and run. Neither seizing and distributing the property of the victim nor even following up of the act with meetings on the spot to explain and propagate their action was contemplated. These were to be taken up only at a later stage. Once the act was completed "the atmosphere will be charged with expectancy of some impending event... people will be elated but still hesitant". At this stage the party cadre were to start their propaganda by telling people how by killing all landlords and other police agents, they could own all the land in the village.[32]

This document was clearly based on the understanding since a revolutionary situation already existed in the country "the fight for the seizure of political power initiated by a few advanced sections is nourished by the tremendous initiative of the masses and actions, and the flames of people's war engulf the whole actions, and the flames of people's war engulf the whole countryside".[33] After the initial secret annihilation the masses would rally around the guerillas and carry out many such acts ultimately clearing their area of all class enemies and establishing liberated zones of their political power. The theoretical backing to the programme of annihilation was subsequently given in the *Political and Organisational Report of 1910.*

In the plains, the first act heralding the new programme took place on 19.5.1969 in Borivanka in the Sompeta area when Balleda Krishnamurthy and his brother were annihilated in broad daylight by the squad led by Panchadi Krishnamurthi, Subba Rao Panigrahi and Tamada Ganapati in an incident in which hundreds of local villagers participated. Property worth one lakh was taken and promissory notes worth three lakhs burnt.[34]

However within five days of this incident the police struck a morale shattering blow to the maoists when in an encounter they killed Panchadi Krishnamurti who was then the party secretary of the maoist party in Srikakulam along with several other militant cadres all of whom were in their early teens.[35]

This incident necessitated a reorganisation in the Sompeta squads and consequently the area organisers of Sompeta met at Metturu on 11th and 12th of June, 1969. In this meeting the squads were reorganised and new areas were demarcated for their operation. The leadership of the squads was entrusted to Tamada Ganapati, Chaganti Bhaskara Rao and Pyla Vasudeva Rao. Within a further two weeks of the incident on June 24, 1969, another meeting of Sompeta area committee was held to review the situation arising from Panchadi's death. In this meeting Tamada Ganapati was elected as the new Secretary and wide ranging discussions were held on the ways and means of securing weapons and of safeguarding the lives of guerillas. Arrangements were made to develop an efficient courier system to coordinate the activities of various squads and the members were warned to be on the look out for police agents and informers.[36]

The squads in the Sompeta area had about five members each. Their *modus operandi* was to fix a target for an annihilation, get together four or five other squads to carry out the task and use the event for an on the spot propaganda. It was expected that in some cases they would be openly assisted by the villagers in the annihilation process while in others they would have only stray sympathisers, and where it would become necessary to conduct on the spot propaganda once the annihilation was completed.

One incident in which the villagers spontaneously participated occurred at Akkupalli village. In this case as many as 400 villagers participated in the annihilation of Konchada Bhuchandra Rao. This followed by several other annihilations like that of Patro of Gowripuram village and Krupa Sindhi of Konaka village.[37] However, the annihilation programme was not followed strictly as laid down by Charu. In a number of cases, especially those concerning the Sompeta squads, avenging Panchadi Krishnamurti's death, was the prime motive. At

Akkupalli for instance, after the annihilation was over Panchadi Krishnamurti's wife Nirmala who was an active participant dipped her hand in the blood of the victim, snatched away the *Mangalasutram*[38] of the victim's wife and is reported to have told the landlord's wife "just as the police made me a widow so shall you become one".[39] Further, in an extension of the same event a raid was conducted on the house of Konchada Dasaratha Ramudu but the person himself was not attacked.[40] Thus even at this stage not all victims of attack were annihilated.

Whatever the actual results, the maoists felt that annihilations were helping their cause. They felt that annihilation helped them to work freely in the area as the terrorized local landlords and police agents got demoralised and the people as a consequence would gain confidence and have faith in the determination and capability of the CPI (ML).[41] Extending this argument further they felt that even an annihilation carried out without local peoples' participation served their purpose. In other words they felt that they need not limit their annihilation activities to areas where they had some support and had previously conducted propaganda campaigns, for annihilation was in itself a way of propagating the ideas and spreading the movement to these new areas. Thus according to them it was essential to carry out guerilla actions and annihilation wherever it was technically feasible, irrespective of any political considerations.[42]

Following this analysis they started extending their activities to Tekkali and Pathapatnam where they previously had no hold. One typical action here was the annihilation of Pratapchandra Padi, President of Devabandupuram Panchayat and a big landlord. This action was carried out by a squad of ten members who were joined by another ten from among the local people who were opposed to the landlord. The annihilation was carried out in a somewhat theatrical manner with the head of the dead landlord being severed from the body, and paraded through the villages.[43] In spite of actions like these and the very optimistic assessments, by the party in regard to the efficacy of the annihilation tactic in mobilising people wherever the party relied only on annihilations, the so called supporters and sympathisers fled at the first sign of strong police action. The Agency areas and, to a lesser extent the Boddapadu region where there was a tradition of mass activity, witnessed greater resilience on the part of the people.

The Srikakulam District Committee meeting's decision of May 14-16, 1969, was simultaneously being implemented in the agency area too. However, given the earlier mass support to the CPI (ML) in the region, none of these activities took place without mass participation. Therefore annihilation was seen here more as a way of driving away the landlords from the agency area and of terrorising the police informers, rather than as an act of propaganda and a way of mobilisation. The first attack consequent on the May 14, 1969 decision was on the landlords of Thumbali village. One of the landlords Gudla Siddhanti was annihilated while three others D. Appalaswami Naidu, M.V. Narasimhamurthi and Seshirekhamma were let off after their houses were ransacked and all promissory notes burnt.[44] In this event not only the party members, but the tribals numbering nearly a thousand from the neighbouring villages also participated. This was followed by the attack on village of Loharjola on 26 May 1969. Here one of the landlords Anguru Induvada Naidu was annihilated while six others were let off after their houses had been ransacked. In this incident about two thousand tribals led by Vempatapu, Choudary Tejeswara Rao and others participated.[45] In a third major incident about seven hundred tribals led by Vempatapu and others attacked a Savara landlord and usurer of Palakonda village, Samburu Naidu. In this attack about Rs. 10,000 was confiscated and distributed among the participants.[46]

Soon after the above incident the CPI (ML) celebrated Vietnamese Solidarity Day by ceremonially annihilating Nethala Balaji Naidu and Koti Chiranjeevi Naidu of village Mallivecdu.[47] This was followed by an attack on the tobacco and tamarind trader, Ramamurthi of Doddukallu village by the *Kendriyadalam* (Central Squad) in the agency area led by Vempatapu on August 8, 1969. Ramamurthi's house was ransacked and he was beaten up and left for dead.[48]

In the Boddapadu area the main target of the maoist attack was Maddi Kamesam the Garudabhadra landlord who had foiled an earlier attack. On August 5, 1969, the day before the Home Minister was due to visit the place, the activists conducted a raid on the village. This time (compared to the five hundred men in the previous attack) only a handful of people were involved. Pyla Vasudeva Rao who had nearly been handed over to the police by Maddi Kamesam on the previous occasion, killed the former in his second attack. On the whole this time there was hardly any participation by the local villagers and they preferred to view the fight as a personal one between Maddi Kamesam and the maoists rather than as one involving the village.[49]

To counter the maoist activities the Government declared the agency area in Srikakulam district as a disturbed area in June 1969.[50] The implication of this order was that the police came to be equipped with extraordinary powers. This order was extended in August to cover the whole area comprising the Pathapatnam, Sompeta, Tekkali, Icchapuram, Palakonda and Parvathipuram taluqs.[51] More Central Reserve Police (CRP) reinforcements were brought in and intensive combing operations were carried out. Orders to shoot at sight were also given.[52] Under the circumstances the maoists were compelled to restrict if not altogether abandon, their strategy of conducting open raids in the villages especially in the plains. In fact the problem of dealing with the Central Reserve Police overshadowed all others and ultimately they had to rely more and more upon squad organisation and squad actions.

The Squad Strategy

Informally, that is without it being accepted as a general policy, various area committees (as for instance the Sompeta committee) had been adopting the technique of organising themselves into squads in order to function more freely and effectively. Such squads had the merit of being more mobile, a factor which was invaluable when it came to avoiding the police dragnet. Towards the end of May the party slowly came to the conclusion that the best way of countering the police was to organise squads which would adopt guerilla tactics.

Guerilla tactics had been made use of even as far back as in December 1968 when one police party had been ambushed and another attacked and the camp burnt down. The general feeling of the leaders was that "the people gained confidence from the activities of guerilla squads. The mood of meek submission to repression, and the attitude that all their troubles vanished with their handing over the leaders to the police is no longer present. Pessimism is gone, and people are now evading arrests by climbing up the hills during police raids and even remain there for a long time when situation demanded."[53]

Committed to analysis of this sort it was decided to adopt a guerilla squad approach more fully. The squads were to have all the responsibilities ranging from making an analysis of the land ownership structure in their area, pin pointing the enemies and friends, to acting as the sentry to the village and watching police movements, and defending the village against police raids by organising ambushes.[54] They were to be armed with bows and arrows and bamboo sticks shaped as spears and at all times the squads were to maintain contacts with others through an elaborate courier system.[55]

The squad members at the village level were not full time members. They had to bear these responsibilities in addition to their normal occupation. The squad as a whole was responsible for the over all well-being of the party members and sympathisers. It had to provide for the families of member who had to leave the village by getting them financial and medical aid besides aiding them in their agricultural activities.[56]

The village defence squads were to be supervised by zonal organisers who co-ordinated the activities of the squads and were also instrumental in recruiting and forming the guerilla squads from among the members of the village defence squads.[57] The organiser was also the commander of the zonal squad. They had the last word as to when and on whom raids be were to conducted. He was also in charge of political and theoretical education of the cadre. In fact, the organisers were "the pillars on which the movement had to be carried forward".[58] The agency area was divided in all into fifteen zones each under the charge of an organiser.[59]

The guerilla strategy for facing the police which was decided upon received a further boost with the visit of Kanu Sanyal and Souren Bose, the two Central Committee members, to the agency area between July 30, 1969 and August 4, 1969. A conference was held in their presence at Etumanuguda in which as many as one hundred squads with all the top leaders participated.[60] During the conference Souren Bose conveyed the views of the Central Committee on the Srikakulam movement to those present as follows :

"We are of the opinion that a people's army can be raised in Srikakulam since the Red Government has aleady been established there. This army should have at least a thousand full time guerilla soldiers who will be used to carry out a mobile and offensive warfare against the landlord Government of India".[61] Commenting further on the lessons of Srikakulam struggle he said, "The Sompeta struggle showed us that we could mobilise a great number of people against the enemy and only through the guerilla warfare".[62] Bose and Sanyal also gave the details of their experience in China where they had military training for three and a half months in Wanking Military Academy.

Consequent on these discussions the following immediate programme was worked out. (1) Armed Struggle was to be intensified by attacks on police and by snatching away arms and ammunition. (2) A peoples liberation army was to be formed, trained and equipped to conduct mobile offensive warfare. (3) The struggle was to be extended to all possible areas. (4) Political propaganda was to be conducted among masses to make them aware of the necessity and the need to support guerilla warfare and (5) to kidnap landlords and hold them as hostages in return for ransom.[63] In this scheme of things, the relation between the guerilla and the people was seen as being similar to the one between the landlords and the army (police) i.e. the fighting arm of the general body. In the present stage (stage of intense police activities) it was felt that the people could hit back at the landlords only through the guerilla. "Without the guerilla the people can do nothing at this stage".[64] The condition of intensified police activities was in fact seen as a positive help to the formation and development of the guerilla units. They further felt that "the more there is repression on the people, the greater is their strength. Without repression, there is no people's army and thus no village revolutionary base. The present Governmental repression makes it easier for us to go forward and intensify the movement. Repression is as natural as waves in the sea, and those comrades who do not see it as such have not yet had a scientific understanding and proper political consciousness".[65]

The main objective of the mobile warfare in the immediate future was not to be that of defeating the enemy forces (police or army, as might the case be) but of inflicting the severest possible losses on them. "Our problem is not to defeat the enemy but as to how many class enemies we can kill. This is a war of annihilation of class enemies. When the situation is convenient we attack them and when inconvenient we withdraw and attack at some other place where it is convenient. This is the substance of mobile warfare".[66]

The organisation for this mobile warfare was to be based on guerilla squads, each having five to seven members. These roving bands were to be fed and supplied with information by the people and would be constantly on the move, ambushing the police and annihilating class enemies (landlords, money-lenders, police informers etc.). It was felt that they had the upper hand over the regular police for, according to Kanu Sanyal, "theirs is a mercenary army needing elaborate arrangements for food, housing etc. They do not have people's support and as such it was difficult for them to communicate with other police units and even to get information about the guerilla squads. For them it was only possible to conduct a stable warfare since they have to return to the camps as the night falls. In these circumstances the guerilla having people's support and sympathy and capable of conducting mobile warfare had an upper hand".[67]

Kanu Sanyal followed up his advice on guerilla struggle with a dramatic and courageous act to prove its effectiveness. He led an ambush on a police group consisting of nearly thirty-six men and after causing wounds to some of them seized their guns.[68]

Throughout in the month of May 1969 the guerillas engaged the police continuously for three days near Jeraduguda in Aviri area and finally forced them to make a temporary retreat. In the same area in June they forced a police search party which had come for the dead body of a landlord, to retreat without gaining their objective. In Podi area they raided the Andhra Pradesh Special Police camp twice and succeeded in creating considerable confusion and anxiety,[69] among the police ranks. The battalion of Andhra Pradesh Special Police which had its camp at Sirikonda was attacked thrice when it went towards Nilakantapuram in search of the maoists.[70] Eight policemen were killed in the Aviri hills in ambushes. On May 26, 1969, the police party clashed with maoists at Diguvavili and in the resultant firing Pyla Bheemudu was killed.[71] On the very next day the police clashed with a hundred and fifty tribal maoists and three tribals were killed.[72]

Government Response

The maoists however never really had an upper hand and once the police was strengthened by the addition of two battalions of Central Reserve Police in mid-July 1969 (which were now freed from their engagements with the separate Telangana agitation), their position worsened. The police brought with them more sophisticated equipment and made good transport and communication arrangements. They effectively prevented supplies coming from sympathisers and party members living in other areas from reaching the guerillas in the agency area. This combined with the disruption caused by the movement to the normal agricultural activity within the agency made the food situation very difficult for the guerillas. With this it became easier for the Central Reserve Police to hunt them down. The task was rendered even more easy by the guerilla's policy of attacking the police rather than defending themselves by retreating and hiding. In the Parvathipuram agency area the police had their first major success when they shot down six guerillas.[73] In another encounter near Elwinpet the guerillas lost their leader Biddika Addai.[74] This was followed by the further loss of guerilla leaders Kurangi Sundari and Addakula Chiranjeevulu in an encounter near Palakonda.[75] A major loss was suffered by the guerillas in an encounter in a mango grove near Elwinpet when ten tribal members of Nirmala Krishnamurti's squad were shot dead.[76] In an another incident five of the maoist cadre were shot dead.[77] The Central Reserve Police continued its operations of clearing the guerillas from the area with ruthless thoroughness. Innumerable arrests were made and they did not flinch even from burning whole hamlets with the purpose of terrorising guerilla sympathisers and forcing them to move into Government camps where they would not be in a position to help the guerilla squads.[78]

These measures were supplemented by various ameliorative and pacificatory steps. The then Home Minister J. Vengala Rao toured the entire area making promises of justice and help to each and all. Food and cattle were distributed among the tribals. In about 60 villages land was surveyed and about two hundred acres of land which was under occupation of plainsmen, and moneylenders was returned to the tribals and a promise was made that in the other villages too similar steps would be taken as soon as law and order was restored. A tribal cooperative bus service and a cooperative *Khandasari* sugar unit were opened.[79] The Girijan Corporation started free distribution of rice gruel and sale of subsidised rice. Fresh employment opportunities were provided for tribal boys as salesmen, inspectors and jeep drivers in the Corporation. Many tribal women were shown gainful employment in leaf-stitching and deseeding of tamarind. Prices offered to minor forest produce collected by the tribals as well as to the firewood felled by them were raised. Interest free short term loans were disbursed liberally and the corporation itself was streamlined in an effort to remove the corrupt officials. Promises were made to the tribals that any kind of harassment by forest guards and police men would be prevented.[80]

Stagnation

As a consequence of all this the help received by the guerillas from the people in the form of food. shelter and information was largely reduced. The guerillas themselves admitted that "the people are taking temporary protection under the Government. Though the masses do not see eye to eye with the Government under the pressure of circumstances they are being neutralised."[81]

The party acknowledged that there was "stagnation" in the movement, and that the cadre was losing enthusiasm. There were no fresh recruitments and the village defence squads were organisationally liquidated.[82] In fact, barring the Central Squad consisting of the hard core party leaders hardly any other squad was in a position to be active.

Questions began to arise among the cadre whether the steps taken by them were correct or not. Some felt that they had unnecessarily invited repression. However, the party opined "Repression after struggle is as natural as the sound following the explosion of a bomb. It is necessary to help the movement to go forward....Just like the pain during the child birth it is necessary to bring about a new system".[83] They felt that repression would "isolate the Government from the people and also enable us first to identify our real friends since at this moment one is forced to choose his sides".[84]

Reviewing their defeats they noted two factors as being mainly responsible for their setbacks. One was their inability to use the conventional methods of warfare (setting of traps ambushes, rolling of big stones from mountain tops etc.) effectively,[85] the other, their haphazard organisational methods. "At present there are practically no village defence squads functioning. Many mistakes took place in the building up of these squads. We acted under the assumption that recruiting members to the village defence squads can be done in the same manner as canvassing for supporters in the elections. Therefore no attention was paid to the individuals' initiative involvement and creativity".[86]

This kind of self-criticism however did not question the general strategic and tactical line which was seen as being correct in general, and which as such was to be continued but with minor changes. The cadre was asked to make the best possible use of the difficult situation. For example they were to take advantage of the growing rift between the landlords and the Central Reserve Police. "The CRP is snatching fowls from the landlords' homes and even misbehaving with their womenfolk. Some landlords are even thinking that the naxalites are preferable to the CRP. We must take advantage of the contradictions arising between the CRP and the landlords".[87]

The pressure of the situation however proved too much and contrary to the resolutions to continue as before, the guerillas were forced to make at least one major change in the mode of their activities. They left the more populous and open areas and shifted to places which provided them with more natural cover. In their search for safe hideouts which could be used as bases for activity they moved towards and even across the Orissa border and to the remote hilly regions within the agency area. In the party circle this was described as the spreading of the movement to new areas while in fact it was nothing more than retreating for the sake of survival and defence.[88] Quite obviously, whatever the compulsions of the situation the party refused to dilute in any way its acceptance of a strategy of offence vis-a-vis the police.

This position was reiterated at the meeting of the Central Organising Committee of CPI (ML) which was held at Calcutta between September 5-9, 1969. The meeting was attended by Mamidi Appalasuri and Choudary Tejeswara Rao from the Srikakulam Committee. It discussed reports from the various states and the programmes to be adopted by the party in each case. In the world context it saw World War looming large over the international horizon with the reactionary forces of the world getting ready to destroy the revolutionary forces in general and China in particular. To prevent such an eventuality from becoming a reality it was resolved that the revolutionaries all over the world were to intensify their struggles. This meant that the Indian revolutionaries were to "seize the day, seize the night and create as many pockets of struggle as possible". To this international imperative the national situation was also seen as providing a favourable opportunity. The country was seen as clearly polarised into two sides with the broad masses of people on one side and on the other side the feudal forces consisting of landlords and the entire bourgeoisie of India which was characterised as being totally comprador in nature. This situation, it was felt, called for starting innumerable small bases of armed struggle. with it was further argued could take a political form only when the class enemy was annihilated.[89] In sum, to the Srikakulam Committee this meant that they were to continue as before and go on intensifying their activities and starting new areas of activity wherever possible.[90]

In October 1969 a conference of squad commanders and party organisers was held in Megada hills of Parvathipuram taluq. In this meeting discussions were held about the Calcutta decisions which were made known to them by Mamidi Appalasuri. The Agency Committee was also reconstituted with Vempatapu as General Secretary and T. Pandu Ranga Rao, Namballa Appalachari, Kurangi Chakrapani and Kurangi Mokhalingam as members.[91] Significantly this was the only time when Vempatapu was given a position of some importance in a party committee.

Brief Revival:

At about the same time as the meeting was being held eleven top maoist leaders escaped from the Visakhapatnam jail. They included among others, Adibhatla Kailasam, Nagabhushan Patnaik and Dr. Mallikarjunudu.[92] This spectacular jail break came as a shot in the arm and boosted the sagging morale of the maoists. also strengthened them organisationally as the leaders quickly re-established their contacts with the movement.

After the Megada hills meeting and the Visakhapatnam jail break there was a revival in maoist guerilla activities. At Peddabhudidi village the maoists led four hundred tribals in an attack on landlords. Property worth Rs. 40,000 was looted, a cloth shop ransacked and Putnuru Satyanarayana the local Sarpanch, abducted and released, after collecting a ransom of Rs. 3,000/-. Among others Vempatapu Satyam and Adibhatla Kailasam participated in the raid.[93] This was followed by the annihilation of Sari Appanna at the village of Banjara-yuvarajapuram, in the plains area bordering Mahendragiri hills. The maoists bore a grudge against Sari Appanna, a rich landlord of this village, because he had previously tried to get Pyla Vasudeva Rao arrested by the police. In this incident a squad led by Tamada Ganapati and Pyla Vasudeva Rao, attacked and killed him. His head was severed and hung up to a beam in front of his house and slogans were written on the walls with his blood. Property worth Rs. 60,000 was looted and many promissory notes burnt.[94] At around the same time in the agency area the maoists Kurangi Vasunarayana and Kurangi Mokhalingam led nearly two hundred tribals in an attack on Himmaraka Mohan Rao and killed him. Mohan Rao was an ex-President of the Sitampet Panchayat Samiti who after having been elected with Communist support crossed over to Congress and was suspected to be helping the police. This period also saw several attacks on the police and according to the maoists following the Megada hills meeting fourteen policemen in all were killed. Eight in an ambush at Nidagallu hill, three in an encounter at Bartangi, two in another encounter at Bandlaguda and one in Orissa.[95]

The 'successes' of maoists were shortlived. They suffered a major loss in an encounter at Kerasingi hills in Tekkali taluq. In this incident one of their most active squads was wiped out and the losses included Tamada Ganapati, the secretary of the Srikakulam District Committee and Dr. Chaganti Bhaskara Rao, a chief organiser of the plains area.[96]

Consequent on this loss a meeting of the squad leaders of Sompeta was held on 15.12.1969 to discuss reorganisation plans. It was decided to streamline the courier system to maintain constant communications between the party centres and squads. Some suggestions were also made regarding improvement in the relations between tribal and non-tribal elements within the movement. To this end the members who had come from outside were asked to shun elitist attitudes which they some time adopted towards the local tribals. The squads were also asked to learn Hindi and Oriya as the movement it was claimed was 'spreading' into Orissa and other regions bordering the Srikakulam area. Finally many suggestions were made regarding the safety of party leaders. They felt that most of their losses were occurring during their movement from one place to another. So the members were asked to avoid travelling by trains, buses and other public transport systems and when forced to travel to carry bombs and other arms. The squads were asked to thoroughly acquaint themselves with the topography of their area of their operation, and to take adequate precautions while going to new places.[97]

Soon after the Sompeta squad meet, the maoists received a crushing blow when six of their top leaders were apprehended and shot dead by the police on 22 December, 1969.[98] On 19th December four squads consisting of sixteen members left the Kerandi den where the Sompeta squad leaders meeting had taken place. They were moving towards the interior mountain ranges, when an accidental bomb explosion caused injuries to two of their members and forced them to halt and camp for the night. They were taken unawares by the police because their sentry[99] was asleep. Subba Rao Panigrahi who was the Secretary of the Uddanam Committee had the previous day dismissed any need for elaborate precautions saying that "there is no need for sentry in distance. The people will inform us of any dangers".[100] Six members including Subba Rao Panigrahi, an Oriya lawyer Ramesh Chandra Sahu, and Panchadi Nirmala were arrested along with three others and later shot dead.[101]

This event caused the movement in plains area to come to a standstill. A squad leader wrote "The cadre are getting frustrated and are scared. Even I am scared. To give others courage I do not show my fear—and try my best to keep up the spirits. But it is not possible to give a concrete programme with the tragedy staring in front of our eyes".[102] With these events several maoist guerillas left for their homes on various pretexts.[103] The plains area committee in its review noted that "there is no enthusiasm; there are no new recruitments. There are no village defence squads. Except for the Central Squad, there are no squads capable of attacking the enemy".[104]

In spite of this major set-back the maoists in Uddanam continued their activities under the leadership of Dr. Mallikarjunudu.[105] His squad managed to capture Latchanna who had given police the information leading to the death of Subba Rao Panigrahi and the death of other five maoists. A people's court was held where eighty people from ten villages attended. In this meeting they let off the captured police agent who had caused inestimable loss to them because "the people said 'leave him'. We will ourselves kill him if he repeats his activity". After this the squad planned to kill policemen to avenge death of their comrades. They got an opportunity when five Orissa policemen came to Bansugaon village. But the squad members who were at this time staying in the nearby Impirisingi village were dissuaded from making an ambush by the local people who pleaded that they had a festival on the next day and as such they should not spoil the atmosphere. In view of this kind of attitude on the part of the people the squad limited its activities to propaganda and meetings. They went round villages forming committees and setting up contacts. For the time being under the relentless pressure of events and local responses (or the lack of it) they refrained from resorting to annihilation. Even when they caught two policemen near Sirankandi village they let them off after delivering a long lecture about maoist philosophy.[106]

Even in this situation Charu wrote a letter to the Srikakulam maoists in which he said "organise the children, teach them politics .....a new man unafraid of death and losses is being created in your area. Enemy's last hours are coming near. So he is becoming terrible......in two or three months Bengal is going to turn into a volcano".

Vempatapu's Criticism of District Leadership

At this stage the effective theoretical leadership of the movement fell into the hands of Vempatapu Satyam, who had already proved himself to be its most succesful and enduring leader. He came out with two documents reviewing the causes of the failure of the movement and the future course of action. This document put the blame for failure squarely on the district level leadership viz. Nagabhushanam Patnaik, Mamidi Appalasuri and Tejeswara Rao. The main points of criticisms were : (1) "The Zilla leadership did not implement Mao's thought in practice" for Mao stressed the need to establish bases in the mountain region and later spread to the plains. The district leadership ignored this completely and prematurely extended the activities to the plains. (2) Some members of Zilla leadership repeatedly gave revisionist and defeatist advice. Appalasuri differentiated between good and bad landlords, between tribal and non-tribal exploiters and suggested alliance with the former type. "They gave slogans like "Respect those who respect us. Reject those who disrespect us. This is Gandhism rather than maoism". (3) The Zilla leadership "behaved like officers, who visited occasionally and point out the mistakes. But they never directed as to how to rectify our mistakes nor even give a correct line". (4) The Zilla leadership is responsible for disarming of the masses which had taken up arms on November 25, 1968 to confront directly the Special Armed Police and restricting struggle to the guerilla squads only. As a result instead of staying in an area, and consolidating the power and gains in that area, the cadre was kept roving without any purpose. (5) The Zilla leadership demoralised the movement by condemning heroic deeds of the people for example the seizure of landlords' property at Mondemkhal and the burning of police camps were characterised as hasty by Appalasuri and others. (6) All initiative of the local units was suppressed and destroyed. They were not allowed to even issue pamphlets, thus preventing any kind of propaganda. (7) The District leadership failed to inform the local units of the actual conditions of movement thus causing confusion and failing to co-ordinate the various activities. (8) The District leadership failed to help the struggle area units with finances, or medical facilities or supply of arms and ammunition or help in recruiting and training cadre".[108]

In the light of his criticism the agency committee decided to fight revisionism and opportunism in the party by setting up a centre in the 'red area' which would co-ordinate various activities and provide proper guidance and help. This area was to be stabilised as a base, using the mountain region as shelter and then slowly spread to the plains area in order carry on the annihilation programme.[108] Based on a faulty reading of this document several people have tried to present it as evidence for Vempatapu having said that non-tribal interference in tribal affairs must stop. In fact, Vempatapu was criticising only the interference of district leadership.

Shift to the mountains

After the severe losses in plains area and following the Agency committee document, most of the maoist hardcore cadre in plains districts shifted to mountainous regions by January 1970. The leadership at this time in the plains regions was with Dr. Mallikarjunudu,[109] along with three other top leaders—Dummu Appalaswamy, U. Malleshwara Rao and Pyla Vasudeva Rao,who moved into the Uddanam area. This area comprised Tekkali and Sompet Taluks which were covered mainly by cashew topes and bordered on one side by the Bay of Bengal and on the other side by the Mahendragiri range of hills. It had a number of places which were not easily accessible and therefore it was in this area that the maoists decided to carry on their activities.

This new centre of their activities is best described in Dr. Mallikarjunudu's own words "There are no landlords here but people are being ruthlessly repressed by moneylenders and traders. The agricultural labourer unable to find work is migrating to industrial area or becoming slaves of moneylenders whose loans they are unable to repay. All the women here are working and as a result quite independent. They show a lot of response to our propaganda. The fishermen are very poor and do not own the implements of their profession—boats, nets etc. These are controlled by the *sowcars* who extract a heavy return for their use. Previously there was no activity of the communists here. All the people here were under the influence of Swatantra Party. We have developed relations with all the villages between Dokalpadu and Baruvavara on the trunk road by the sea"[110]

The *modus operandi* of the maoists at this stage seems to have been to station themselves in safe regions of mountains, establish contacts with villagers, enquire of their problems and to preach that the solution lay in annihilation. If they felt that this propaganda had a good response from a particular area, they would conduct a foray into the village, carry out an annihilation and follow it up by some more speeches and propaganda. Then they would again withdraw into the mountain region to surface at another village at a later time.[111] In one typical action of this type which took place on January 18, 1970 in the village Bavanapuram, Voona Savariah the local moneylender was killed, his head severed and hung from the beam in front of the house. Rs. 30,000 was seized and promissory notes worth one lakh burnt.[112] The maoists claimed that this action relieved hundreds of indebted peasants in about fifteen villages of the surrounding area. However, the participation in the actual act was limited to the maoist guerilla cadre. Another such action took place on February 2, 1970 at Ambati-Kambaram where a moneylender Narayana Gowda was killed in a similar fashion and Rs. 10,000 seized.[113] In this action it is claimed by the maoists that many local people also participated.[114]

In May 1970 the Central Organisation Committee of the CPI (ML) met at Calcutta. Vempatapu, Nagabhushan Patnaik, Adibhatla Kailasam and Appalasuri represented Andhra Pradesh. In spite of three of these being closely connected with the Srikakulam movement there was hardly any concrete discussion about the specific situation in Srikakulam except for paying homage to the martyrs and commending the glorious people of Srikakulam. No note was taken of the defeats and no discussion was made on whether any modification in strategy and tactics was necessary.[115]

Disaster and Downfall

June and July 1970 were disastrous for the maoists in Srikakulam. The May Draft Programme of CPI (ML) had called for offensive action, painting a rosy picture of the present and future. In spite of nagging doubts many local leaders continued to be optimistic. On 13 of June, Dr. Mallikarjundu wrote in his diary, "We can seize arms on a large scale and soon form the peoples' army. So in a short time we will be in a position to march to Bengal".[116] Such a false sense of optimism led to further attacks on the police and this proved fatal for them in the face of intense combing operations by the C.R.P.

The first major casualty for the maoists came early in June. In the Polla Area of Agency region, their top leader and organiser Medavarapu Ramanamurthy, was shot dead in an encounter with the police. Ramanamurthy, a school teacher of Badevalasa, was the main maoist organiser in Bobbili Taluka. Consequent on the severe losses in plains areas, he was shifted to the mountain regions on Polla, in consonance with the agency committee document which advised withdrawal from plains and building of base areas. Functioning in the same fashion as the Uddanam squads he had annihilated five landlords and was killed while he was returning from this campaign.[117]

On 9.6.1970, Simhachalam a member of the Uddanam maoist squads was arrested and he turned a police informer. This caused many losses to the maoists. "He showed them all the places which are used by us, he got arrested the people who were making guns and ammunition for us. He exposed all our sympathisers, many of whom including all the villagers of Tangaruputta were arrested. He showed the police the hideout of Pyla Vasudeva Rao, who escaped just in the nick of the time. Here a whole lot of equipment - SBML gun, country bombs, explosive substances, electric detonators, gelatine, cartridges etc. fell into police hands. He also exposed our Kondalogam centre, but since we were careful nobody was arrested. Now the police have all the information and our whole organisation in Uddanam area is exposed".[118] Five days after the Simhachalam affair, Jutti Umapati who was incharge of couriering in the Uddanam area was killed by police.[119] They suffered losses in other areas also for example on June 25, 1970, in an encounter near Jonaga hills in the agency area Mandali Sangamesu was killed.[120]

Even amidst these reverses the maoists of Uddanam carried on a raid on the landlord of Attukota village on 10 June. Promissory notes worth Rs. 90,000 were seized and burnt in front of the villagers. No annihilation was carried out as the landlord managed to escape from the backdoor. Reviewing the success of this raid they felt that they had established contacts with local people and had taken the help of those who were directly benefited by the action—the indebted peasants.[121] This was followed by two other annihilations in the agency area– one at village Tulasivalasa, another at Naiduvalasa on 11 June.[122]

In July 1970, the Central Reserve Police inflicted two fatal blows to this campaign, one of which destroyed almost the entire maoist leadership of the agency area and the other did the same to the maoist leadership in the Uddanam area. On 10.7.1970 the police were informed by a broker of Gottivada Sarpanch (who was supporting Tadangi Naidu for the post of Panchayat Samiti President) that Vempatapu Satyanarayana and Adibhatla Kailasam were camping in Bori hills, reportedly to canvass support for Thati Raju, a follower of maoists who was contesting for the Panchayat Samiti Presidency. Acting on this information the police led by PVV Stayanarayana, DSP of Parvatipuram, surrounded Vempatapu and Adibhatla and a group of sixteen other maoists and in the resultant encounter both were killed.[123]

On 30.7.1970 the police wiped out the entire maoist leadership of Uddanam area in a single blow. Dr. Mallikarjunudu, Dummu Appalaswamy and Urlam Malleswara Rao were surrounded when they were camping on the Ramrai hills. The police report says that all of them lost their lives in the resulting encounter.[124]

Around this time (July 22, 1970) Nagabhushanam Patnaik and Appalasuri both of whom were members of the CPI (ML) Politbureau and in charge of the Srikakulam movement, after their escape from the prison in October 1969, had gone to Calcutta and met Charu Majumdar, reportedly to plead the view that isolated killings of 'jotedars' were alienating the maoists from the rural masses. Before they could return they were arrested in a clinic at Calcutta.[125]

Thus the Srikakulam movement was hardly left with any of the old leaders who had started the movement. Only Pyla Vasudeva Rao was surviving among the old cadre. Due to pressure of police he seemed to have gone to Calcutta for a couple of months during this period. In these circumstances a teenaged engineering student from Nellore, Rajaram Reddy was elected as the Secretary of the Agency Area Committee and given the responsibility of continuing the movement. By this time the guerillas who had nearly 8000 men with them at the height of their operation[126] were reduced to hardly 20 or 30.[127] Around a hundredmaoists had been killed in encounters,[128] and nearly three thousand were in jails. Most of those who had come from the plains had left the area. The police on the other hand were present in full strength. There were twenty-two DSPs (as against only one before) with two Central Reserve Police battalions, eight companies of Andhra Pradesh State Police and six platoons of District Armed Reserved Police stationed in Srikukulam to suppress the maoist movement.[129] The police had established three new police stations in areas where the maoists were strong –Sitampet, Nilakantapuram and Donubai. These were supplemented by many police outposts in forest areas and police pickets in villages which were maoist strongholds. They had also established many protection centres on the lines of Vietnam's strategic hamlets, into which the tribals were moved from their hill-top hamlets thus cutting off the guerilla's contact with the tribal masses. In these circumstances, the maoist activity came to a complete standstill at least for the time being in their old strongholds in spite of the energetic campaigns of Rajaram who used to tour the area extensively trying to arouse the people into guerilla action again. With his command of the tribal language and his ability to totally identify himself with the local population by using their language, clothes and customs etc. he was able to escape the police until January 1973 when, according to the police version he died in an encounter near Donubai hills. The maoists alleged that he was shot by the police after being arrested at Kotturu on 30 January.[130]

This left only Pyla Vasudeva Rao among the old cadre. He seemed to have an inordinate knack for survival. Thrice he escaped by hair's breadth. First in the Garudabhadra incident[131] and again in the encounter at Mattlaipet where Tamada Ganapati and Bhaskara Rao were captured[132] and finally in the police raid on his hideout following Simhachalam's revelations.[133] He was later joined by Appalasuri who escaped from police custody for the second time by jumping from a running train but neither could do much thereafter. The Srikakulam movement had finally run out of steam.

Conclusion

If anything the foregoing description of the progress of events at Srikakulam shows how tricky the entire business of analysing the movement really is, for, unlike the theoretical formulations, the actual implementation of the policies does not fall into rigid slots or phases. Of course it would be too much to expect that this would in fact happen especially when one notices the wide variety of conditions in which these policies were sought to be implemented. In fact because of these variations in conditions, even within the confines of Srikakulam itself, one finds that the manner in which the movement progressed in the agency areas was somewhat different from the manner in which it did in the plains areas.

One thing that emerges clearly is that the implementation of any policy followed the dictates of compulsion and expedience as much as that of principle. For instance the shift from mass action to action by squads took place not merely because the party leaders after careful analysis advocated it but also because the local leaders were not in a position to engineer mass actions once police repression reached a certain level. Thus, in the plains areas the leaders unable to mobilise the masses to any great extent found it extremely convenient to adopt the changed line and did so with considerable alacrity. In fact in certain areas of Boddapadu, squad action was in operation even before the party formally advocated it. At the same in the agency areas where the movement always enjoyed the support of the people mass action continued to be adopted with several hundreds of villagers participating in each action even after the party line had changed. In both cases, the party line really had very little to do with the methods adopted by the leaders and to view the activities as instances of adherence to party line would be somewhat farfetched because there never was any choice and the leaders even if they had so desired would not have been able to implement any other line.

The pattern of development of the movement within Srikakulam also had a lot to do with the leadership in each area. There was one set of leaders who were thrown up during the organisational crisis which enveloped the communist party when the maoists broke away. This included among others persons like Choudary Tejeswara Rao, Panchadi Krishnamurti and Mamidi Appalasuri, who operated almost entirely in the plains areas. On the other hand, there was what may be termed as the "*traditional*" leadership of Vempatapu, Adibhatla Kailasam and others who had been operating in the agency areas for over a decade and who had achieved a position among the tribals which none of the other activists could hope to match. Over the years these leaders had painstakingly built up a movement which involved almost all the tribals in the area and when they finally did join the AICCCR in preference to the APCCCR it was a conscious and deliberate decision taken not only because of the support that would accrue to them in terms of finance and organisation but also because they genuinely felt that the stand taken by the AICCCR was the correct one. In a sense thus, the '*traditional*' leaders adopted the AICCCR as much as the AICCCR adopted the movement. This being the case it is somewhat strange that the leaders of the AICCCR never bothered to induct either Vempatapu of any of the other agency area leaders into the decision making bodies of the party. By and large the party bosses tended to depend on the newer leaders operating in the plain areas and as a consequence it was they who dominated the various party committees including even the Srikakulam district committee. Initially this situation was apparently of little consequence as no friction was generated between the two sets of leaders, but obviously all was not well. As the movement faltered Vempatapu Satyam launched a scathing attack on the Srikakulam district committee accusing the members among other things of behaving like "officers, who visit occasionally and point out the mistakes".[134] Significantly enough, Vempatapu Satyam's charges were all against the District Committee leaders and he voiced no complaint against Charu Majumdar himself.

One can also discern a difference in the attitudes of the district leaders and the CPI(ML) party leaders towards the movement in Srikakulam. To the leaders of the party in West Bengal, the Srikakulam movement was just one more movement and any setback which it received was not viewed with the same seriousness as did the district leaders. In fact they were more worried about the impact which such a setback could have on other movements, mainly the one in Bengal, than on the movement in Srikakulam itself. So much so that in December 1969, Charu Majumdar went to the extent of dissuading the Andhra representatives to the CPI(ML) Central Committee from revealing the real extent of losses suffered in Srikakulam on the plea that given the national mass upsurge, such revelation would preach moderation and caution when in fact the need was for going ahead and unleashing struggles everywhere. The losses were explained away as an inevitable price to be paid and it was even argued to be beneficial in the long run because it would arouse class hatred. The only comment which the COC of the CPI(ML) made was "our grief is immense, our grief is great. But Comrades we must turn this great grief into deep hatred towards the class enemy... We call upon the entire party to annihilate as many of the class enemies in the countryside as possible and thus avenge the despicable murders of the valiant comrades of Srikakulam".[135] All this was actually linked to the basic premise of the existence of revolutionary upsurge everywhere which the CPI(ML) leaders accepted unequivocally. With this premise in view the setbacks were seen as only being temporary and as arising out of organisational and operational weaknesses which could be overcome. At no stage did the CPI(ML) leaders consider re-evaluating this basic premise of theirs and because of this they were inexorably drawn towards adopting a more and more extreme stance.

Despite the reverses in Srikakulam, Charu Majumdar continued to voice his optimism regarding the progress of the movement in general and the atmosphere was seen as not only favouring but actually demanding immediate revolution in India. In this he found encouragement from the political developments both national and international which were taking place at that time. In the international arena the intensification of the Vietnam war and the precipitation of an international monetary crisis were viewed as further signs of weakening of the enemies of revolution. Charu Majumdar, writing in *Liberation* in October 1969, expressed the view that Imperialism hedged in on all sides by the surging struggles of the people, was frantically plotting to launch a war of aggression on China, which after the cultural revolution had emerged as the bastion against the reactionary forces of the world. In this situation, he wrote, war could be prevented from becoming an inevitability only by consolidating the forces of revolution. He exhorted his cadre to "seize the day, seize the hour, exert yourself to the utmost, do not lose a single moment in starting armed struggles in India."[136] Satyanarayan Singh expressing similar opinions felt that India with its vast manpower and immense resources occupies a very important position in the imperialists' global strategy to destroy China. This meant 'for us in India that we must mobilise all our efforts to unleash the revolutionary people's wars throughout India and we must create hundreds of Naxalbaries... This would help us not only in besieging the enemy at home but would also frustrate the imperialist plot to use India as a base for aggressive war".[137]

The national situation too was perceived as being extremely favourable for starting armed struggles everywhere. The continuing anti-Congress wave and political instability as indicated by the results of the 1969 mid-term elections coupled with the split in the Congress Party was analysed as indicating that "political stability has now become a thing of past. All the ruling parties present a picture of disintegration. Faced with the ever deepening economic crisis they can hardly deceive the people any longer".[138] No significance was attached to the new socialist slogans of Indira Gandhi. In their opinion these slogans only enabled one to see "more clearly the crafty reactionary features of Mrs. Gandhi and her party".[139] In general they felt that the "puppet character of the present regime and hollowness of the Parliamentary system are becoming clear to the entire people... The necessity of the battle of annihilation against these butchers is felt by vast masses of the people and the struggle is spreading to rural areas with tremendous vigour".[140] It was also noted that "the present armed struggles have engulfed more than twelve States in India and have already become a motive force of the history. The onward march of the armed struggle of the peasantry will continue unabated".[141] They thus saw success and progress all around for their armed struggle.[142] Continuing in this highly optimistic vein they maintained that "the new year held promises of still bigger victories"[143] and called upon their followers to "Make the 1970s the decade of Liberation".[144] In fact Charu Majumdar even went to the extent of prophesying the liberation of India by 1975 after formation of a Red Army and a Long March over India during early seventies.[145] Clearly then, there was, at no stage any perspective of a long drawn out struggle.

Considering all this optimism, which on hindsight looks quite exaggerated, it is obvious that the AICCCR bosses saw no reason to alter their stance on annihilation and guerilla warfare. A closer look at the progress of the movement would have revealed that their optimism was misplaced. The implementation of the annihilation policy in Srikakulam for instance was at best erratic. While a majority of incidents occurring immediately after the announcement of the policy did result in annihilations this was no longer so after a while and annihilation as a matter of policy ceased to be implemented and we find several instances in which the victim was let off for no apparent reasons. With their belief in the existence of revolutionary upsurge everywhere the party never saw the need for either propaganda or for large participation from the people. They only sought to provide the "spark" to set the "prairie fire" of revolution going. But in the end all that they achieved was alienation from the masses, a fact which became even more pronounced when police repression grew. So much so that in the later stages of the movement they did not receive any cover when they resorted to action from the villagers whom they were supposedly benefiting. In fact the villagers on their part tended to view the whole thing as a personal affair between the maoists and the victim. This in a sense was perhaps inevitable because the villagers were often not consulted on the issue of who was to be annihilated and the victims were chosen more for the danger they presented to the activities of the cadre rather than to the villagers themselves. In other words it was more a policy of annihilation of party enemy rather than one of annihilation of class enemy.

The party's advocacy of guerilla warfare everywhere irrespective of whether there was a strong movement existing in the area or not was also based on their stubborn acceptance of the existence of an upsurge everywhere. Clearly in this respect their strategy failed. In fact even Vempatapu was constrained to remark that "The Zilla leadership did not implement Mao's thought in practice – for while Mao stressed the need to establish bases in the mountain region and afterwards spreading to the plains, the district leadership had ignored this and prematurely extended the activities to the plains".[146]

To a very great, there was thus a certain rigidity about the attitude of the CPI(ML) in general. Whenever faced with a choice of either revising their over optimistic assessment of the favourability of the conditions for a revolution or of changing their strategy they always plumped for the latter. As a consequence they were forced to adopt a more and more extremist line which in the end they were unable to maintain. In this regard the approach of the maoists in the Telangana area, represents a total contrast and it is to them that we shall devote the next two chapters.

NOTES & REFERENCES

1. "Ryotu Karyakarta," *Amara Veerula Charitra*, Pilupu Publications, Hyderabad 1973, p. 147.

2. *Charge Sheet* of Parvatipuram Conspiracy Case, also known as Naxalite Conspiracy Case (NCC) p. 14.

3. *The Hindu,* December 19, 1968.
4. Crime Sheet of NCC, *op. cit.* p. 15.
5. Crime Number (Cr. No.) 117/68 of P.S. Elvinpet First Information Report (FIR) of 20.12.1968.
6. Cr. No. 118/68 of P.S. Elvinpet, FIR of 23.12.1968.
7. Cr. No. 119/68, of P.S. Elvinpet, FIR of 23.12.1968.
8. See for example Cr. No. 6/69 of P.S. Kurupam, FIR of 16.1.1969 and Cr. No. 4/69 of P.S. Nilakantapuram.
9. *Agraharamdar* is a kind of land tenure system in which the management and ownership belonged to the local priest.
10. *Charge Sheet* of NCC p. 15. The news of Charu's visit reached the police after some days and they raided Gangannadoravalasa. In the resultant clash with the local tribals the maoists suffered their first casuality—Renjim a Savara peasant, the leader of the local squad died.
11. *Charge Sheet* of NCC p. 17.
12. *Ibid.*
13. *Ibid,* pp. 16-17.
14. *Ibid.*
15. Cr. No. 13/69 of P.S. Kasibugga, FIR of 16.12.1969.
16. Document A-4 of NCC Panchadi Krishnamurty's diary.
17. Cr. No. 17/69 of P.S. Baruva, FIR of 24.3.1969.
18. Cr. No. 27/69 of P.S. Sompeta and FIR of 31.3.1969.
19. Cr. No. 21/69 of P.S. Mandasa, FIR of 24.4.1969.
20. Cr. No. 19/69 of P.S. Mundasa, FIR of 19.4.1969. This was the first incidence of killing by the maoist squads.
21. Cr. No. 45/69 of P.S. Bobbili, FIR of 7.3.1969.
22. Cr. No. 45/48/69 of P.S. Bobbili, FIR's of 10.3.1969.
23. Document 4-9 of NCC.

24. For example Cr. No. 3/69, 18/69 and 19/69 of P.S. Nilakantapuram, Cr. No. 22/69 of P.S. Elvinpet.

25. See Cr. No. 10/69 of P.S. Elvinpet, FIR of 5.4.1969 and Cr. No. 23/69 of P.S. Kothuru, FIR of 10.5.1969.

26. Cr. No. 9/69 and 11/69 of P.S. Nilakantapuram.

27. Cr. No. 7/69 of P.S. Donubai, FIR of 12.3.1969.

28. *Charge Sheet* of NCC *op. cit.* p. 21.

29. Besides the ***Political and Organisational Report, op. cit.*** several articles in *Liberation* also elucidate the theory of annihilation. For example, see "Flames of Guerilla... struggle spread to New Area". *Liberation,* January 1970 and "March forward by summing up the experience of Revolutionary Peasant Struggle", *Liberation,* December 1969.

30. "Flames of Guerilla...etc." *op. cit.* p. 61.

31. *Liberation*, February 1970. This article called by some as the ***Murder Manual*** is compared to Carlos Marghellas *Mini-manual Urban for Guerillas.* This was circulated among the maoists and became the basis for all their actions during 1969-70, particularly in West Bengal.

32. "A few words about guerilla actions", *Passim.*

33. *Ibid,* p. 23.

34. FIR of Cr. No. 31 and 32/69 of P.S. Ichapuram.

35. This included among others Tamada Chinna Babu who often used to play female roles in Subba Rao Panigrahi's cultural troupe, Dunna Gopala Rao, Bayanapalli Papa Rao, and the 13 year Niranjan Rao. Many of them were students of Boddapadu High School and had come under the influence of their radical. headmaster FIR of Cr. No. 37/69, P.S. Sompeta states that they were killed in an encounter. This is strongly contested by the party circle among others. A pamphlet (Document E-6 of NCC) says that they were arrested while travelling in a train, and taken to the hills and shot dead. In Vempa-

tapu's book (*op. cit.* p. 46) it is maintained that they were arrested on May 27, 1969 at Kanchali railway station near Sompeta, taken to village Jasantarkot where they were shot dead.

36. Document E-9 of NCC, Minutes of Sompeta Area Committee Meeting of 24.6.1969.

36. See Document D-1 and U-9 of NCC, *op. cit* and Cr. No. 39/69 of P.S. Sompeta, FIR of 1.7.1969.

38. *Mangalasutram* is a sacred thread worn by the wives during the lifetime of her husband and a attaining widowhood is removed.

39. Document D-1 of NCC.

40. Cr. No. 39/69 and 40/69 of P.S. Kasibugga, FIR of 20.6.1969.

41. Document M-1 of NCC Summary of Sompeta Taluq Cadres meeting discussions.

42. Document D-1 *op. cit.*

43. Cr. No. 71/68 of P.S. Pathapatnam, FIR of 18.7.1969.

44. Cr. Nos. 31/69, 32/69 33/66 and 34/69 of P.S. Kurupam and relevant FIRs of 17.5.1969.

45. Bhaskar Das, "Srikakulam Vimukti Porata Vaastavalu". *Prasarita*, July—September 1972, p. 31, also Cr. Nos. 26/69 and 36/69 P.S. Pattapatnam.

46. Cr. No. 9/69 of P.S. Sitampet.

47. Cr. No. 64/67/69 of P.S. Palakonda, FIR of 20.8.1969.

48. Cr. No. 51/69 of P.S. Kurupam, FIR of 20.8.1969.

49. Information based on interview.

50. Under section 3 of Andhara Pradesh Suppression of Disturbances Act of 1948. G.O.Ms. No. 371 of GAD, Govt. of Andhra Pradesh.

51. G.O.Ms. No. 626, August 20, 1969 of GAD Dept. of Section General A, Government of Andhra Pradesh.

52. Document U-62 *op. cit.*

53. Document U-31 of NCC.

54. Documents K-4 and C-2 of NCC.

55. Documents C-9 and C-1 of NCC.

56. Document C-2 *op. cit.*

57. *Ibid.*

58. *Ibid.*

59. These 15 zones and their organisers are (1) Kurangi Vasunarayana for Sirikonda, (2) Bora Appala Narasayya for Marripadu, (3) Narayana Rao for Doddukallu, (4) Kumar for Peddakharja, (5) Malayya for Palakonda and Polla, (6) Mokhalingam for Killada, (7) Prabhakar for Manapuram, (8) Ranga Raju for Chinnakambha, (9) Pandu Ranga Rao for Kaliki and Dobba, (10) Appala Chari for Podi, (11) Chakrapani for Jammuvalasa, (12) Laxminarayana for Kuntubai, (13) Brahma Reddi for Gujjuvayi, (14) Jarada Somulu for Aviri and (15) Krishna Rao for Merangi. Eleven of these fifteen were plainsmen.

60. V.M. Nair, "Extent of Naxalite Revolt in Andhra Pradesh". *The Statesman* December 10, 1969.

61. Document C-2, *op. cit.*

62. In *Ibid*—Tejeshwara Kao's Provincial Committee Report.

63. *Ibid.*

64. Document E-3 of NCC "On Guerilla Warfare".

65. *Ibid.*

66. *Ibid.*

67. *Ibid.*

68. Document C-2 *op. cit.*

69. '*Amara...etc*', *op. cit.* p. 159.

70. Cr. No. 14/69, 15/69 and 16/69 of P.S. Nilakantapuram.

71. Cr. No. 12/69 of P.S. Nilakantapuram and Document N-4 of NCC.

72. See Cr. Nos. 17/69 of P.S. Nilakantapuram and also Cr. Nos. 34/69 to 36/69 of P.S. Elvinpet.

73. Cr. Nos. 16 to 18/69 of P.S. Elvinpet.

74. Cr. No. 36/69 of P.S. Elvinpet, FIR of 13.7.1969.

75. Cr. No. 69/69 of P.S. Palakonda, FIR of 24.7.1969.

76. Cr. No. 37/69 of P.S. Elvinpet, FIR of 3.8.1969.

77. Cr. No. 79/69 of P.S. Elvinpet. See also Cr. Nos. 49/69, 54/69, 75/69 and 73/69 of P.S. Kurupam, Cr. No. 14/69, 15/69, 20/69, 21/69. 25 to 27/69, 31/69, 1/70 and 2/70 of P.S. Nilakantapuram, Cr. No. 37/69, 43/69, 47/69, 51/69, 8/70, 14/70 and 17/70 of P.S. Elvinpet for description of clashes between the CRP and the maoists. Excepting in two of these cases the casualty suffered was invariably by the maoists.

78. Document S-6, *op. cit.*

79. See Subba Rao, "Revolt in Srikakulam", *op. cit.*

80. "The Healing Touch", *Free Press Journal*, December 26, 1970.

81. Document R-1 of NCC.

82. *Ibid.*

83. Document E-2, *op. cit.*

84. Document E-3, of NCC.

85. Document Z-2 of NCC.

86. Document Y-8 of NCC.

87. Volume 7 of NCC, p. 120.

88. Document S-6, *op. cit.* The police immediately reacted to the new situation holding a joint meeting of Andhra and Orissa forces and made efforts for combined activity to curb guerilla movement, *Indian Express*, August 11, 1969.

89. *Passim*. The Draft Programme of CPI (ML).

90. It is alleged from Satyanarayana Singh a member of the Central Organising Committee (COC) of the CPI (ML) that these decisions were taken and the advices given to Srikakulam Committee by the COC because they were not fully aware of the situation, in Srikakulam. He maintains that Appalasuri and Tejeshwara Rao informed Charu Majumdar, the Chairman of CPI (ML) about the state of disorganisation, intense police activities and innumerable arrests in the Srikakulam area. But Charu Majumdar suppressed the information from reaching the other members of the COC—See *Self-critical Report, op. cit*.

91. It is claimed that 150 CRP men were successfully held at bay for three days when they had tried to surround the meeting and capture the leaders. See *Amara......etc. op. cit.* pp. 160-161.

92. *Indian Express*, October 10, 1969.

93. Cr. No. 60-69 of P.S. Parvathipuram.

94. Cr. No. 66/69 of P.S. Mandasa.

95. Document U-62 *op. cit.* "The Political Report of Agency Area Plenary Committee Meeting". According to them following the Megada hills meeting 14 policemen in all were killed. 8 in an ambush at Nidagallu hills 3 in an encounter at Bartang, 2 in another encounter at Bandlaguda in Orissa.

96. The Srikakulam Zilla Committee alleges contrary to the Government report that Dr. Bhaskara Rao and Ganapathi were arrested at Madalapeta—when they were travelling towards the agency area and later shot dead.

97. Document N-2 of NCC.

98. Cr. No. 83/69 of P.S. Mandasa.

99. A lired young boy of 14.

100. Document S-2 *op. cit.*

101. Document M-4 of NCC.

102. *Ibid*, 25.12.1969.

103. Document S-7 of NCC.

104. Document R-1 of NCC.

105. Dr. Mallikarjunudu had left pursuit of higher studies at the prestigious Jawaharlal Institute of Medical Sciences at Pondicherry to join the maoist movement as a physician and soon took up active political duties and after Panigrahi's death became responsible for the movement in the plains area.

106. D. Narayan Rao, No. 503 and Brindaban Chari No. 339. The relieved policemen gladly contributed Rs. Six towards the party fund out of which they again received Rs. Four for expenses for their return journey.

107. Document N-4, *op. cit.*

108. Document S-2, *op. cit.* 108. a *Ibid.*

109. Though no clear evidence is available of his being officially elected as Secretary it is quite evident from committee meeting minutes and diaries that he was in charge of organisational matters.

110. Document C-2, *op. cit.*

111. See Document No. 1 of NCC, Pyla Vasudeva Rao's notes describing their activities at this time.

112. Document No. 15 of NCC and also Cr.No. 4/70 of P.S. Kasibugga.

113. Cr. No. 9/70 of P.S. Mandasa, FIR of 13.2.1970.

114. Document N-15 of NCC.

115. Document S-36 of NCC.

116. Document C-1 of NCC, Dr. Mallikarjunudu's diary.

117. *Amara... etc. op. cit.* p.43.

118. Document D-1, *op. cit.*

119. The police say that he was killed in an encounter following bomb throwing by the maoists. See Cr. No. 53/70 of P.S. Kasibugga. The maoists' claim that he was arrested following Simhachalam's revelation and then killed. See Document D-1, *op. cit.*

120. Cr. No. 5/70 of P.S. Sitampet.

121. Document No-1, *op. cit.*

122. *Ibid.*

123. Cr. No. 55/70 of P.S. Kurupam, FIR of 10.7.1970. Some reports ascribe dejection and frustration of Vempatapu at the time of his death. He is quoted by C. Subba Rao in "The Bullet Beats the blow" *Times of India* (Weekly) March 21, 1971 as saying "We have killed many people, we have looted a lot of gold and money. But will all this benefit the poor girijan. I am caught in a vicious circle. I cannot call off the movement and cannot see much purpose in continuing the movement". Such reports are unauthenticated and are not borne out by a study of the diary and other writings of Vempatapu. He as well as rest of the leadership seems to have been of the opinion that guerilla struggle must continue, albeit with certain tactical changes.

124. Cr. No. 54/70 of P.S. Mandasa, FIR of 30.7.1970.

125. Based on interviews. This was the period when the Bengal followers of Charu had declared that anybody who differed with Charu was not a maoist and as such can even be annihilated.

126. Erhard Haubold, "Srikakulam— Model of a Guerilla Uprising", in *Swiss Review of World Affairs*, March 1971, reprinted in *News and Views Gririjan Co-operative Corporation Ltd.*, Govt. of Andhra Pradesh.

127. Based on interviews.

128. Erhard etc. *op. cit.*

129. Based on interviews.

130. *Amara... etc. op. cit.* p. 76.
131. *vide p.* 118. In this incident Pyla Vasudeva Rao, who was locked up in the landlord's house managed to escape by removing tiles from the roof and climbing out. See Cr. no. 120/68 of P.S. Kasibugga, FIR of 25-11-68, p. 118.
132. *vide p.* 139
133. *vide p.* 145
134. Document S-2 *op. cit.*
135. "Avenge the murder of Heroic Martyrs of Srikakulam", *Liberation* January 1970.
136. See Charu Majumdar "Develop Revolutionary War to eliminate war of aggression against China" *Collected writings of Charu Majumdar* Volume 2 (West Bengal CPI(ML) 1972).
137. Satyanarayan Singh, "Possibility of World War and the task before Indian Revolution", *Liberation,* February 1970, p. 36.
138. "As we greet the New Year", *Liberation,* January 1970.
139. Manav Mitra, "Indira Gandhi's Radicalism," *Liberation,* February 1970, p. 16.
140. "*Political and Organisational Report*", *op. cit.*
141. *Ibid.*
142. For example, see "Flames of Guerilla Struggle Spread to New Areas", *Liberation,* January 1970, and "Peasant Guerilla Struggle spread to New Areas", *Liberation,* February 1970, and also "*Political and Organisational Report*", *op. cit.*
143. *Liberation,* December 1969.
144. "Peasant Guerilla... etc." *op. cit.*
145. For example see "Flames of Peasant Guerilla Struggles Spread to New Areas", *Liberation,* January 1970, and "March Forward by summing up the experiences of revolutionary peasant struggles", *Liberation,* December, 1969.
146. Document S.2 *op. cit.*

CHAPATER 6

Telangana-I

Telangana-I

The differences between the approach of the leaders in the APRCC and that of CPI (ML) already apparent in theory were even more evident when it came to practice. While setting forth once again some of these differences, we shall in this chapter describe in brief as to how they tended to affect the tactics deployed by the Andhra maoists and contrast them with those of the CPI (ML).

While the Srikakulam movement proceeded on its course, elsewhere in Andhra and Telangana the maoist movement under the control of the APRCC was following the line of graduated and protracted struggle advocated by the party high command led by T. Nagireddy (T.N.), C. Pulla Reddy (C.P.) and D. Venkateswara Rao (D.V.). Unlike the Srikakulam leaders the above three had considerable experience in the organisational and leadership politics of the erstwhile CPI and CPI (M). All three had been members of both the Secretariat of the CPI (M) in Andhra Pradesh and also of the Central Committee of the party. Even more, all three had been members of the Andhra Pradesh Legislative Assembly and in contrast to their counterparts in AICCCR they were all older and in their fifties when the movement picked up in 1968.

While T.N. was the mass leader, fund raiser and the general popular symbol of the Andhra maoists, C.P. was the typical organisation man in the leadership of the Communist Party,. Sxtremely popular among the party militants this lanky and tough organiser from Kurnool district had been in the forefront of many struggles led by the Communist Party in Andhra and had been prosecuted by the government many times.

In contrast to T.N. and C.P. both of whom came from the Rayalaseema, D.V. was from Telangana. D.V. was primarily a theoretician and a party ideologue during this time. Way back in 1948-51 he had been one of the members of the five man committee which had led the Telangana armed struggle.[1]

These three leaders formed a coordination committee for communist revolutionaries within the CPI (M) in March 1968 and barely three months later, on 30th June after the Burdwan meeting, precipitated matters by converting themselves into an independent organisation, the APRCC.

The different attitudes which the APRCC and CPI (ML) adopted as regards the tactics and strategies to be employed arose from their differing assessment of the existing situation. While the APRCC agreed with CPI (ML) that there was a revolutionary situation in India it refused to accept that it was in the form of a "nationwide upsurge which had reached the stage of armed struggle everywhere". To the APRCC the revolutionary situation was an objective fact in the sense that the productive forces in India had reached an impasse and could not under any circumstances develop any further without a social revolution taking place. This revolution could be carried out only through an armed struggle directed against the state and not through the existing electoral mechanisms. The subjective situation however had not matured to the extent the objective forces had. The people, because of the illusion they had about bettering their situation within the existing political structures, were not yet conscious of the fact that the revolution they needed would come about only through an armed struggle. In other words the felt needs of people had not taken shape into the people's demands. Further, there was no revolutionary working class party in India which was strong enough to be an effective medium and institutional channel through which the requirements of history could fulfil themselves.

In view of these facts, the APRCC put forward the concept of uneven development which was based on the premise that

India with its size and socio-cultural diversities presented not just one but several stages of development of a revolutionary situation.[2] It was as a consequence of the acceptance of this concept of uneven development that the APRCC went in for variable tactics depending on their assessment of the regional variations. The areas were classified by them as (i) areas with active struggles, (ii) areas with a party organisation and a lull as far as the movement was concerned and (iii) areas where both were absent. In the years following the establishment of APRCC movements were organised in all three types of areas. Before going into a description of the progress of the movements it would be instructive to know at a broad level, the region where the party operated.

When the maoists broke away from the CPI (M) they carried along with them large sections of the party members even in Coastal and Rayalaseema districts.[2] In these areas new committees were formed and T.N. and other leaders toured extensively propagating among the party members, the APRCC line. However, in spite of having a strong organisation of experienced communist cadre they were unable to start any militant mass movement here and in these areas the party was more successful in generating funds than anything else. To a certain extent the reason for this lies in the fact that much of these areas had been settled according to the ryotwari tenancy system which did not allow glaring disparities in land holding to arise. Secondly, and this was more true of the Coastal areas, because of earlier communist activity the labour was already receiving comparatively higher wages and to that extent they had lesser cause to be aggrieved. Further, the very fact that the maoists were more successful in Telangana than in these regions suggests another explanation for their failure. Unlike in Telangana which during the pre-independence period had been under the feudal political and administrative set up of the Nizam, the Coastal and Rayalaseema areas had experienced some sort of liberal democratic politics from as early as the second decade of this century. Further, having been a part of the British Madras province the people of this region, had greater awareness of the governmental administrative machinery. This awareness coupled with the greater exposure to party politics had caused among the people of this region a tendency to adopt constitutional rather than extra legal methods especially violent methods, to solve their problems.

While the movement floundered in the Coastal and Rayalaseema areas it received support from several areas in Telangana notable among these being the forest areas of Warangal, Khammam and Karimnagar. In fact apart from the forest area of East Godavari district there was no non-Telengana area under the party influence. The fact that the movement flourished in the districts having considerable areas under forest where the tribal population was concentrated indicates a certain similarity with demographic terrain of the Srikakulam movement. In a sense this was true. The general nature of the tribal problem involving the monetisation and commercialisation of tribal economy, land alienation and forced labour, and penetration of unscrupulous plainsmen and moneylenders was the same in both areas. The difference lay in that in the Telengana area these issues affected the local non-tribals as much as it did the tribals and thus while in Srikakulam the rank and file of the maoists comprised mostly tribals in these areas a number of non-tribals were also involved.

Apart from this there were several differences between the movements in Srikakulam and the Telangana area concerning the areas of operation and issues involved. In the first place both Warangal and Khamman had more than double the forest area which Srikakulam had.[4] At the same time the density of population in these areas was much less than in Srikakulam.[5] This meant that the maoists had greater room to manoeuvre while the police had greater difficulty in carrying out combing operations. In other words, technically these were areas where prolonged movements could be sustained.

Secondly, compared to the Srikakulam forests the Telangana forests were richer by far and consequently in these areas the extent of commercialisation was also greater. For instance the value of bamboo and beedi leaves from just the one taluq of Bhadrachalam in Khammam alone was over Rs. 8 lakhs in 1967-68, whereas in the same period the Srikakulam forest yielded Rs. 60,000/- worth of the same materials.[6]

Not only was the forest poorer in Srikakulam but the area under cultivation too was much less than in the forest of the Godavari belt of Khammam, East Godavari and Warangal districts. Once again comparing the statistics pertaining to Khammam and Srikakulam one finds that the net sown area in the two tribal blocks of Khammam was nearly twice that in the Srikakulam tribal blocks.[7] When one considers this aspect along with the fact that in Khammam and adjoining districts the tribals, in contrast to the tribals of Srikakulam rarely resorted to shifting cultivation, it becomes apparent that in these areas the pressure on land was much lower than it was in Srikakulam.

These differences had several implications. Greater commercialisation of the forest economy in the Telengana belt implied an increase in the number of persons employed by the timber merchants and the forest contractors. As a consequence wage struggles assumed much greater significance in these areas than it did in Srikakulam. At the same time the lower pressure on land relegated the issue of land occupation to one of an act of defiance rather than of immediate need.

In this context it must also be noted that in these areas there were few monopolist land holders cultivating large holdings within the forests. Most of the cultivation, especially of commercial crops, was being done along the river Godavari by landlords who had come from the Coastal areas of Krishna and Guntur comparatively recently, i.e. in the early 1940s. Originally a part of the Nizam's dominions, these areas had never been settled as had the Srikakulam agency tracts. Consequently, in these areas the new land holders were looked upon as oppressors more for their exploitation through low wages and money lending at very high rates of interest than for the reason that they had alienated tribal land and occupied it. In fact in certain areas especially in Warangal, where the APRCC was particularly active, the Andhra Pradesh Land Transfer Regulation was never even treated as an issue.

The initial stronghold of the APRCC was in the Mulug area of Warangal district. Here a militant mass movement of tribals and peasants had been organised even before 1967 under the leadership of Ramanarasayya who had been active in the communist movement from the Telangana days. At one stage he was the secretary of Mulug Taluq CPI(M) and also the Vice-President of Mulug panchayati samithi. He resigned from both these posts to join the APRCC and had taken up its maoist line. Despite the fact that it had conducted several mass struggles in the area against *vetti*, bribes and other forms of local evils, and despite the fact that it had a strong organisation manned by dedicated cadre the party put up a miserable show in the elections, Failing to poll even a reasonable percentage of votes. The Warangal district committee which met soon after the fourth General Elections thus felt that militant mass movements could not be carried forward, unless the Parliamentary path was abandoned. In future it was decided to concentrate party activities in the forest areas and mobilise the people for militant mass struggles. It was with this understanding, that they continued their struggles in the forest areas against forest officials, contractors, *patels* and *patwaris* and moneylenders. By June 1968, the party claimed that it was entrenched in the whole of Mulug area.

Around this time the newly formed APRCC sent a circular to the various units of the CPI(M) asking them to direct the people's movements towards the path of armed struggle. The maoists in Warangal District Committee promptly separated themselves from the CPI(M) fold and held a meeting at Vadlakonda. This meeting was addressed by D.V. and Nalla Narasimulu of Nalgonda, another old hand from the Telangana days. Both of them explained the stand of maoists on various national and international issues, present situation and the proposed path of revolution for India. At this meeting Ramanarasayya was made the area Secretary and he was to be assisted by Appanna a forty eight year old (in 1969) veteran CPI(M) organiser, who was at that time working in Warangal town, Bhaskar Reddy, the right hand man of Ramanarasayya and Anthi Reddy a militant from the neighbouring Nalgonda district. The meeting decided upon mobilising people to occupy *banjar* and *poramboke* lands,[9] and to conduct the struggle in such a way as to take it to more militant forms.

Efforts to implement the above decisions met with immediate success. Many local youths were attracted to the party and many village committees were established. In all, about 30-40 village committees were organised. The secretaries of these village committees formed themselves into an area committee to co-ordinate the movement. The Telangana armed struggle with emphasis on its "uncompromising nature" was hailed. The politics of CPI(M) were attacked and those remaining in CPI(M) were castigated as 'cowards.'

With the increase in party strength the programme for occupation of *banjar* lands was implemented. In Mulug taluq at Royyuru, Rampuram and Ramnagar villages the land of some merchants cum landlords like Tappa Ramaswamy, Tungaturthi Venkata Sastri and Vadde Rajeswara Rao was forcibly tilled. In Veerannapeta two hundred acres of leased out land was occupied. The programme of land occupation was also carried out in Eturu, Katapuram, Chintagudem, Lakshmipuram, and Tupakulagudem. On the whole in ten villages, the party claimed the people occupied 2500 acres of land belonging to landlords.[10] Other struggles, by agricultural labourers for increase in wages, struggles against forest guards who took *mamuls* frequently for allowing the cattle to graze in the forest areas followed.[11] On their part the landlords retaliated by implicating many party workers and sympathisers, in criminal cases, especially in the villages of Dumpalagudem, Pasra and Venkatapura. Professional *goondas* were employed, and many attempts on the life of Ramanarasayya's life were made.[12]

The impact of the movement in Mulug area was soon felt in Nugur Taluq adjoining Mulug across the river Godavari, in Yellandu taluq, south of Mulug and also in Manthena taluq of Karimnagar district situated in north of Mulug and West of Nuguru.

On July 1, 1968 the important maoists of Khammam area formed a District Co-ordination Committee. The APRCC Secretariat had already sent C.P. to this area to lead the movement and to develop it along the new party line.[13] In the meeting it was decided to mobilise people on the issue of land alienation, collection of *mamuls* by forest and government officials, wages and a host of other Issues. It was also decided to impart political and military training to young militants from villages. While the over all leadership was to be with C.P., the movement was organised by different people in different areas. In Boorgampadu, Palwancha and Yellandu taluqs the main organiser was Bathula Venkateswara Rao.[24] He was a native of Madhira taluq in Khammam and had taken active part in student politics. At the time of the split in CPI(M) he came out very strongly against the present organisation. Subsequently he became the Secretary of the Khammam District Committee owing allegiance to APRCC. The major struggle which he launched initially was in Aswaraopet block of Khammam in which it was claimed by party that thousands of acres of land was occupied by the tribals. He carried out similar struggles against *vetti*, low wages and exploitation by landlords in the Bayyaram and Kodavatancha areas of Yellandu, Venkatapuram, Pagideru and Jaggaram areas of Boorgampadu and in Bhadrachalam and Sattupalli areas of Palwancha. In the Nugur area the most charismatic of the party activists was Nirmala alias Radhakka who hailed from a family of party sympathisers and who had been sent to this area at her request. In Nugur too the main issues related to land and wages.[15] The tribals were being exploited heavily by the rich land holders who had migrated to this area from the Andhra district of Godavari, Krishna and Guntur. The wages paid to them as agricultural labourers was paltry and some times only Rs. 60/- was paid at the end of eight months work. The first action indulged in by the party was a strike by about 4000 people against *vetti* and the corruption of forest officials. This was then followed by a strike of agricultural labourers in the Dharmavaram group of villages.[16]

In the Manthena taluq of Karimnagar, in the regions bordering Mulug taluq the main APRCC organisers were Panduranga Rao a 35 year old lecturer from Tenali college and his wife Jhansi (sister of of Radhakka). Besides these two, Datla Venkata Rama Raju and his brother Krishnam Raju were also very active in this area. In the initial stages the most notable incident in Manthena was the struggle following the call of the party to disregard the government's drive to collect four years' arrears of land revenue and to pay only the current year's demand. According to the party it had the support of the villagers from 40 villages on this issue.

During this time the APRCC also mobilised people on various issues in the plains areas notably in in Jangaon, Nalgonda and Warangal town.

In formulating the nature of operation the APRCC was guided by a couple of factors which was implicit in their understanding of the situation. The first was the inevitability of a long and protracted struggle and the second, the regional specificity of the issues involved. Both factors immediately made it necessary to adopt an approach which was flexible. This flexibility was related both to the tactics to be employed and the class of people to be mobilised, and even to the issues on which the people were to be mobilised. It is this aspect of flexibility which characterises the entire theoretical framework of the APRCC and makes it stand out in contrast to the somewhat rigid posture of the CPI(ML). As one follows the line of thinking of APRCC it is this distinction between it and the CPI(ML) which becomes more and more apparent.

The primary task according to the APRCC in proceeding with the movement was the creation of a mass base which would isolate and weaken the enemy. This was to be done by building a united front of the working class, students, middle classes and the large masses of the peasantry. Within the peasantry itself the peasant was to be united initially against the "big land lords and the big usurious merchants".[18] Subsequently the small landlords and the small merchants were to be neutralised, in order to completely isolate the landlords. Each one of the sections in the united front was to be mobilised on the basis of its day to day demands and immediate problems. For example, the workers were to be led into struggles on issues like wages, better working conditions and participation in management as well as struggles which had a clearer political content like, solidarity campaigns with peasant movement and protests against government and 'imperialism'.[19] With this perspective in view the APRCC disputed the CPI(ML)'s formulation that the principle contradiction was the one between the landlords and peasants. Acceptance of this formulation they felt, would lead to abandoning work among workers, students and other classes and giving them idealistic and impractical calls like asking them to abandon their present mode of life and "go to the villages" and "integrate with the peasants". The APRCC instead put forward a broader characterisation of the Indian situation, as one in which several contradictions existed for example between the workers and the bourgeoise, between the middle classes and the system in general and among the capitalists and imperialists themselves. This enabled them not only to justify and pursue their United Front line but also to advocate mobilising of various classes of people by appealing to their specific problems.

The APRCC also realised that for the United Front to be effective it would have to be given an organisational shape. This organisation they split into two categories. In the first were the student organisations, organisations of the workers and agricultural labourers, *girijan sanghams,* civil liberties groups and cultural organisations. These were to be utilised to mobilise and educate the masses. The second category of organisations consisted of gram sanghams and village militia which would provide alternative institutions for people's government and also act as defence squads. These mass organisations were not to be abandoned even during repression and only their form was to be changed to adapt to new situation.[20]

As a starting point the masses were to be mobilised on partial struggles. Unlike the CPI (ML) which viewed economic struggles as nothing more than economic inducements, the APRCC adopted the line that the "political and revolutionary consciousness of the workers is raised only through a process of economic and partial struggles".[21] But this would only be the starting point. Each partial struggle, the APRCC argued, would ultimately develop into a political struggle. This would become possible because in the course of the struggles the participants would be exposed to the true character of the State and the people whom it supports. Thus if the struggles were to be combined with propagation of revolutionary politics they would be made to realise the need to overthrow the state through armed struggle and that it is only through overthrow of the rulers by armed struggle that the real freedom can be achieved".[22] The APRCC felt that it was only due to the misuse of partial struggles in the past by revisionists that the party and the people were led into the morass of economism and therefore this should not be utilised as an argument for abandoning partial struggles altogether. In sum the APRCC's view was that partial struggles were the instruments and medium through which the revolutionary potentialities of the underdeveloped subjective conditions could be realised.[23]

One illustration of this line of thought of the APRCC is the issue of land occupation. According to the APRCC the question of struggle for occupying land of the landlords was the keystone of agrarian revolution. It was not to be regarded as being merely another economic struggle. In their view the question of land could not be separated from that of seizing political power and armed struggle.[24] Land occupation was the first step towards armed struggle. It was only in the process of defending the occupied land that the broad masses of the people could be mobilised to carry out armed struggle for seizure of political power. Only by occupying land could they realise the necessity of overthrowing the state, which being the defender of the landlords would automatically try to wrest back the land from them. In fact land occupation was seen by the APRCC directly as seizure of power, since the feudal relations and feudal power which characterised the State were dependent on the pattern of land distribution.[25] For these reasons they disagreed with CPI (ML)'s view that "agrarian revolution must await the smashing of state power" and that "to attempt an agrarian revolution without first smashing the State machinery is straightforward revisionism."[26] They also rejected the CPI (ML)'s view that the agrarian programme exposed the revolutionary workers, invited police attacks, bogged down the peasant masses in the mire of economism, and finally the setbacks suffered during the conduct of the struggle would only lead to demoralisation of peasant masses. The APRCC's reply to these was that in a protracted struggle set-backs were common. The masses would, therefore, be prepared to overcome these set-backs and this would be done by increasing the consciousness and awareness of the people regarding the "relation between the struggle for land and struggle for political power".[27] The question of land the APRCC felt was so vital to the peasants, that "if the enemy were able to seize the land by employing overwhelming force, the peasant masses would be fully prepared to recover the land no matter how many times they have to do it."[28] One cannot fail to notice that the assumptions of the inevitability of a protracted struggle and of the efficacy of partial struggles is implicit in the APRCC's reasoning.

The APRCC also called for flexibility in the sphere of tactics. It refused to accept the CPI (ML) line that guerilla struggle was the only tactic to be adopted. According to APRCC "though guerilla struggle was the main form of struggle any other form of struggle whether it be legal or illegal, open or secret, should be taken up if it is useful for mobilising the people and leading them towards armed struggle."[29] This did not mean however, "that every form of struggle must be followed, but that every necessary form of struggle had to be followed"[30] Guerilla tactic was seen only as a tactic which appeared at a particular stage in the revolutionary process and not as being applicable at all times.

As far as the area of operation was concerned the APRCC gave preference to mountainous and forest region. The poor transport and communication facilities in these areas, they argued, would make it difficult for the police to operate. At the same time the local population, in the absence of proper links with the bigger towns, would tend to be more self-sufficient than in areas which are easily accessible. Both these factors enhanced the possibility of holding out against police attacks even over prolonged periods. Thus they felt "if we could mobilise the people of the forest areas on the basis of a concrete political and military line, we could develop the area soon into a guerilla zone and then a liberated area."[31] Specifically they pointed out to the forest area around the Godavari river which spread over the four states of Andhra

Pradesh, Orissa, Maharashtra and Madhya Pradesh as a good starting point.

This however did not mean that the APRCC abandoned the need for developing struggles in the plains area, as alleged by CPI (ML). The APRCC felt that in the plains areas adjoining the forests, efforts to intensify class struggles and limited guerilla resistance at the present stage was possible. In case of severe repression the party cadre and militants could seek refuge in the forests, and return when conditions improved. By following a policy of advance and retreat, the movement in the plains and forests could be co-ordinated and taken to higher forms of struggle. In case of those areas, where the movement had already reached a higher stage of struggle temporary base areas could be established and as "armed struggle advances, wherever necessary conditions develop, we must try to establish stable base areas in the plains area also".[32] The CPI (ML) criticised the APRCC's line of limited guerilla resistance in the plains and sending the cadre to the forests as resulting in isolation from the people and called it a jungle theory. The APRCC felt that the CPI (ML) criticism did not take the APRCC's total perspective of developing the movement, which was "It is incorrect to think that plains areas are not useful for resistance, though they are less favourable than forests and other mountainous areas in terms of armed resistance".[33]

Taken together all these aspects of APRCC's framework of operation developed into their scheme for successful conduct of revolution. The first step was to implement a programme of economic demands along with land occupation and once this programme was started, it was they felt that severe police and landlord repression would begin. The people would then resist and come forward to defend their gains causing an open confrontation between government's armed forces and people. At this stage, the peasants would be armed and the APRCC would organise its cadre and militants into regular squads which would go underground. The entire area would be made a guerilla area of constant activity and raids. Any area possessing natural advantages like forests or mountains would, as the movement progresses, be converted into a guerilla area.[34] These were the bases to be utilised by the cadre when it had to attack or stage a retreat in the face of State repression. Out of this guerilla war would arise a regular Red Army which would have the capacity to deal hard and decisive blows to the armed forces of the ruling classes.

With all the guerilla areas engaging and bogging down armed forces of the ruling classes, one or two liberated areas would be created. These liberated areas would be self-sufficient in all respects. In their stronghold "the existing government machinery would be smashed...a red area and parallel government would be formed". With such a step, they believed a qualitative change would come in the national scene. After this, guerilla warfare would be supplemented and soon the whole country would be liberated.

One fundamental idea to be kept in view throughout the process, was that the whole struggle had to be conducted with a defensive perspective. The struggle was based on defence of people's rights and of people's gains. People were to understand that they were defending their just rights against exploitation and oppression. The enemy on the other hand was to be branded and made to look like the aggressor.[35]

The APRCC did not visualise any quick victory. They saw ahead of them a long period of struggle involving many ups and downs. "We should not clamour for immediate victory...This is a protracted struggle...victory is certain. But, we should remember the cruel truth that it would depend not merely on our efforts and wishes but on many national and international conditions".[36] However, they were confident of victory and believed in their historical destiny. They had implicit faith in Mao's saying that, "All reactionaries are paper tigers. In appearance they are terrifying but in reality they are not so powerful. From a long term point of view it is not the reactionaries but the people who are really powerful".

Criticism of CPI (ML)

The APRCC line of thought was clearly at variance with that of CPI (ML). It was fully conscious of this and at every stage took pains to point out these differences and to justify their own stand. As mentioned earlier, it dismissed as wishful thinking, the CPI (ML) assessment of the existence of a nationwide upsurge and the need to unleash Naxalbari type of struggles everywhere. They also rejected outright the CPI (ML)'s line on United Front which was that it could be built only after some areas had been liberated because it was only then that the principal contradiction *viz.* between the landlords and peasants, would be eliminated. According to the APRCC the abandoning of mass struggles and partial struggles based on economic demands in favour of guerilla action alone by the CPI (ML) resulted from the latter's lack of patience to nurture a movement. It was, they felt, only out of rationalisation of their isolation from the masses that the CPI (ML) had adopted the strategy of operating through guerilla squads and without mass contacts.

The CPI (ML)'s line on annihilation of class enemies as being the highest form of class struggle also came in for severe criticism from the APRCC. According to the APRCC it was not by annihilating the class enemies in large numbers but by destroying the State machinery that seizure of power is possible.[37] The annihilation of class enemy does not annihilate the system nor the forms of exploitation.[38] Nor would annihilation disperse the enemy's armed forces. It would only lead to an increase in their armed concentration and resulted in demoralising the people. It would certainly not lead to the creation of liberated areas as the CPI (ML) claimed.[39] It might be that through annihilation, people in that particular area get some relief temporarily, but this would not help the progress of the movement, and in fact it would not even help to start a revolutionary movement unless the people had been organised and made conscious of the need to effectively resist the opposition. Thus annihilation only invited repression and scared the people, and terminate the opportunity to organise the people for armed struggle.[40] It created illusions among them, that without their own efforts and just with a handful of individuals working, they would be liberated from the present system of exploitation.[41]

The CPI (ML)'s claim that repression lead to an increase in political consciousness of the people was also denied by the APRCC. It stated that "it was only repression which was an outcome of the necessity to suppress the united and militant political and economic struggles that created political consciousness and not the repression which was the result of annihilation campaigns."[42] They also felt that annihilation usually degenerated into indiscriminate killings, disrupting the united front and alienating the party from people.

The APRCC also criticised the CPI (ML) for its wrong understanding about creation of base areas, which was a result of its wrong estimation of national upsurge all over the country. CPI (ML) made no distinction between different types of terrain and stated that a base could be created any where and every where simply by conducting raids. The APRCC also denounced the CPI (ML) for saying that liberated areas could be created "when the guerilla units begin to act in this manner (meaning annihilation) in any area the class enemies will be forced to flee from the countryside and villages will be liberated".[43] It was felt wrong to equate the movements of the guerilla squads from one area to another with mobile warfare, because mobile warfare developed only at a higher stage when the guerilla army increased in number, in arms, training and when it forms into a regular armed force.

NOTES & REFERENCES

1. This five-man committee had only two members from Telangana region – D.V. and Bhim Reddy Narasimha Reddy.
2. *vide* Chapter II.
3. Document N—2 of Hyderabad Conspiracy Case (HCC).
4. In Warangal the forest is distributed over 3914.43 sq. kms. and in Khammam 3033.43 sq. kms. while in Srikakulam it is 1550.2 sq. kms. *Statistical Handbook* (cyclost-

yled). Tribal Cultural Research Training Institute (TCRTI Table 8.1, p. 57.

5. Whereas the density of population is 600 per sq. mile in Srikakulam district, it is only 76 per, sq. mile in Mulug 188 per sq. mile in Narsampet Taluqs of Warangal District and 110 sq. mile in Yellandu of Khammam district.
6. *Statistical handbook, op. cit.* "Value of Forest Products". Table 8.2, p. 88,
7. *Ibid* Table 6.1.
8. Document W—2 *op. cit.*
9. *Banjar* lands are village fallows, and other common lands not yet occupied and brought under cultivation.
10. "The Struggle for Agrarian Revolution in Andhra", *Liberation*, Vol. 8, February—March 1975, p. 28.
11. Document W-2, *op. cit.* Minutes of Guerilla Area Committee Meeting, 8.12.1969.
12. *Ibid.*
13. Document C-28 of "Hyderabad Conspiracy Case".
14. "*Amara Veerula...etc.*" *op. cit.* pp. 107-109.
15. Document C-28 *op. cit.*
16. *Ibid.*
17. *Ibid.*
18. *Some Problems concerning the Path of People's War in India*, APRCC (printed, probably 1970) p. 45.
19. *BharataViplava Karula Ativada Dhorani*, APCCR (printed) October 1970, p. 70.
20. *Ibid.*
21. *Ibid.* p. 19.
22. *Ibid.*
23. *Ibid.*

24. *Some Problems of People's War*, APRCC (mimeo) p. 2.
25. *Ibid.* pp. 1-2 and Bharata Viplava...etc. *op. cit.* p. 24.
26. *Liberation*, November 1969, p. 80.
27. *Some Problems...etc. (mimeo) op. cit.* p. 3.
28. *Ibid.*
29. *Bharata Viplava...etc. op. cit.* p. 35.
30. *Ibid* p. 37.
31. *Some Problems...etc.* (mimeo) *op. cit.* pp. 6-7.
32. *Ibid* p. 11.
33. *Some Problems...etc.* (printed) *op. cit.* p. 5.
34. *Ibid.*
35. *Bharata Viplava...etc. op. cit* p. 50.
36. *Bharata Deshamu Praja Yuddha Pandha*, APRCC (mimeo) 14.3.1972.
37. *Bharata Viplava...etc. op. cit.* p. 47.
38. *Ibid.* p. 48.
39. *Some Problems...etc.* (printed) *op. cit.* p. 41.
40. *Bharata Viplava...etc ,op. cit.* p. 47.
41. *Ibid* p. 48.
42. *Ibid* p. 47.
43. *Some Problems...etc.* (mimeo) p. 5.

CHAPTER 7

Telangana II

Telangana II

Despite the Andhra Pradesh Revolutionary Communist Committee's (APRCC) criticism of the Communist Party of India, Marxist-Leninist (CPI-(ML)) and of the manner in which the movement in Srikakulam was being conducted there was no denying that they were fully aware and even anxious of the popularity of the Srikakulam movement. In fact as we have seen in their initial efforts to draw away the Srikakulam District Committee from the All India Co-ordination Committee for Communist Revolutionaries (AICCCR) they had gone to the extent of aligning themselves with this committee inspite of their reservations. But even after they had reconciled themselves to the loss of the Srikakulam Committee and had broken away completely from the AICCCR the successes and the consequent popularity of the Srikakulam movement continued to haunt them. This in no small way contributed to building up of pressures within the party to adopt a more militant approach. There were of course other reasons for this development, the main one being the need to cope with increasing police repression. How this effected the policies of APRCC and how it ultimately led to a split within the party arc some of the issues that will be discussed in this chapter which also describes in detail the activity of the party during this period.

From the very beginning, the APRCC had to keep adjusting to meet the demands of the more radical elements in the party.

Very often, however, these adjustments were only gestures and did not result in any genuine change of line. Thus for instance in November 1968 they entered into an alliance with the AICCCR just to please certain elements in their group.[1] But neither these elements nor the main group was particularly satisfied with this arrangement. Matters came to a head within one month and in December 1968, after failing to make the APRCC pass some resolutions in support of the AICCCR the 'rebels' led by Kolla Venkaiah left the party to join the Srikakulam group.[2]. Later the uneasy alliance lasted only two months and in February 1969 the AICCR expelled the APCCCR. The matter however did not end with this. Rumblings within the APRCC continued against alleged revisionism and cowardice and arguments in favour of adopting a more militant stance continued to be propounded. In fact in the December 1968 meeting referred to above Bathula Venkateshwara Rao, who was later to become an important APRCC activist, also accused the party of not applying people's warpath in India.[3] At that time, D. Venkateshwara Rao (D.V,) who was the party ideologue replied that it would not be practicable to implement those ideas of Mao which he had developed in regard to the programme in liberated areas, since Indian people were unarmed, while the counter-revolution was to the teeth. D.V. further cautioned Bathula that it was armed not enough to arm a few conscious people but it was necessary to bring the broad sections of masses into anti-government movements.

The Manthena Incident

What really brought this debate into the forefront was the incident that occurred in Manthena after the party began its programme to implement its line. The sequence of events which brought about this incident has the following description by the party report itself.

In Manthena and Nugur, "the growing atrocities of landlords were resisted by the party. This resulted in severe police repression. It was becoming impossible for the party workers to remain in the open and work among people. The legal opportunities to work. were lost. With this the party workers also could no longer function as individuals but had to form into squads and work on the basis of squad organisation in order to defend themselves from attacks of landlords and police".[4] There was an initial opposition to the formation of squads by Appanna. Ramanarasayya though initially against the idea came to accept it later.[5] Soon it was felt that it was necessary to arm themselves for purposes of self-defence and thus armed squads had to be formed. In such a situation the local cadre appealed to the Mulug area committee for arms. This was placed before the Rashtra Committee for discussion by C.P. and Ramanarasayya. The Rashtra Committee agreed to give arms to the squads there—one rifle and a sten-gun.[6] But even before this was implemented the cadre in Manthena grew impatient and on their own initiative without consulting the higher committee seized two weapons from an American hunter on March 12, 1969.[7] Following this incident the maoists in both Manthena and Nugur Taluqs had to face further intense police repression.

By the end of March the more moderate sections in the APRCC were under heavy pressure. The Srikakulam movement by now had caught the imagination of many in the State and was being constantly referred to in the press and other media. At the same time many of their own cadre were vociferously demanding acquisition of arms and formation of squads to raise the pitch of the struggles in their area. Thus when the first state conference of the APRCC was finally held on April 10, 11 and 12, 1969 at Atlapragada village near Vijayawada the party was forced to grant certain concessions.

The first was in regard to the issue of participation in elections. The earlier view that elections were to be boycotted depending on the situation was discarded. It was now categorically stated that under no circumstances would the party take part in elections.[8] By now T. Nagireddy had already resigned from the Assembly stating that it had degenerated into a talking shop incapable of solving any problem.[9] C.P. too underwent self-criticism and considered the views he had expressed earlier as wrong. On the issue of raids on police stations in Kerala, T.N. retracted from his earlier view that it was merely a Congress and CIA plot. While not commending it outright, he stated that his incorrect assessment earlier had arisen because he had not heard the Peking Radio broadcasts on this issue. The conference also took a firm stand on the manner in which the separate Telangana agitation was to be viewed. Rather than dilute its own movement the party passed a resolution denying any role to the separatist agitation and calling for a completely independent movement of the maoists.[10] The most important manifestation of this APRCC's "leftward deviation" however was in the *Immediate Programme* that was formulated in this conference outlining the manner in which the party led struggles were to proceed. At several places in the programme statements were introduced which convey the impression that the authors expected armed struggle almost overnight. Thus for instance we have statements like "The activities of the people should be taken to the higher levels (armed struggle) by the end of April 1969".[11] ; "Launch counter attacks on landlord class by May 1969".[12] ; "Be prepared for armed struggle in the coming rainy season—June 1969"[13]

A second look at these "concessions" however shows how illusory they really were. More than anything else they represented sops to the militants and did not reflect an authentic change in line. Issues like participation in election had already been cleared when the communist party failed to make a showing in the 1967 election. The change of stand on the Kerala attacks too was not a significant concession and for all its optimistic allusions to the starting of armed struggle almost immediately, the *Immediate Programme* was basically in consonance with the moderates' stand of the need for graduated and protracted struggles. In fact, that all these deviations resulted only from internal pressures was acceded to later on by the leaders of the APRCC.

The Immediate Programme

The *Immediate Programme* was a very broad programme outlined by the APRCC. It laid down the framework within which the movements conducted in the party's name were to be operated. The key role was given to land occupation programmes which were seen as the crucial step in the progress towards armed struggle. For this purpose land was divided into six types (1) forest land, (2) cultivable government waste land under occupation of landlords, (3) temple and endowments land under occupation of landlords, (4) landlords' pasture lands, (5) tenant cultivated lands and (6) the self cultivated lands of the landlords. Keeping in view the level of preparedness of the people it was proposed that in the first instance only forest lands and lands illegally occupied by landlords should be occupied. Once the people were fully prepared then even the self cultivated lands of the landlords could be taken over, but for the present this was only to be a slogan. Similarly it was decided to tackle small landlords only after dealing with the bigger ones.

The main programme of land occupation and distribution was to be supplemented by other struggles relating to local issues. As mentioned previously the crux of APRCC's line was the greater flexibility it envisaged vis-a-vis the issues to be taken up. Thus forced labour, corrupt officials, usury and unreasonable wages were all to be resisted. Whereas the AICCCR condemned any struggles on economic issues the *Immediate Programme* permitted struggles to be started on even specific issues like free access to palmyra trees to tappers or to tanks for fishermen. Again, even in the forest areas, the *Immediate Programme* listed out such specific issues like prices of minor forest produce, role of GCC and so on which were to be taken up. Finally the *Immediate Programme* rounded off by cautioning the cadre, that while importance was to be given to the problems of tribals and forest areas, they were neither to neglect the non-tribal poor nor the movement in the plains area.

The *Immediate Programme* also proposed a boycott of the Panchayat elections which were to be held in June 1969. It was felt that greater purpose would be served if the opportunities were utilised to expose the futility of the Parliamentary system. To this end the corruption in Panchayats was to be highlighted and it was to be proposed as a positive alternative that only village committees which could help solve the real problems of the villagers should be formed.

On the issue of defence of people from the attacks of landlords and police the *Immediate Programme* advised the formation of "volunteer squads" consisting of youth from the village. These squads were to use locally available weapons like sticks. It was only at a higher level that "local squads" were to be formed and given some basic training in defence methods. The over all emphasis was on defence activities and that too by the people themselves and not by a few party members. All such actions were to be mass actions only and was never to be allowed to degenerate into adventurists acts of a few people. The *Immediate Programme's* answer to the question of defence raised by the controversial Manthena incident was thus ambiguous. In fact in suggesting such a "equivocal" scheme of defence it plainly sought to avoid the entire issue of what should be done for the defence of the cadre if the police repression began even before the people could be fully mobilised. Subsequent events show how time and again the cadre was faced with this problem and how grossly the APRCC had under-estimated its importance and did not attempt at any explicit answers.

The Kondamodalu Movement

No where was the *Immediate Programme* as closely adhered to as it was in the Kondamadalu forest area of East Godavari. The APRCC enjoyed considerable popularity in this area and when it split from the CPI (M) it carried along with it most of the party members and student federation activists. Just as C.P. had been sent to organise the movement in Khammam district the East Godavari district was left to Vasanthada Ramlingachari. As in the other districts the forested areas *viz.* Rampachodavaram and Yellavaram taluqs, were chosen as operational zones and an area committee to attend to each area was created, to mobilise the people. For example, Dr. Ankamma Choudary and his wife Veena were assigned to organise in the Palem area, Somachari a seasoned Kisan Sabha activist was to mobilise people in Kota and Gujjimamidivalasa areas, Shanti Raju—a local tribal militant was to be responsible for the Pullangi area and Simhadri Subba Reddy a student federation leader to the

Kondamodalu area. Several other enthusiasts like Paulus and Stalin Babu were also sent to help them.[14] The strategy adopted was to take advantage of existing disputes in the area and utilise them to motivate the people to start a general movement. The Kondamodalu group of villages were ideally suited for such a strategy because there were many standing areas of conflicts between the tribals and plainsmen who were the local moneylenders and landlords. At the same time considerable tension also existed between the tribals and the petty forest and revenue officials who extracted bribes and illegal levies. The emphasis was on a graded approach. For example when the people in the Kondamadalu area were organised to refuse to pay taxes to the *karnam* and agitate against the illegal extractions of forest officials they were allowed to represent to the Tehsildar, who subsequently visited the area and asked the tribals to submit a petition to the Collector. But when in spite of this being done no action was taken by the administration, the APRCC members moved in and spread their message that petitioning would not solve any problem and it was only by preparing themselves through armed struggles to defy government, that oppression could be terminated.[15] Again after March 1969, when the party embarked on a programme of land occupation the people were not prevented from approaching the Collector for redressal of their grievances. Here too, in spite of conclusive proof of their rights to the occupied land, the people were not able to extract much from the Collector and the problem remained as it was. This situation was once again fully exploited by the maoists who gave a call for general seizure of land and stepped up the propaganda against the government.

The *Sangham* set about raising the level of the people's political consciousness and conducted schools not only with the purpose of improving literacy but also for educating the people regarding their rights. Efforts were made to develop revolutionary enthusiasm among them, by telling them about the struggles of oppressed people throughout the world as for instance in Vietnam and conducting cultural programmes, which propagated revolutionary ideas. These were then coupled with agitations on various local issues and problems. It was expected that in the process of these struggles a movement and an organisation could be built up to carry out armed struggles at later stages.

While the first demand that was taken up concerned the indebtedness of the tribals and their exploitation by the moneylenders who made them repay amounts many times the principal, the issue on which the movement really picked up was farm wages. During March 1969, the *sangham* raised a demand for the enhancement of wages from Rs. 200/- to Rs. 400/- per annum along with extra food, clothing and cancellation of accumulated debts. Responding to the *sangham's* call the farm labourers of Kondamodalu went on strike enmasse catching the landlord unawares as they had not anticipated this step. The party then raised the slogan of "land to the tiller" and tried to link up the farm servant's issue with that of land alienation and usury. Most of the farm servants were in fact erstwhile independent tillers who had lost their lands and become servants because of their inability to repay loans. The party's demands of cancellation of debts and abolition of the farm servant system enthused the people considerably and despite threats and intimidation on the part of the landlords they came forward in large numbers to participate in the strike. The intervention of the administration at this stage did not alter the situation substantially as it was unable to find a solution. This strengthened the hands of the maoists even further and they gave a general call for seizure of lands.[16]

The strategy proposed for seizing the land was that tribals from several villages were to gather carrying ploughs and arms, and go to each village and occupy the lands. Such a combined effort would clearly indicate their unity, generate confidence amongst the participants and enthuse those who were vacillating. Tribals were to be fully prepared for any kind of resistance by landlords, and they were even supplied with some crude bombs by the maoists.

The lands that were to be seized were those that had been alienated to the non-tribals, those that had been mortgaged by the tribals for raising a loan, and did not include the "self-cultivated lands" of the landlords over which the tribals as yet felt they had no claim.[17] Once occupied the land was to be distributed among the tribals as equitably as possible. All disputes regarding the distribution would be settled by village committees only. Interestingly enough, it was also decided that tribals who had not actively participated in the struggle would not be granted any seized land, even if he had a rightful claim to it on account of having cultivated it prior to its alienation.

The programme was implemented in the third week of June 1969. It elicited massive response. Big crowds of tribals gathered hoisting red flags on lands and ploughed them and declared its occupation and seizure. The police in the area was hardly in a position to deal with such a mass upsurge in which militant tribal groups of about a thousand members each were showing all signs of being willing to resist if attacked by police. Even then the police made some attempts to arrest the leaders but backed out when faced with resistance.[18]

This programme was carried out through the months of August, September and October.[19] Led by Ramalingachary the tribals concentrated mainly on occupying the lands of landlords Mulla Venkata Kameshwara Rao, and Lanka Venkateshwara Rao.[20] They also singled out tyrannous landlords like Karre Somanna Patrudu, who had alienated vast stretches of land from the tribals, and taken them on 'tenancy' basis from them. His land was occupied at least about four times, in four different places.[21] Similarly they occupied the lands of Kondamodalu *sarpanch* Pothulu Sayanna Pantulu who was a big landlord and owned big tobacco farms,[22] and the lands of the local *karnam*.[23]

One factor which greatly helped the maoists was that conflict over land was not a new phenomena in this area. In fact on an earlier occasion the tribals struggling for their rights had even killed a landlord. Many of them had participated in violent confrontations and had even served sentences in jail. The maoists found many recruits among these people and after giving them a political perspective used them to lead occupations of land.[24]

The outburst in Kondamodalu area helped them to expand to Nelakota area, where land was forcibly occupied and tilled.

In this area, almost all the landlords whose lands were occupied were absentee landlords, in possession of the land for over sixty years.[25] Their attempts to bring labourers from the neighbouring villages were also foiled by the tribals by threatening the landlord and his supporters.[26]

While the plan of land seizure was in operation the APRCC activists were busy organising village volunteer squads and conducting propaganda. A number of non-political activities were also taken up. The women were grouped into *mahila sanghams*, and age old prejudices especially those relating to caste and superstitions were attacked.[28] The *sangham* also settled many local disputes by holding local courts and this enhanced their reputation considerably as they meted out quick and immediate justice.

The success of their programme in Kondamodalu and Nelakota areas led the APRCC to make efforts to extend the movement to the neighbouring villages of Manturu, Gonduru and Madipalli. But before they could proceed ahead they were suddenly confronted with a situation for which the *Immediate Programme* did not advocate any solution—*viz.* severe repression by the police. The maoists were neither armed nor trained nor were they programmatically and ideologically prepared to physically resist the police squads and threaten the police agents. Operating as they were by touring from village to village they were particularly susceptible to informers who were able to spot them easily and convey information regarding their movements to the police. The "mass defence" tactics advocated by the *Immediate Programme* was of no use during this initial phase of the movement and thus even while the movement was picking up many of the leaders were arrested. Ramalingachary, Bhaskar Rao and Nakka Appala Rao were all picked up by the police with ease. Even in later stages when learning from their initial set-backs the maoists tried to organise a guerilla squad under the 18 year old Stalin Babu, they did not succeed. Though some initial training including making of crude bombs, was given to them, at no stage did they seriously implement the squad form of organisation as was done in Khammam and Warangal areas.

Organisationally too the party was in no position to face the situation. It had absolutely no finances and after a time it became extremely difficult to procure food grain even for day to day needs. On top of all this there was the extra burden of the families of persons who were arrested to be supported. The increasing money and food constraints demoralised many and even full time workers began leaving the area. In the party's own words "there were no squads, no squad training, no weapons, and the local girijan squads became inactive due to lack of proper technical training. Though the people were willing to fight there was nobody to give them a lead or proper guidance".[28]

It was thus that in Nelakota within two weeks the landlords organised themselves and reoccupied all the lands seized by the tribals. They then utilised the stranglehold they had on the local economy and which the maoists could not break in the all too short a period they were active, to blacklist all those who had participated in the movement. They refused to give seeds during the ploughing season and also refused to buy the minor forest produce collected by them. Once such drastic measures were taken the movement quickly fizzled out.

The situation in Kondamodalu was better but only slightly so. The confrontation between the people on the one hand and landlords and police on the other stretched for a longer period as the people did not lose the will to fight. Although they had no fire—arms the tribals were quite willing to fight with bows and arrows and some efforts were even made at organising guerilla squads. However, no one had sufficient training for the purpose and before anything could be done news filtered in that most of the leaders of the Provincial Committee had been arrested. With this demoralisation set in and the movement came to an end.

More than any thing else the Kondamodalu movement emphasised the major lacuna in the *Immediate Programme* which was that it provided no answer to the question of how to deal with state repression if this had to be faced even before "mass defence" could be organised. It is indeed quite perplexing that such a major point should have been left unconsidered in the programme. It is a moot point that this neglect was deliberate and each area was to chose its own solution. More likely, the old guard T. Nagireddy and D. Venkateshwara Rao were afraid that if squad action was given official sanction the movement would develop with same lines as the Srikakulam movement. In any case, sooner or later, faced with repression some thing along the lines of squad action ultimately had to be resorted to and while this attempt proved abortive in Kondamodalu it crystallised in Warangal and Khammam where the movement continued long after it had died down in East Godavari.

The Pagideru Incident

The day after the State conference ended (April 13,1969) the Khammam and Mulug area committees met to chalk out a course of action. Unlike the case of Kondamodalu the question of finances and of defence were raised right at the start mainly because the movement existing in these areas had already faced those difficulties. It was straight away decided that in these areas the party would be reorganised on the basis of squads. In other words the party members were no longer to function alone but in groups of 4-5 each comprising a commander, one deputy commander and a political propagandist. For the purpose of finances raids were permitted to be conducted on rich persons but only in areas where the party had no base.[29] This would ensure that the party supporters do not bear the brunt of the inevitable police repression that would follow.

The incidents at Pagideru indicates the manner in which these squads acted. There had been some initial efforts in the area to mobilise the masses on the problems of food scarcity but even as the efforts were bearing fruit news came in that the police were due to arrive in the area soon. On receipt of this information Bathula and several other local members pressed C.P. to grant them permission to conduct raids and acquire some arms. Although C.P. realised that such a decision would go against the advice of the State Commitee which had stressed that under no circumstances should squad actions be permitted, he gave in to the pressure of the local cadre. Later on he justified this decision saying that he did not want to disappoint the local cadre who were not only enthusiastic but also adamant. In fact, several cadre and even those like Manikyam- a veteran of Telangana Armed Struggle days stated that unless they were given arms they could not trust the leadership's intentions. Under the circumstances C.P. felt that rigidity on his part might even have alienated the cadre. He also felt that the raids would also give the squad members, much needed experience.

Between 16th and 18th of April 1969, the pagideru squad along with twenty other party members including C.P. Bathula, Radhakka and Mohan Rao raided the houses of the landlords and moneylenders in and around the village.[30] On the whole they seized three shot guns, two burmars and some cash. The incident triggered of a series of other raids (all in Khammam) and by lst of May some fifteen attacks took place mainly on landlords, moneylenders, and officials like *Patwaris* and *Patels*. In the Kodavatancha area one Veeraswamy Appadu a well known moneylender was "annihilated" and according to the Party's claims, Rs. One lakh worth of promissory notes, seized and burnt.[31] Similar raids took place in Nugur taluq at Jagannadhapuram where the sarpanch described as a "collaborator with plainsmen from outside" was one of the victims. Here again promissory notes to the tune of Rs. one lakh were burnt.

Once squad action began in Khammam its influenc espread to the adjoining Mulug area where the area committee under the leadership of Ramnarasayya started to conduct raids almost on a competitive basis. Thus within a short space of time after the State level conference the cadre in these two areas completely gave in to militant pressures.

It is now quite clear that the Khammam area committee of C.P. in particular was committed to squad action even before the state conference. There can be no other explanation to the fact that despite endorsing the *Immediate Programme* the committee resorted to squad action within just a few days of the conclusion of the conference. The Pagideru incident for instance occured just four days after the conference and the incidents at Nugur occured after a lapse of only about ten days. This is further confirmed by the fact that barely twenty days after the State Conference on May 1, 1969 the leaders of the area committees of Mulug and Khammam *viz.* C.P. Rammarasiayya and Bathula met at Katapuram in order to give these raids a programmatic form. It was announced here that with the Pagideru incident the armed struggle had begun and a ten point programme as guideline for future action was laid down. This included conducting of raids on landlords and police stations in order to collect arms, annihilation of police agents and, if necessary, even landlords, occupation of lands including forest land, attacks on forest officials and so on.[32] The most glaring feature of the programme was an absolute lack of emphasis on the need to build up mass movements, a fact which had been stressed time and again by the APRCC leaders.

The influence and pressure of the Srikakulam movement on the programme is quite apparent from the fact that such a heavy emphasis is laid on guerilla type of actions. Even annihilation of landlords seems to have been accepted as a part of the over all strategy. However, this did not acquire the same theoretical importance as it did within the CPI (ML) theory. Annihilation in this instance was mainly as an inevitable event in the course of a struggle arising out of a tactical need. In other words some thing which need not be avoided if the situation demands such an action.

Rapid dissolution in Khammam :

In pursuance of the programme several raids were conducted in the Khammam area but with the intensification of police action the squads fell into disarray and the strategy collapsed. The police, according to the party adopted every trick in the book to isolate them. Their sympathisers were harassed, villages giving shelter to them were threatened to be razed and even counter propaganda, denigrating the party members as dacoits in comparison to C. Rajeshwara Rao of CPI and P. Sundarayya and of CPI (M) respectively, who it was claimed were "real communists" was resorted to. In areas where the party was weak many local men were recruited as home guards and cash awards were announced for catching the maoists.

Even more important than the activities of the police, which in any case was only to be expected, and th e fact which forced the area committees to reconsider operation through squad action was that it was beginning to get isolated from the masses. This was forcefully brought to light in the Gondigudem event when the central squad of Khammam area consisting of C P., Bathula and Radhakka besides nine others was attacked by a local mob of villagers who had been organised as homeguards. While, C.P., Radhakka and five others barely managed to escape, Bathula was among those captured and it is alleged that all those captured were subsequently killed by the police.

Two factors saved the Khammam group from total extinction at the time and for neither was the party itself responsible. The first was the early setting in of monsoon that year (1969) which made it difficult for the police to carry out extensive combing operations. The second was the reduction of the police pressure in the area on account of the shifting of some of the forces to deal with the separate Telangana agitation, elsewhere in the state. If nothing else, this respite gave the local leaders an opportunity to take stock of the situation, reorganise themselves and chalk out alternative strategies.

The activities in Mulug Area:

Soon after the meeting on May 1, 1969, the Mulug area committee reorganised its cadre on the basis of squads and squads each with about ten members were formed. One of these was led by Ramnarasayya and it was to operate in the Katapuram area of the Mulug taluq. Another was led by Bhaskar Reddy and was to operate in the Gurrevula area of the same taluq while the third, led by Datla Venkatram Raju and Panduranga Rao was to function in the Manthena area. All these were to work under the immediate supervision of the Mulug area committee.

The activities of the squads began almost immediately thereafter. The first few raids were mainly meant to acquire arms. In one raid on Sarvapuram village they managed to capture four burmars.[33]

In the next stage they set about attacking and even annihilating "local tyrants" and police informers. Their first victim, one Ahmed Khan was killed, more by mistake than by intention. He was mistaken for his father Sheikh Mohammed, the *sarpanch* of Kondai village who had been instrumental in disturbing many of their meetings earlier.[34] The *sarpanch* of Gurrevula was annihilated on 27.5.1969 for the same reasons.[35] In this case many local people who had disputes regarding land with the *sarpanch* participated. Similar such attacks took place on a number of others most of whom were either landlords or *sarpanch* . The squads were particularly severe on police informers inside the organisation and on one occasion killed a close friend of P. Ramnarasayya for having betrayed them to the police.[36]

Corrupt village level police and revenue officials were also not spared. At least two police *patels* including one at Govindaraopet are known to have been killed in this period.[37]

However, these attacks were not always successful and perhaps their biggest failure, as also their most adventurous was their raid on the Perur police station which ended in a fiasco. The plan was to attack from two sides and surprise the guards but the sentry proved to be more alert than expected. Once the element of surprise was lost the raid degenerated into a disorganised shooting affair and ultimately the attackers beat a hasty retreat. After this event the squads left the police station alone.

One trend which became very popular in subsequent months and which was started by the squads during this period related to raising of finances for their maintenance. The usual method was to kidnap the forest and beedi leaf contractors operating in the area and extort ransom from them. In one instance they held Kamal Mohan Rao a landlord cum beedi leaf contractor, his partner Srinivasa Rao who was also Panchayati Samithi President, Mahadevpur Block and Tulja Singh a timber merchant hostages at Bayyakkapet in Parkal taluq and raised Rs. 20,000/-as ransom.[38]

As in the Khammam area, in Mulug too the activities of the squads attracted a lot of police attention. On 7th November 1969 the entire area comprsing Mahaboobad, Narayanpet and Mulug taluqs was declared as distrubed area.[39] Police reinforcements were sent in and in a short space of time 22 squad members were arrested. In one crippling attack on the party cadre in the Mulug area the police seized 15,000/- rupees and large volume of documents.[40] Ramnarasayya and several other top leaders had a providential escape but all the same the squad activities dwindled sharply thereafter as the party members took refuge in the thick forest along the river Godavari.

It was thus that the first phase of total dependence on squad action irrespective of mass participation came to an end It had lasted for a mere month or so in Khammam while in Mulug where there already existed a fairly well entrenched movement it lasted a little longer till November 1969. In resorting to this sort of tactics i.e. of squad action the area committees of Mulug and Khammam fell into the very trap which the *Immediate Programme* was seeking to avoid. In the absence of any mass participation squad actions tended to be viewed by the police more or less as straight forward robberies and dacoities and dealt as such. In other words these incidents could and in fact were treated as plain law and order problems. It was also easy for the police to act because of the fact that the squads were isolated from the people and this meant one line of defence less for the police to handle. Ultimately both in Mulug and in Khammam the movement floundered badly and in places the scheme of action was reorganised to meet the situation.

The Second Phase: Re-assessment and Response:

As early as in June 1969 the Khammam area committee reassessed the situation in the light of the events since the May meeting at Katapuram where the ten point programme was formulated. A fresh six point programme,[41] restricting squad actions to some extent, was proposed. Significantly it was decided that the squad activities must take cognisance of the level of people's consciousness.[42] Further, these activities were to be coupled with economic struggles and accompanied by intense propaganda.

The response to this programme was greater than to the earlier one. In the border areas of Manukota and Yellandu taluqs at Bawajipet some 300 acres of forest land was cleared and occupied. At Gopalapuram village in the Narasampet taluq and at Vantaguduse in Yellandu *banjar* lands were occupied. In regard to wage struggles the party claimed responsibility in the increase of the rates of tree cutting from 75 paise to One rupee in the Kanigiri area of Narasampt. Apart from this the wages of the agricultural labourers also rose from 4-$5^{1}/^{2}$ measures of rice per acre of land to six full measures in Bayyaram where the party was particularly active. The activities against corrupt forest and revenue officials also continued. In fact in the absence of any dramatic response from the masses it was this particular aspect of immediate punishment to harassing officials which generated support to the party. In many areas especially where the party was just taking roots it was through such action alone that the link with the people was maintained.[43]

Ultimately however, the fact remained that the people were willing to move only on economic demands and not for political struggles. This was a crucial factor because at some stage of the movement or the other confrontation with the police was inevitable. In the present state of preparedness the party was not in a position to repulse any concerted action from the police. In fact the only reason why they had survived so far was that the terrain in which they operated provided abundant cover. The argument that had been advanced at the state conference in April was that the defence against State repression would be provided by the people in a mass movement. But as has already been noted this provided no solution at all. The situation became even more aggravated between 1969 May and 1969 November, a phase during which the Mulug and Khammam area committees resorted to squad action in a big way. Although an ambitious programme of training squad members in fire arms was mooted and a lot of notes circulated about how to counter police attacks it became increasingly apparent to the squad members and the area committee that the real answer lay in avoiding confrontation with the police and not in engaging in running battles. Subsequent events show how this reasoning was ultimately accepted in the next phase of the movement.

Response in the Plains Areas:

The movement in plains areas hardly got off the ground, except in some scattered areas in Jangaon taluq of Warangal, Nalgonda, Kurnool and Anantapur districts. In Jangaon the movement was mainly for foodgrains, and increased wages. These were complemented by several localised struggles for restoration of alienated lands. In Nalgonda district Alugupalli Narasimha Reddy and Sankara Lakshmi Narasayya organised several struggles for occupation of alienated lands and eviction of landlords from village common lands and Government fallows. They also conducted several raids on moneylenders and traders.[44] In each of these raids though more than hundred persons participated, they were not natives of the village in which the raids were conducted, most of them being maoist sympathisers collected from several neighbouring villages. However, they enjoyed quite a bit of local support and the victims of their raids were hesitant initially, even to complain against them to the police. Under the circumstances, the police were forced to book cases *suo motu.*[45] However, the situation changed as soon as two special police camps were set up in the area and started patrolling the villages. They quickly rounded up most of the local cadre sympathetic to the APRCC. The same was the case with Anantapur—T.N.'s home district. Here the APRCC quickly succeeded in making people occupy several disputed lands in the Garladinne area and under the Tungabhadra river canal. But the movement fizzled out with the entry of police.[46] In Kurnool also they had some initial response. In Nandyal, Koyulakunta and Nandikotkuru taluq about one thousand acres of *banjar* land was forcibly occupied by people led by APRCC. In the village even barricades were set up to prevent police from entering.[47] But once again the movement dissipated by July when large police camps were set up. Another plains area in which APRCC got some response was in West Godavari district where some lands belonging to an agricultural co-operative were forcibly occupied by the local peasant leader under the maoist influence.[48] In all other plains districts the APRCC activity was limited to organising meetings and distributing party literature.[49]

A significant fact is that pressures for more radical actions was visible even in these areas. For example, the Kurnool Zilla Committee passed a resolution in December 1969 in which they recommended formation of squads and leaving the plains areas temporarily to take shelter in the nearby Nallamalai hills. Similarly, the Nalgonda Zilla Committee also passed a resolution in July 1969 which recommended seizing of guns from landlords, and sent a provincial committee member to survey the terrain of the nearby Amaravati hills with a view of forming squads and conducting armed activity from that base. Even the Guntur district where there was hardly any movement the District Committee requested the provincial committee to grant permission for conducting raid in the town with a view to gathering money.[50] More than anything else these resolutions show how squad action seems to have been uniformly viewed as a solution wherever the party was faced with a situation when it was neither able to occupy fresh land nor able to hold on to land already occupied.

The end of the second phase:

By November 1969 the movement in Khammam, Warangal and Karimnagar forest area reached a dead end. Notwithstanding some initial gains in Khammam area, they had suffered severe losses in the Mulug area which had been their initial base. They were also thrown out from the Pagideru and Palwancha areas which had been their initial strongholds in Khammam. As a consequence of these set backs several cadres got disillusioned and left the movement and went back to their homes. These losses were compounded by personal differences and misunderstanding among the forest squads which at one stage became so serious that there was absolutely no contact between the squads of Khammam and Mulug between May 1969 and April 1970. The Mulug Committee went so far as to write a letter to the Rashtra Committee in which it characterised C.P as a "degenerate betrayer" and narrated several alleged incidents which substantiated their charges. C.P. was potrayed as being arrogant, bureaucratic, anti-Chinese, factional and authoritarian and even of being immoral.[51] The movements losses also led to severe criticism by Rashtra

Committee leadership which was quite unhappy with the local leadership's squad based activity (which were quite contrary to the understanding in the *Immediate Programme*). The State Secretary wrote a letter to C.P. castigating his activities as adventurist and irresponsible and demanded to know in what way his activities were different from those of CPI (ML) in Srikakulam. The movement further suffered from total organisational disruption when almost the entire Central Committee members were arrested in Madras, as a result of the information given by one of the Central Committee members who was in fact a police CID.[52] The only positive factor (for APRCC) at the end of this phase was that the core of their forest area leadership and their squads were not totally annihilated.

Renewal of Activities:

In a concerted bid to assess the situation and recoup losses the Khammam and Mulug area committees held a joint meeting at Katanagar in July 1970.[53] At this meeting they admitted their mistakes and criticised themselves for their rash actions in the period April 1969 to April 1970. Raids on moneylenders, traders and landlords, they decided whether for arms or for money did them more harm than good. Inspite of the fact that they had formed themselves into squads the primary task which the committee set upon themselves was that of mobilising and organising people.[54] The only acts of aggression they permitted themselves was in regard to police informers who were to be dealt with severely.[55] They were to engage with the police only in cases of supreme urgency when for self defence this became essential. The Katanagar meet also contributed a good deal towards reorganising the party which had almost been demolished by the police in the December 1969 swoop. The meeting formed a regional committee to co-ordinate the activities of all squads, established a party centre to direct the movement throughout the State and made plans for publishing a paper and organising committees in various districts.

With this background the *modus operandi* of APRCC completely changed during the third phase. As proposed in the meeting their squad completely gave up raids, and now concentrated on propaganda for mobilising people. Instructions were given to the squads that they were to tour villages, conduct meetings, and after properly investigating the conditions in the village explain to the people, how their local problems were connected to national and international issues. After gaining some sympathisers in the village they were to run night schools, conduct cultural shows and study circles and organise *Praja Sanghams* (a mass organisation of villagers). All these were to be used to propagate their views and exhort people to resist and rebel. As and when people got ready to participate in the struggles militant groups and volunteer squads were to be organised. There were to be equipped with traditional weapons and act at the front line of people whenever they went to seize landlord's crops or had to face attacks from the landlords, men or even the police. They were also to be incharge of punishing police agents in villages. From these groups and squads, the more mature and committed were to be taken as party members and formed into party committees. Every effort was to be made to concentrate on a cluster of villages which should be turned into "Party Centres", with village committees which would function as local self governing bodies replacing the regular Government institutions. These committees would look after various problems in the village like redistribution of lands, defence of the village and so on. In such a situation liberated zones would be formed where the Red Rrmy would ultimately be developed to aid the liberation of other areas.[56]

While this was the theoretically advocated model for functioning in forest regions the practice was somewhat different. This difference can be seen in the functioning of their squads. While theoretically they were assigned only two distinct tasks *viz.* to act as propaganda units and to provide defence for party members, in reality they took over a third task—that of acting as the 'Big Brother' or Guardian Angel' to the local tribals. It is this role of squads, that seems to have become the cornerstone of the APRCC movement in the forest region. In many instances the squads effectively intervened to get the tribals' demands fulfilled. For example they threatened the moneylenders to lower rates of interests ; they scared some landlords into vacating lands unjustly taken away from tribals ; they thrashed forest guards to prevent their taking bribes or reporting to police or to higher ups regarding reserve forest lands 'illegally' occupied by the tribals they pressured various contractors to raise wages, and so on while propaganda and mobilisation of masses and development of peoples initiative participation were neglected or given up, that and independent actions of APRCC squads were often a part of the whole process, at certain times substituting for peoples, participation, at others initiating peoples participation and most of the time giving confidence to and generating enthusiasm among the masses. However squad activities of the earlier variety *viz.* raids on the houses of moneylenders, and direct confrontation with police parties and even attacks on police stations were completely abandoned in this period.

This phase also saw the APRCC giving comparatively much more importance to propaganda. Though there were not many public meetings in villages, due to police pressure, squads constantly met groups of villagers to politicise them. Political classes were held in several areas for the sympathetic and militant among the local people.[57] These were capped now and then by massive public meetings in the forest areas which at times was attended by as many as 15,000 people.[58]

These activities were visible mostly not in their original strongholds of Mulug and Yellandu but in the newly extended areas—Narasampet, Palwancha and Yellavaram.[59] This was perhaps due to the fact that they had already gone through this process in the old areas. Land also came under forcible occupation by the people during this period and this included mortgaged and forest land. What qualified any piece of land for such occupation was the fact that its present owner had no legal right over it. Subsequently, the APRCC also began encouraging the people to occupy unoccupied land like government wastes, fallows, village commons and reserved forest lands. In the last case the tribals were somewhat hesitant initially and after cutting a few trees here and there they waited to see the reaction. When nothing happened they went ahead and cut some more of the forest. The APRCC squads often beat up any forest guard who dared to complain. During this period (1971) the government also was not too keen on pressing the issue as the elections were round the corner. In fact even ministers toured the area and promised to disreserve some forest land for the purpose of occupation by tribals. Emboldened, the tribals went ahead in a big way with the programme of occupation of forest land and according to APRCC's claims nearly 5 lakh acres were occupied between 1971 and 1974.[60] These figures are no doubt exaggerated but they give an idea of the importance attached to this programme by the APRCC.

A significant aspect of the land occupation movement conducted by the APRCC throughout was that at no stage was any claim made on the "self-cultivated" lands of the landlords inspite of repeated theoretical assertions in all their documents that armed struggle would really start only when such lands were occupied by the masses who would be willing to defend themselves and hold possession of the lands so occupied. The explanation for this discrepancy according to the APRCC was that the movement was strong in the tribal areas where there were no big landlords possessing large tracts of land while in areas where such landlords did exist the movement was weak. In this situation the APRCC seems to have settled for a 'semifriendly' relationship with the rich peasants in the area and in return for a fair deal to the tribal and regular contribution to the party they were allowed to cultivate unmolested.

Daring this phase, the APRCC, continued to mobilise people on the issues of usury and wages. The squads came to be particularly useful in these cases by acting as 'protectors'. A recalcitrant moneylender or a corrupt forest guard was made to toe the line by these squads who were not averse to using force.[61] But by and large the activities of the APRCC in this period was marked by an element of moderation. For instance in cases of moneylending they no longer asked for a total writing off of loans but only demanded more reasonable rates of interest. This seems to have been the result of a realisation that the moneylender formed an essential part of the local economy for there was as yet no alternate source of credit. The theoretical justification for this, however, was expressed more euphemistically and the moneylenders were described as being potential allies in the united front against imperialism and feudalism.

The most ambitious wage struggle launched during this period was the one against Birla bamboo coupes in the Palwancha area. A strike was called and for nearly three months the workers, some 25,000 of them, struck work. In terms of realisation of demands the strike was somewhat of a failure.[62] However, it provided the APRCC an excellent opportunity to conduct propaganda and project themselves as the champions of the worker, cause.

In another case the APRCC led a wage struggle against beedi leaf contractors. While the rate fixed by the government was six paise for 100 leaves the contractors were paying only three paise. After the party entered the field the wages rose to the prescribed level. This was in 1971. In 1972 a demand was made to double the existing wage rate. This proved too much for the contractors. They felt that they were on the one hand being forced to pay contributions to the party funds and on the other raise the wage rates to inordinately high levels. The net effect was that the party killed the goose that laid the golden eggs. The contractors to gain at least minimum profits bid very low and the government decided not to award the contract to any one but take it up themselves. Once the government took over even the wage struggle fizzled out and the party lost on both counts.

In both cases viz. the Birla bamboo coupe strike and the beedi leaf workers wage demand, the lesson driven home was that there was the need for moderation. In the very next year the party brought down its wage demand so that the contractors could bid again and take over the beedi leaf. trade.

Countering Police Repression :

A problem which the APRCC solved with a certain amount of success during this period was that of preservation from police attacks. They realised that their earlier tactics of attacks on police was only leading to increased police pressure on common people who were being intimidated by the former to withdraw their support to the party. Instead they adopted a two pronged approach. Realising that the police were heavily dependent on informers for information regarding the movements of the party members it was decided to take severe action against all such informers. At the same time direct confrontation with the police was completely avoided.

The APRCC distinguished between, class enemies and police agents in the matter of the methods to be employed in dealing with them. The former were to be dealt with only through mass movement while the latter could be dealt with summarily by the squads. Theoretically however, mass participation wherever possible was to be resorted to even in the case of police informers who were to be "watched, warned, brought to open trial and told to live in peace with the village."[63] While this may have been adopted in a few areas where the party was particularly strong and when the offence was not serious the general practice was that the squads themselves dealt with the informers. Twelve incidents where informers were killed by squads are definitely known to have occured between 1973 and 1975.[64] In cases where the informers were rich landlords or forest contractors they took action by burning their property and thereby rendering it unprofitable for them to co-operate with the police.[65]

A significant drop took place in the number of cases of direct confrontation with the police in this period. Upto 1974 some 150 clashes are reported to have occured between the party and the police resulting in 50 casualities to the maoists and four to the policemen.[66] However, of the losses tomaoists only eight had occured between 1971 and 1974 which was the period when the party had adopted defensive tactics. Even these losses the maoists felt, was the out come of lack of proper training and would not occur once this defect was overcome.[67]

Government Response :

The Government's reaction was a mixed one. On the one hand they set up police camps in the affected areas and on the other they stepped up propaganda on development programmes in the hope of winning over the people. Finding the existing police strength unable to curb the maoists the government decided on 1971 to launch operation on a military scale. Freed from the political constraints of mid-term elections they set up nearly 100 police camps employing 15,000 policemen in the Khamman and Warangal forest area. Thereafter each camp was set up within two to eight miles of the next one covering all the areas where APRCC was active. All roads were carefully watched and all the major water sources of the forest area guarded. Section 144 was declared in the whole of the forest area and partial curfew imposed preventing the villagers from leaving their houses between 6 p.m. to 6 a.m. Watch was kept on all shops and traders in the area, and villagers were banned from taking food or water into the forests. Efforts were also made to utilise the services of the officials of the forest department, the malaria department and teachers to get information about the squads. These measures were supplemented by many welfare schemes. Loans ranging from Rs. 500/- to Rs. 1000/- were given to several tribal families. Agricultural equipment including oil engines were distributed as were sheep units, milch animals and the like. But inspite of all this the 1971 operation was not a major success. In this period only three guerillas were killed and seven others apprehended by the police while several police informers were known to have been killed.[68] Further the welfare activities of the government were not an unqualified success. In the first place they were not of the magnitude required and in the second they were to some extent nulified by the tensions created by the police activities. Above all, the maoists put forward the convincing argument that all welfare activity was an outcome of their presence in the area and that once they felt government would no longer bother about the people here On the whole the party policy of a defensive strategy against the police was a success and even in 1974 when a fresh offensive against them was launched using the CRPF they lost only two leaders while two others were arrested. Throughout this period their underground journals continued to be printed and circulated.

Revival in the Plains area:

Having consolidated and somewhat extended their movement in the forest region, the APRCC turned its eye to the extension of the movement in the plains. In August 1970 they formed the regional committee for the plains. This committee consisting of Neelam Ramachandrayya as Secretary, Madala Narayanaswamy and Nukalapudi Rama Rao were given the task of building party organisation as well as of organising mass movements and class struggles in the plain areas. They were to build an underground party centre to run a paper and to distribute party literature besides establishing a courier system for helping the movement in the forest areas.[69] This committee gave an immediate programme for conducting struggles on the demands of minimum wages for agricultural labour, fair salaries for *palerus*, *banjar* land distribution and abolition of old debts.[70] The organisational methods were similar to those in forest areas *viz.* first organise struggles on these issues and out of the struggles develop units of militants.[71] Several difficulties were however envisaged in the style of functioning in the plains area. First of all it would not be possible to operate on squad basis at all because the terrain offered no protection. The party workers would therefore have to operate in utmost secrecy and conduct struggles from behind the scenes rather than from up front. Secondly, given the somewhat lower level of militancy in the plains areas more use would have to be made of legal methods.[72] The issues too would have to be of a general nature.[73] With this programme and tactical line the APRCC soon succeeded in resurrecting "district committees or district organising committees in nine districts and strong contacts in four districts".[74] After forming these committees the party held district wide "Congresses" of its members. These were meant to be "schools in our party's political struggles".[75] The APRCC also held eighteen party schools in different areas of the State to train and recruit members. Nearly three hundred workers were covered in this program. These lasted fifteen to twenty days and consisted of physical training, training in making bombs, besides imparting ideological education.[76]

The APRCC gave instructions that the emphasis was to be laid upon organising the basic classes—workers in town, agricultural labour and the poor peasants in villages. Importance was also to be given to organising youth who were seen as providing the militant content to the party activity.[77] They succeeded in this task to a certain extent in areas like Warangal,[78] Visakhapatnam, Nalgonda,[79] Kurnool, Guntur[80] and Nizamabad.[81] By and large, they held sway in their old strongholds like R.T.C. union in Warangal and B.H.P.V. in Vizag. They were also popular among certain groups of unorganised labour like the Nizamabad beedi workers and the Nalgonda toddy tappers. In most cases some progress can be attributed to the presence of charismatic leaders rather than to the popularity of the programme. For instance they had Neelam Ramachandrayya in Kurnool, Madala Narayanaswami in Guntur and Gurunatha Reddy in Nalgonda.

Even in the plains area the main thrust of APRCC activity was directed at developing land occupation struggles. The main area of activity was in Jangpaon where nearly 700 acres were reported to have been occupied in the villages of Santapuram, Bammera and Padidapalli [82] In Nizamabad too some 300 acres of *banjar* land was occupied[83] and so too in Warangal, Karimnagar, Nalgonda and Kurnool.[84] The strategy in the main was exploitation of factional quarrels between the big landlords in the area.[85]

The Split in APRCC:

On comparing the manner in which the Kondamodalu movement developed with the movement in Mulug and Khammam, it becomes obvious that the approaches of the leaders in these two areas was quite different. This difference was not something which had developed overnight. In fact, as has been pointed out earlier the Mulug and Khammam leaders deviated from the *Immediate Programme* right from the start. This was particularly true of C.P. and his followers. The only fact that kept the APRCC as a single group till as late as 1973 was that in December 1969 itself T. Nagireddy along with a number of the then Rashtra Committee members were arrested and removed from the scene. With this C.P.

got a free hand and when the call was given by the existing Rashtra Committee members in jail to form a new Rashtra Committee he promptly became one of the three members, the other two being Ramnarasayya and Neelam Ramachandrayya. Subsequent events clearly indicate that the *Immediate Programme* was not given much support by the new Rashtra Committee. By 1971 the difference was so great that T.N. and others in jail began asserting that they were the official Rashtra Committee and refused to accept the legitimacy of the three man committee outside. The fact that the latter committee was allowed to run unhindred for so long is only an indication of the lack of contact between the jail leaders and their followers. Ultimately, T.N. gave a call to his followers in the state to form their own committees and not to obey any directives from the C.P. group. But they could get only the Hyderabad and Guntur committees on their side. In the forest area only a fraction of a squad consisting of five men opted for T.N.'s leadership and very soon even they retracted and went over to the C.P. group. The C.P. group put forward several proposals for unity in which they said that a fresh plenum should be held and a new Rashtra Committee elected to decide the basic course of action. The T.N. group rejected such "formal democracies" and asserted that unity would be possible only on the basis of acceptance of the documents *Immediate Programme* and "*Ma Moulika Pandha—Aikyata Samasya*" (Our fundamental line—question of unity). With this it was clear that a separation of ways was inevitable.[86]

APRCC & Unity Centre

The attitude of C.P. and his followers towards the *Immediate Programme* was not the only reason for the parting of ways between him and T.N. The 1971 general elections to Parliament and the events leading to it seem to have decisively affected a small section of the party which consisted of such top leaders as T.N. and D.V. This section while broadly agreeing to the general maoist assessment of the national and international situation as favourable to the movement, emphasized and described those aspects of the situation which should be viewed by the maoists with caution. They declared that "any overestimation of the weakness of the ruling class and strength of the revolutionary organisation would lead to losses".[87] In various documents they described the different aspects of the situation which necessitated caution on the part of the maoists. They stated that though there was an economic crisis in the country the Government was taking serious steps to alleviate the problem. For example, it was nationalising banks, taking over those industries which were running at a loss and in general expanding the State sector. Further, they felt that inspite of severe competition and several internal contradictions, the ruling classes in India were united. There were several comprador sections in India for example those which represented the interests of Soviet imperialism and the public sector through which the Soviet imperialism exploited India and those which represented U.S. imperialism and its ally the private sector in India. Though these interests were competing with each other for a bigger share of the cake, their interests in general were reinforced and complementary to each other. It was wrong therefore to view either the Congress split or regional agitations as evidence that the Indian ruling classes had fallen out among themselves. The struggle between the leaders of the Congress party was viewed by this section as a factional one, aimed at acquiring power and that as such it did not have any far reaching consequences. The split could not be held as an indication that the pro-Soviet and pro-American sections of the Indian compradors had irretreivably broken with each other. In fact according to them Indira Gandhi represented the interests of both Soviet and U.S. imperialism. Though she leaned slightly to the Soviet side, she was not anti-U.S. and the statements of American leaders and news media supporting Indira Gandhi proved this.[88] Similarly it would be wrong to derive from separatist agitations like the one in Telangana that the contradictions within the ruling classes were reaching a breaking point.[89] The sections also felt that there was general political stability in the country and with the elections of 1971 "the instability of 1968 has turned into stability".[90] Slogans like *garibi hatao* were creating illusions among people and getting good response.

Any instability in the political situation was only a temporary phenomenon and could have been turned into a permanent one only if there was a revolutionary Communist Party and a wide spread revolutionary movement. They could have utilised the temporary political instability to deala crushing blow to the ruling classes and turn the instability into a permanent one. Since in India neither such a party nor a movement existed, the ruling classes could regain their stability at least for the time being. The rule of the exploiters in India it was felt was still based on the illusions of people. The situation was not one of simple brutal suppression. In fact, compared to the days of Telangana armed struggle (1947-51) the situation at present was more difficult for revolutionaries. Tactically the Indian ruling classes were stronger, parliamentary illusions had spread among people, the vocal sections of the people were corrupted, there was no single united revolutionary party[91]. And finally, India was of such a strategic importance to the imperialists that they would be prepared to take any steps to suppress revolutionary movements here. The intention of T.N. group in emphasizing these unfavourable conditions was not to deny the existence of a revolutionary situation but only to demand moderation.

On the other hand C.P. emphasised the more favourable aspects with a view to proposing a slightly more aggessive tactical line. In his view the strength of the ruling classes in India was fragile. The country "is in the grip of serious economic and political crisis. People of various classses were fighting against the policies of exploitation of the ruling class".[92] An "excellent revolutionary situation" was developing day by day and even a few armed squads could paralyse the general governmental machinery (in the Godavari forest area), given the correct political line and determination.[93] He felt that the Indian ruling classes "are split on policies to be followed and are beset with internal contradictions and as a result are getting weakened"[94] and that the split in the Congress could not be seen simply as a power or factional quarrel but should be viewed as a deep and clear division on basic policy matters between the group supporting U.S. imperialism and the one supporting Soviet imperialism.[95] The 1971 elections were not seen by C.P. as bringing stability. Thus according to him "the continuing President's rule in many States, the victory of Jana Sangh in Delhi Metropolitan elections indicate otherwise".[96] The conditions which created permanent instability, he felt had not disappeared with the electoral victory of Indira Gandhi. The so-called stability was only a temporary phase within the frame work of permanent instability.[97] On the whole compared to the situation in 1947, C.P. felt that the conditions were more favourable for a revolution now. People had no illusions about Congress; the internal contradictions of bourgeoise had matured; not only the communists but many others were also conducting armed struggle for e.g. the Nagas, Mizos etc.; the financial and monetary situation was relatively worse and the country was beset with border problem which it never had before.[98]

The differing assessments of the situation was reflected in (and was probably to some extent caused by) their different perspectives of the tactical line to be followed. The main dispute seemed to be centred around the party's relation with masses. T.N. repeatedly stressed the mass line—the need to rally masses and to completely depend on their strength for otherwise the ruling classes were too strong to be faced. The C.P. group on the other hand for various reasons advocated a more positive role for the party.

Once the split crystallised differences of opinion on various tactical issues was inevitable. According to the T.N. group "armed struggle is a peoples, struggle. Only when people participate in it directly can the armed struggle be started. Since we are in the state of agrarian revolution, only when the revolutionary peasant movement had developed to a certain stage can the armed struggle be started".[99] For the C.P. group on the other hand, armed struggle started much earlier, "When the people launch struggles against feudal exploitation, the landlords and the reactionary governments come down heavily upon them. In such a case the people are prepared to resist, armed struggle can be started".[100] Thus the C.P. group neither accepted the stipulation of direct participation, nor was willing to wait until the peasant movement had developed. For them the armed struggle began almost simultaneously with the launching of the movement. Again the T.N. group saw a symbiotic relation between land distribution and armed struggle. This was to them the lesson of 1948, the teaching of Mao Tse Tung and the experience of Kondamodalu struggle. They felt that unless people came forward to occupy lands, they would neither have the stake nor capocity to develop the consciousness necessary for conducting a protracted armed struggle against the State. This was particularly important in India because Indian revolutionaries did not start with a 40,000 man army as Mao did and had to totally depend upon the people's support and strength.[101] The C.P. group did not agree with this analysis. They thought that to stay armed struggle until land distribution had taken place was to "bind our hands and legs and expose the people and the movement to the enemy's repression and torture. It is to make us helpless in the face of enemy's actions".[102] In C.P.'s view "Government would not wait until people get ready for land distribution. Long before that they would attempt to suppress the peoples, movement with force. So armed struggle is to be started in the earlier stages of the movement based upon partial struggles. These can be slowly developed into armed agrarian revolution. It is only when people gain confidence in our squads, ability to face Governments armed forces, that they will be ready for land distribution but not otherwise".[103] In contrast to this the T.N. group felt that "partial struggles cannot provide the organisation and mass consciousness necessary for guerilla struggle".[104] They did not oppose militant steps including armed resistance by people during partial struggles. But "we oppose calling such militant armed acts as guerilla struggle. We oppose organising guerilla struggle for conducting of partial struggles"[105] C.P group also laid great stress on self-defence of the cadre. In their view if people were not prepared to directly resist repression in the initial stages of the struggle "we must adopt necessary tactics for self-defence of the cadre and mass movement. The form of self defence would depend on the degree of preparedness of the people and the terrain of the movement etc".[106] They characterised such struggles as the first step towards armed struggle. It was on this basis that they supported formation of squads and their activities in the Godavari forest area. The T.N. group severely criticised these concepts. They said that if self-defence of the type proposed and implemented by the C.P. group was taken up "people will become spectators. Their consciousness will never rise. Their self-confidence will suffer. They fall into apathy and dependence".[107] Further the group felt "it is wrong to say cadres' self-defence is necessary for the defence of movement. You think of defending the people and the movement and because of the fear of you the landlords etc. may not exploit the people for some time. But such victories are self-defeating. They will crumble like a house of cards as soon as the attack of enemy begin."[108] T.N. felt that cadres' self-defence could never become a substitute for peoples' self-defence, and, that in Khammam, the party had lost all contact with people only because of armed acts which were not related to peoples participation. It was only by depending on the mass line and on volunteer squads raised from people and equipped with local weapons could mass participation be assured. He was not opposed to self-defence as such but to the calling of self-defence as the first step of armed struggle.[109] He compared such statements to the CPI (ML)'s view of annihilation being the initial stage of guerilla struggle. The C.P. group rejected T.N.'s advise of limited self-defence and self-defence without weapons. They said that it would amount to capitulating to the enemy. They laid more emphasis on squad action which were stultifying peoples' revolutionary consciousness and leading them to inactivity. According to the latter, economic struggles combined with propagation of armed struggle could not lead to revolutionary consciousness. It was only through mobilisation of masses in militant struggles which, would give them practical and first hand experience, that one could develop revolutionary determination among people.[110] The C.P. group maintained that they were not substituting squad actions for mass initiative. They gave a detailed account of their activities in the forest showing how squads were participating only alongside and in support of people, movement and not in place of them.[111] At the same time the C.P. group refused "to stop actions on peoples, enemies by squads in the name of mass mobilisation being the key issue, and under the excuse of causing more repression.[112]

The T.N. group accused the C.P. group of taking to adventurism by depending on squad actions, neglecting land occupations and by not concentrating on any particular area but roaming aimlessly in the form of squads and thus weakening and destroying the movement in the forest area. They also blamed C.P. group's factional and bureaucratic methods, and disobedience of Rashtra Committee directives as being the root cause for losses in the movement. They held the Kondamodalu movement as an example of what might have been achieved in regard to moving people for land occupation if proper methods were followed and attributed the failure of the movement in Kondamodalu to inept and immature leadership.[113] The C.P. group in their reply to these charges said that their squads were not roaming but concentrating on a set of villages and that they were not totally dependent on squad actions but made every effort to form volunteer squads and people's committees. They further asserted that the movement on the whole had shown striking progress by spreading to nine taluqs and increasing the squad membership tenfold. They asserted that they were not neglecting land occupation but were only handicapped by lack of land concentration in the forest areas where they were acting. What euer losses there had been in the movement were a result neither of the conspiracy of a few persons (particularly C.P.) nor of the self-defence line, but because of the general over estimations of the movement, the pressures for greater militancy and deviations in the beginning, lack of clarity in leadership (T.N. D.V. etc.) on tactics and the vaccillations of the leaders. They also held that the Kondamodalu movement failed because the cadre continued to function in villages as individuals and did not take to squad form of organisations.[114] The C.P. group accused the T.N. group of capitulationism, of failing to build the party centre, or helping the movement with various kinds of assistance which was their responsibility as the central leaders. The group chacterised the leaders as being personally weak in not going underground as required by the party rules and accused them of trying to encourage factionalism in the party and satisfying themselves with passing resolutions like bureaucrats.

The C.P. group formally held their first statewide general conference in September 1973 and the C.P. group rechristened themselves as Andhra Pradesh Revolutionary Communist Party (APRCP). In this Conference they issued three documents. *The Party Programme*, "*Rajakiya Tirmanam*" (Political Resolution), *Bharatha Deshamlo Sayudha Poratam-Gamanincha Valasina Konni Vishayalu* (Some problems concerning peoples warpath in India). The first document systematically summed up their analysis of Indian social structure, its contradictions and classes, and presented an alternative system of institutions and policies which would be introduced after revolution. The second document presented a comprehensive assessment of national and international situation which had been developed during their debates with the CPI (ML) and the T.N. group. The third document summarised their views on the strategy and tactics to be adopted. The only fresh aspect in this was their emphasis on overcoming the disunity among the Indian maoists and establishing a united party. This was specified as their first duty.[115] The T.N. group which did not have enough strength in the State to hold a state-wide conference were content to release several documents under the name of the Communist Party of India (Revolutionaries). They issued a *Draft Programme* which was almost similar to that of APRCP except for stressing here and there on several hindrances to revolutionary movement. In general the programme and analysis of CPI (R) avoided the overoptimism of APRCP. The CPI (R) also published a document *Draft Path of Indian Revolution* which comprehensively presented the strategy and tactics of T.N. group as they developed in opposition both to the CPI (ML) and APRCP. While accepting, like others, that armed struggle would be the main form of struggle they added a rider, "at an appropriate level of the movement".[116] The T.N. group did not show any enthusiasm for uniting with other maoist groups. On the other hand it declared itself as an All India organisation—the CPI (R) and invited others to join it on the basis of its documents which would not be open to alteration as a condition to unity. They received some response in Kerala from the K.P.R. Gopalan group and in West Bengal from the Promod Das Gupta and Asit Sen groups with whom they even started publishing a common English paper—*The Proletarian Path.* However their largest strength cadrewise was in Punjab where both their students and Kisan organisations developed some following.

With the formal breaking up of the C.P.T.N. group another phase of the maoist movement in Telangana can be said to have been completed. In subsequent years, until the arrival of the CPI (M.) People. War Group led by Kondapalli Seetaramaiah (K.S.) it was the C.P. group which dominated the field in Andhra Pradesh while the group led by T.N. played a progressively subordinate role. But whichever the dominant group, the fact remained that unlike in Srikakulam, the movement continued to survive in Telangana and whereas it has shown little signs of revival in Srikakulam, it has not only persisted in the latter areas but has actually gained strength in recent years.

From start to finish the Srikakulam movement derived its mass support mainly from the tribals. When it began in 1957 it was conceived of essentially as being a struggle to achieve certain social and economic demands of the tribals who had been driven to a corner by the relentless onslaught of unscrupulous plainsmen traders, landlords and moneylenders. It was with this sole intention that the movement progressed upto 1968 and issues such as capture of political power and so on never figured on the agenda. In 1968 events took place outside Srikakulam which altered the shape of the movement considerably. The events, which led to the creation of a separate party by the maoists and the subsequent developments have all been described in some detail already. The net results of these developments on the Srikakulam movement was an increase in the scope of the movement by firstly extending it, in terms of activities, to areas beyond the Agency tract to which it had largely been confined till then and secondly by integrating it in terms of ideology with movements elsewhere in the country. Despite all this, however, even after 1968 it was the tribals if not exactly tribal issues, who dominated the movement in the sense that it was they who supported most enthusiastically all actions mass, squad or guerilla proposed by the party and throughout it was they who offered the strongest and most sustained resistance to police repression. As a consequence even long after the maoists "took over" the movement it continued to be strong only in the agency areas where it had initially begun and but for the support received from this area would have collapsed altogether much earlier than it actually did.

In short, then, despite the claims of the maoists of widespread support in Srikakulam for the movement, the support came mainly from the tribals who were, as they had been prior to 1968, fighting not for seizure of political power but for redressal of grievances. To the government which was desperately trying to put down the movement, the fact that the tribals formed the backbone of the movement meant that all they had to do in order to achieve their objective once the top leaders were eliminated, was to somehow neutralise this single group of active supporters. This they did quite effectively by offering them concessions which were mainly economic in nature. Had the maoists concentrated and achieved a broader mass base it would not have been possible for the government to suppress the movement by merely neutralising one group of supporters. The situation in Telangana indicates how differently the movement could have progressed in Srikakulam if groups other than tribals had also been mobilised.

The roots of the movement in Telangana go back to as far as the Telangana Armed Struggle and it is quite interesting to note that when the movement picked up initially in the early sixties, it did so in precisely those areas which provided the setting for the armed struggle in the final stages of the Telangana Armed Struggle in 1951. Equally significant is the fact that many of the leaders who were associated with the movement both at its commencement in the early 60's and in the latter part of the decade were persons who had actively participated in the Telangana Armed Struggle.

When one takes a closer look at the Telangana Armed Struggle it emerges that while it was subdued in 1951 by the police action it was never put down totally in the sense that the results which the struggle sought to achieve were not all achieved. Thus while the struggle was motivated by the combined demands of a broad range of classes ranging from the rich peasant to the agricultural labourer the post police action policies of the Congress government as we have already seen served the purposes of only the rich peasant class. It was, therefore, only a matter of time before the discontent among the other classes resurfaced and it was this that fuelled the maoist movement later on in the 60's.

When the movement picked up in the forest areas of Telangana in the 60's it too did so on a wide range of issues and while the tribal problem of the form that existed in Srikakulam did exist here also it was neither the only one nor even the dominant one. More often than not the tribals participated more as members of the agricultural labour class than as tribals. As a consequence in dealing with the movement in Telangana both before and after it entered the maoist phase the government found the demands far too broad based to concede and the only consistent course of action that it followed has been one of repression.

As we shall see later, developments in the post emergency period resulted in more diverse elements joining the movement and this has only served to heighten its broad based character. The impact that such a development has had on the government can easily be guessed and in retrospect therefore it appears that the inability of the maoists in Srikakulam to broaden the base of the movement there turned out to be their greatest disadvantage.

NOTES AND REFERENCES

1. Kolla Venkiah, *Viplava Senulalo Aikyata*, Guntur 1974, p. 35.

2. Document J-40 of Hyderabad Conspiracy Case. (CHCC)
3. Kolla Venkiah, *op. cit.* p. 38.
4. *Andhra Pradesh viplava Communist Party lo vibedhalu-Nagi Reddy group longibatu pandha*, APRCP (printed) 1974.
5. Document J-1 of Hyderabad Conspiracy Case, Minutes of Rashtra Committee Meeting, 6.7.1969.
6. *Two Years of Armed Struggle and our experiences*, APRCC (printed) July 10, 1971, p. 8.
7. Cr. No. 8/69, P.S. Mahadevpur, FIR of 13.3.1969.
8. See *Tactical Line*, APRCC (Mimeo. 1969) and C.P.'s opinions expressed in State Conference, Document J-1, *op. cit.*
9. Andhra Pradesh Legislative Assembly debate, 11.3.1969
10. Document J-1, *op. cit.* Incidentally D.V. belongs to the Telangana region and C.P. to Andhra.
11. Emphasis in the original, *Immediate Programme*, APRCC April 1969, p. 6.
12. *Ibid.* p. 11.
13. Emphasis in the original, *Ibid.* p. 14.
14. See prosecution witness statement of Stalin Babu in HCC.
15. *Kondamodulu ryotanga udyama sameeksha*, APRCC, (mimeo, probably 1970) p. 4.
16. *Ibid.*
17. *Ibid*, pp. 11-13.
18. See *Ibid*, p. 9, Cr. No. 17/69 of P.S. Devipatnam, FIR of 20.8.1969 and Cr. No. 16/69 of P.S. Devipatnam FIR of 19.8.1969.
19. For details see Cr. Nos. 15/69 to 70/69 of P.S. Devipatnam and Cr. Nos. 40/69 and 90/69 of P.S. Nelakota.
20. Cr. No. 21/69 of P.S. Devipatnam, FIR of 23.8.1969.

21. Cr. No. 21/69, FIR of 27.8.1969, Cr. No. 44/69, FIR of 3.10.1969 Cr. No. 49/69 FIR of 8.10.1969, Cr. No. 86/69, FIR of 18.11.1969 all of P.S. Devipatnam. Each time 20-40 bags of paddy were also seized.

22. Cr. No. 37/69 and 47/69 of P.S. Devipatnam.

23. Cr. No. 38/69 of P.S. Devipatnam.

24. Cr. No. 20/69 and 25/69 of P.S. Devipatnam.

25. For example the lands of Kaltapu Satyanarayana Rao, Vemulapalli Pulla Rao, Kalagala Veeranna, and his kith and kin who owned most of the land in the area. See Cr. No. 50/69 of P.S. Devipatnam.

26. FIR of 20.10.1959 of P.S. Devipatnam.

27. *Kondamodalu op. cit.* p. 11.

28. Document J-20 of HCC, 17.10.1969.

29. Document J-33 of HCC.

30. Cr. Nos. 20/69 to 26/69 P.S. Bayyaram.

31. Document J-27 of HCC.

32. *Two Years of Armed Struggle. op. cit.* p. 14.

33. Document J-21 of HCC.

34. *Ibid.*

35. Cr. No. 14/69 of P.S. Mulug.

36. Cr. No. 38/69 of P.S. Ghanpur and FIR and 13/14.9. 1969

37. See Document J-21, *op. cit.* and Cr. No. 25/69 and 37/69. See also Cr. Nos. 8/69, 70/69, of P.S. Etunagaram, and Cr. Nos. 39/69, 47/69 and 31/69 of P.S. Mulug.

38. Cr. No. 22/69 of P.S. Ghanpur FIR of 6.6.1969.

39. Government of Andhra Pradesh, G.O. No. 910 of 7.11.1969.

40. See Cr. Nos. 41/69, 56/69 and 43/69 of P.S. Mulug.

41. These were "(1) cut the forests contiguous to forest areas (2) cultivate the land ; (3) occupy banjar lands, (4) fight

forest contractors for higher wages; (5) increase the wages of agricultual labour (6) permit the free use of minor forest produce" Document J-21 of H.C.C.

42. Document J 27, *op. cit.*

43. *Ibid.*

44. See Cr. No.s 53/69 and 54/69 of P.S. Suryapet rural and Cr. No. 22/69 of P.S. Munugala.

45. See Report of Special Branch Circle Inspector submitted in HCC.

46. See the section of T. Nagi Reddi in Charge Sheet of HCC and *Party lo mitavada avakasavadam*, APCC (R) December 1973. (Vijayawada) p. 48.

47. *Ibid.*

48. Cr. No. 34/69 of P.S. Elore and also Document C 25 of HCC.

49. See Charge Sheet of HCC.

50. *Andhra Viplava Communist Partylo Vibedhalu*, APRCP (printed 1971) p. 108.

51. Document J 5 of HCC.

52. See *Partylo ativada peda dhorani* pp. 104-105, *Immediate Programme*, *op. cit.* Madras Central, FIR of 18-12.19.1969. Except for C.P. and Ramanarasayya all other Central Committee members were arrested. They had been unable to leave the forest area and sent Chalapalli Srinivasa Rao to represent them.

53. *Rajakiya nirmana sameeksha*, APRCP, (printed) submittted at their first Conference in September 1973.

54. *Vyavasaya viplava karyakramam-Ma acharana*, APRCC (printed) 1974 p. 33.

55. *Ibid.*

56. *Janasakti*, May 1974, pp. 2329.

57. Khammam, Warangal, Karimnagar Forest Area Report, APRCP, 1973 (mimeo) p. 18.

58. *Janasakti*, April 1974, p. 11. The APRCP seems to have taken advantage of a tribal mela to hold this meeting.

59. *Ibid*. pp. 23-24, and also *Janasakti*, May 1974 p. 3.

60. *Ma acharana, op. cit.* p. 35. The local officials agree to it though they cannot supply any precise figures.

61. See *Forest Area Report, op. cit. Liberation*, June 1975, *Rajakiya etc. op. cit.*, Janasakti, April 1974, p. 11 and *Praja Yudham*, July to August 1973. The later details of the movement in the forests have been taken from this source.

62. *Praja Yudham*, January 1971, p. 14.

63. *Janasakti*, April 1974, p. 25.

64. See *Janasakti*, July 16, 1974, *Janasakti*, January 1975, *Indian Express*, October 1, 1975.

65. For example, *The Hindu*, January 25, 1974 reports the burning of forest contractors property worth Rs. 50,000 in January 1974 and *Indian Herald*, December 16, 1975 reports the burning of Rs. 30,000 worth property of a contractor in Dharmapuram.

66. *Janasakti*, April 1974.

67. *Forest Area Report op. cit.* pp. 20-23.

68. *Deccan Chronicle* June 6, 1975, July 7, 1975 and November 20, 1975 and also, *Janasakti* January 1975, p. 24.

69. *Janasakti*, May 1974.

70. Rashtra Committee Resolution—December 14-15, 1970, *Janasakti*, January 1971.

71. *Janasakti*, May 1974.

72. *Rajakiya*...etc. *op. cit.* p. 42.

73. *Janasakti*, May 1974.

74. *Janasakti*. April 1974.

75. *Janasakti*, May 1974.

76. *Janasakti*, April 1974.

77. *Rajakiya...etc. op. cit.* p. 37.

78. *Vimochana*, May 1, 1975.

79. *Janasakti*, May 1974, p. 19.

80. *Vimochana*, November 1, 1974, and *Janasakti*, April 1974.

81. *Vimochana*, October 10, 1974.

82. See *Janasakti*, January 1971.

83. *Janasakti*, May 1974.

84. *Janasakti*, April 1974.

85. See *Vimochana*, July 1, 1974, p.16. Because these quarrels gave the party activists a starting point for launching their struggles. Thus for instance the quarrels involving the landlords like Rajeswara Rao, Santosh Chakravarti, Yathiraja Rao and Madhav Reddy in Jangaon was fully utilised. Again in Nimapalli for instance the dislike which the people had for the local landlord was fully harnessed.

86. *Ma Moulika......etc. op. cit.*, pp. 90-100, *Jailu Nayakulu Pampina...etc. op. cit.*, pp. 60-68, *APRCP lo Vibedhalu op. cit.* pp. 114-140.

87. *Partylo ativada peda dhorani*, APRCC, (mimeo) 9.6.1971, p. 13.

88. *Ibid*, pp. 14-22.

89. *Ibid*, p. 26.

90. *Ibid*, p. 16.

91. *Ibid*, p. 28.

92. *Defeat party splitting activities and capitulationist policies of T.N. and D.V.*, APRCP, p. 3.

93. *Andhra Pradesh Viplava Communist Party lo Vibedhalu* APRCP, *op. cit.* p. 23.

94. *Defeat...etc. op.cit.* p. 3.

95. *Jailu nayakulu pampina partylo ativada peda dhorani ane documentuni Tiraskarinchandi*, APRCP (mimeo, *1973*) pp. 7-8

96. *Ibid.*

97. *Parliamentary Ennikala Tadanantara Paristhiti—Mana Kartavyalu*, APRCP.

98. *Jailu nayakulu pampina...etc.* APRCP, *op. cit.* p. 20.

99. *Partylo ativada...etc. op. cit.* p. 24.

100. *Defeat...etc. op. cit.* p. 3 .

101. *Partylo ativada...etc. op. cit.* pp. 36-37.

102. *Jailu nayakulu pampina...etc. op. cit*, p. 30.

103. *Ibid.* pp. 26-27.

104. *Ma moulika pandha—aikyata samasya*, APCCCR (Printed) March 1972, p. 12.

105. *Ibid.* p. 13.

106. *Defeat...etc. op. cit.* p. 4.

107. *Partylo ativada...etc. op. cit.* p. 38.

108. *Ibid.* p. 41.

109. *Ibid.* p. 73.

110. *Ibid.* p. 46.

111. *Jailu nayakulu pampina...etc. op. cit.* pp. 38-49.

112. *Ibid.* p. 34.

113. *Partylo ativada...etc. op. cit.* pp. 106-107, *Ma moulika ...etc. op. cit.* pp. 35-55.

114. See *Jailu nayakulu pampina...etc. op. cit.* and also *APRCP 10 Vibedhalu op. cit.* and *passim.*

115. *Bharata deshamlo sayudha poratam, ‡gamanincha valasina konni vishaalu, op. cit.* p. 17.

116. *Draft Path of Indian Revolution*, CPI (R) (Printed) p. 17.

CHAPTER 8

Breaking up of the CPI (ML)

Breaking up of the CPI (ML)

By mid-1970 it was clear to the members of the CPI (ML) that the movement they had supported in Srikakulam and even elsewhere in the country had not progressed in the manner envisaged by them. To the critics of Charu Majumdar who had so far kept quiet, this provided on ideal opening to launch an attack against the policies he advocated. The first signs of discontent came during the Second All India Party Congress held in May 1970. Thereafter the fragile unity of the CPI (ML) which composed of a large number of leaders all having very strong views on various issues began to crumble. With the arrest of Charu and his subsequent death in jail in July 1972 the flood gates of fragmentation opened. This chapter deals with the emergence and the process of alignment and realignment of the various groups that came to be formed in the period starting from 1970 upto the declaration of Emergency in 1975.

The Rumblings of Discontent :

In the Second All India Party Congress of the CPI (ML) held in May 1970 the U.P. and Bihar groups tried to muster support, albeit half heartedly, to oppose the total dependence on guerilla action. However, despite the somewhat erratic manner in which the movement was progressing and despite the fact that most of the policies had been formed by Charu

Majumdar, the latter's personal image remained surprisingly untarnished. Strong opposition to the U.P. and Bihar groups came from the very quarters which had suffered the most from the set backs in the movement *viz.* the Andhra and Bengal groups and this was perhaps due to the high esteem in which Charu Majumdar was held by the leaders of both the groups. Vempatapu Satyam who was representing Srikakulam where the movement had all but fizzled out and who had earlier castigated the district party leaders for their lackadaisical attitude and wrong policies even went to the extent of now describing Charu Majumdar the "leader of the universe".[1] In fact so strong was this feeling of Charu's infallibility that those who opposed the U.P. and Bihar groups went one step ahead and demanded that Charu be declared as "the *authority*".[2] Souren Bose told the conference that "no revolutionary party can exist without revolutionary authority, and in India this authority is Charu".[3] In this he was supported both by Khokon Majumdar who quoted Mao as saying that Charu was the greatest Marxist-Leninist outside China and by Ashim Chatterjee who quite explicitly stated that if ever differences of opinion arose between Central Committee and Charu, the former must bow. The question of *authority* came to the fore in the context of Charu group's suspicion that the Uttar Pradesh, Bihar and Kashmir members of the Central Committee were attempting to moderate the party line. Though the latter were not in a majority they could achieve majority with support from just two more members, which would then give them a free hand to alter Charu's policies. The question of *authority* was raised to forestall such an eventuality.

The Second Congress ultimately ended with concessions from both sides. The Charu group withdrew (at least formally) on the *authority* question, and on such issues as forms of struggle, United Front and main contradiction in the Indian society. *The Draft of Party Programme* was somewhat ambiguously written. For instance the statement on United Front did not mention rich peasants and national bourgeoisie as partners but introduced a new category, the middle bourgeoisie and thereby left it to the members to interpret it in their own fashion. The proposal on the forms of struggle was contradictory—in that it referred to guerilla struggle at one place as the only form of struggle and at another as being the basic form of struggle. This implied that there were other forms to be contemplated. Similarly the main contradiction was mentioned as being the one between "landlords and peasants, that is between feudalism and vast masses". The two parts of this sentence were open to opposite interpretations. This effort to patch up however, did not last very long and the accumulated dissent led to the formation of groups and their subsequent break up with the parent organisation. This can partly be attributed to the fact the group's differences with Charu Majumdar as in the case of Bihar and Uttar Pradesh groups were by now articulate and open and also due to the depletion of Charu's following as in the case of the Andhra group where the top leaders like Vempatapu and others—who had all along supported Charu and his line—got killed in encounters with the police. Finally in 1972 when Charu died, the party completely broke up into various units with some claiming to be the true successors of Charu and others modifying Charu's theories as they thought fit. Of all the groups that split the one that adhered to Charu's line closest was the 'Pro Lin Piao group'. The other groups like the Central Organising Committee (COC) and the one led by Satyanarayan Singh followed Charu's line to a lesser extent.

The Charu line in Calcutta

Between 1970 and 1972, that is before the split in the CPI (ML) had actually taken place, the movement was conducted along Charu's line in the urban centres of Bengal, predominantly in Calcutta and in certain areas of A.P. This exercise led to the exhaustion of the movement rather abruptly in both the cases. Calcutta experienced the effects of frenzied activity by the CPI (ML) between 1970 and 1971 when the youth took over the movement completely. By mid 1970, faced with the restlessness and urge for action among his youthful followers in Bengal, Charu abandoned whatever conciliatory attitude he had at the Second Conference of CPI (ML). He now took an extreme position that revolutionary overthrow of existing power structure was to be immediately accomplished. He went on to draw up a set of tactics to suit the situation which was one of total offence. He exhorted the cadre to "forget self-defence and depend on offensive actions only",[4] and to carry out "direct and hand to hand confrontation".[5] He saw no need to concentrate on the building up of armed forces for "bases are required by enemy who operates in hostile surroundings not by our cadre who are like fish amidst water",[6] or for that matter unity with rich peasants for "that would only make the party's class line weak and the struggle would lose its determined character".[7] Glorious visions of victory were raised and the party was said to be in an impregnable position. Thus it was stated that "it is impossible to encircle and annihilate us even if they (the Government) gather 500 lakhs of soldiers since the enemy is tactically weak".[8] The people were, it was said, so enthusiastic that "without arms they will destroy the war devil with nails and teeth. A revolutionary cyclone will visit India. By end of 1975 the people will complete writing the epic of liberation."[9] However, after a brief burst of hectic activity in the city of Calcutta and in Birbhum district the movement ran aground.

Further Developments in Andhra Pradesh :

In Andhra Pradesh which was the other state in which some significant activity was taking place things were no different. Here the suppression of the Srikakulam movement put in front of the maoists the question about the next step. Unlike in Bengal they did not move to urban terrorism. The reason for this was that the urban centres in Andhra Pradesh were caught up in the throes of the separatist Andhra agitation. In these circumstances the *immediate revolution* directives from party leadership led mostly to bandit like activities in the rural areas. However, these varied in intensity and the response it evoked. This is evident when we examine these activities as they took place in various areas.

Their activities in Visakhapatnam district which took place almost concurrently with the latter phase of the Srikakulam movement (1968-69) present a preview of the shape the movement was to take in future. In October 1968 the maoists leaders Dr. M. Venkataratnam of Guntur and Y. Koteswara Rao of Nellore recruited two batches of volunteers from the coastal districts [10] and sent them to the Chintapalli agency area in Visakhapatnam with instructions to establish themselves there as teachers, forest labourers or in whatever other way possible and try to whip up a movement like the one in Srikakulam. [11] These volunteers contacted two local influential persons [12] who were sympathetic to the movement and with their help started holding meetings in the weekly local shandies in an effort to try and influence the tribals with their propaganda and collect the names and addresses of those who were responsive. Two of the volunteers joined as teachers, two more became stone cutters, a few of them set up tobacco business while some others opened small restaurants. These activities were to cover their financial needs as well as give them a legitimate guise to contact people. However, the true nature of their aims was an open secret and the police who had already been alerted by the happenings in Srikakulam did not have any difficulty in flushing them out. The few who escaped the police dragnet left the agency area and went to work in the neighbouring Anakapalle and Chodavaram plains areas where the young maoist cadre Nagella Sekhar, Sheik Bude and Dr.Ramakrishna had already won some amount of following. These leaders had utilised quarrels between tenants and landlords to build up support for themselves. At this time Nagabhushanam Patnaik who had been deputed by the State leadership to conduct the movement, came with instructions to abandon all open activity and to take up squad organisation and conduct annihilations. On May 14, 1969 at a meeting of Visakhapatnam district maoist activists Nagabhushanam Patnaik explained the new policies and expressed the desire to implement them by conducting an annihilation on the very same day. He over-ruled the advice of his followers that they should wait a few days so that the local people could be mobilised to participate in the annihilation. He chose the landlord of Nakkavanipalem as victim, against whom the local peasants under Nagella Sekhar's leadership had previously conducted several violent raids. Thus on the same night (May 14, 1969) Patnaik led a squad consisting of all the main maoist workers in the district and killed the landlord. On the whole this murder proved counter productive. Very soon there was an increase in police concentration. Desertions, betrayals and arrests followed leading to the disorganisation of the movement. all the leaders including Patnaik fell into police hands and the movement was effectively wiped out.

By the middle of 1970 the movement in Srikakulam was suppressed. This indirectly caused a spate of maoist activities in the circar districts of Krishna, Guntur, Godavari and Nellore. These districts form the richest and most modernised part of Andhra Pradesh. There were no big landlords in this area and at the same time these areas had the highest incidence of landless labourers. This area was populated by highly active and politically conscious people. Though the maoists had the largest number of cadre in these areas they could in no way implement their *anti-feudal* policies here, because the kind of *feudalism* in its most exploitative shape did not exist here. There was neither a high incidence of bonded labour, nor of largescale moneylender extortions nor of heavy land concentration. So initially these areas were used more as grounds for recruiting cadre, collecting finances and doing propaganda and organisational work like publishing newspapers, arranging for arms and ammunitions for the Srikakulam area and so on. Even when they conducted several raids and murders it was basically with the view to collect finances for the Srikakulam movement or to train the batches of cadre who were being sent to Srikakulam. [13] However, once the policy of annihilation was taken up, the maoists in these districts formed themselves into secret units and became roving murder squads. In Guntur throughout 1970 a maoist squad led by Bikki Ramulu—a school teacher, created terror. However, this squad was hunted down by police and most of its cadre were killed in the ensuing encounters. [14] In Krishna district too several murders and raids were conducted under the leadership of D.V. Ramana and T. Venkataratnam. The *modus operandi* was to conduct an action, disperse, hide in forests or far off places and gather together again to conduct another action. However, faced with intensified police activity the maoists could not sustain themselves and collapsed after just a couple of actions. In the Godavari districts the maoists under Raja Gopala Rao's leadership tried out similar activities but, here too they collapsed after just two annihilations. They had relatively greater success in Nellore district where they were led by Intha Ramana Reddy, a popular local lawyer and the Vice President of Panchayati Samithi and Dama Chenchiah, a rich landlord These persons had set up youth and cultural organisations which attracted many people. They had also organised agricultural labourers and had done a good deal of work among the harijans. Now the activists from this area under their leadership gathered and organised themselves on squad lines. They surveyed the neighbouring Udaigiri hill region and decided to make that their base. Activities were started by killing the landlord of Tollapalem village to whom they had previously sent a letter conveying the news that the District Committee of maoists had passed a death sentence. They committed several other murders and also set up a workshop for manufacturing bombs. However, the movement was soon disorganised due to desertions and 'betrayals'. People who had joined on the spur of the movement could not sustain their convictions when faced with prolonged periods of underground life, constant harassment by police and isolation from relatives and people in general. [15]

Though the nature and content of activities was similar, they had somewhat more success with their activities in the Telangana districts. Most of the erstwhile CPI (M) cadre in these districts had gone over to the T.N. and C.P. group. However, two teachers' union activists K.G. Satyamurthy and Kondapalli Seetharamaiah [16] joined the Charu Majumdar group and organised squads and annihilations in the Telangana area. One of their squads led by Bedida Chinnayya a veteran communist activist had thirty members and it committed more than forty raids [17] for acquiring guns, money and sometimes for annihilating moneylenders and landlords. This squad was active in the Mahboobabad Taluq of Warangal. Armed with crude bombs, guns and axes they conducted raids and took shelter in the neighbouring forest areas on completion of the raid. None of the raids were accompanied by any speech-making or any other kind of propaganda. They did not even concentrate on burning promissory notes or land deeds as had been the case in Srikakulam and West Bengal. Most of the raids were conducted on people against whom one or other of the squad members had a previous grievance, and were often conducted in broad daylight. This squad's activities lasted for more than a year until its strength was slowly eroded by dessertions and losses to the police. The activity and fate of various other CPI (ML) squads in Telangana *viz.* K.G. Satyamurthy's squad which was active in Jangaon taluq of Warangal and Jagtial area of Karimnagar, and the squads under Kondapalli Seetharamaiah in Adilabad and Karimnagar areas was identical. [18] The relative success of squad actions in Telangana as compared to the Circar districts can be attributed to the existence of a tenant problem in this area resultant constant tensions in the rural areas causing much dissatisfaction against landords. Further the members of squads in the Telangana region were mostly from rural areas and had a history of participating in communist led struggles. They were generally from the poorer classes in rural areas and thus capable of facing the rigours of underground life. On the other hand, the members of squads in Andhra regions mostly came from unemployed student sections of urban population.

With Charu Majumdar's death this phase of maoist activities may be said to have come to an end. The continuous losses to the movement apparently made even Charu Majumdar rethink about his policies and estimations. He is said to have revised his opinions on an alliance with rich peasants, on the primacy of annihilation and on the slogan proclaiming China's Chairman as India's Chairman.

Charu Majumdar's death brought the debate into the open and his followers split into various factions. All of them claimed to be the true heirs of Charu Majumdar. The most important factions were (a) the Pro-Lin group, (b) the Central Organising Committee (COC) group, (c) the Anti-Lin group and (d) the Assam-Tripura Zonal Committee (ATZ) group. Of these only the first two had some amount of following in Andhra Pradesh and as such the origin, theoretical formulations and activities of only these two groups will be examined.

Pro-Lin group

After Charu's death, a group of maoists emerged, who implemented his line without any change. This was the Pro-Lin group. There were three reasons for their persistent reverence to Lin-Piao inspite of his fall from grace even in China. Firstly they wanted to continue the line of guerilla struggle as in Birbhum i.e. attempting to build a red army by snatching guns etc. from police, and Lin's name was most closely linked to such a guerilla strategy. Secondly, in the Tenth Congress of CPC Lin Piao's address mentioned India as one of the countries where guerilla struggle was possible, while Chou-En-Lai's speech at the same venue pointedly omitted India. Thirdly, Lin's name was linked to a more radical and revolutionary foreign policy for China and those maoists in India who did not toe Mao's line in Bangladesh, preferred to identify themselves with Lin's foreign policy line. This was particularly important to those who depended on highly emotional young and raw cadre.

The pro-Lin group followed Charu's line almost unaltered. If anything they adopted on even more extreme stance than the one advocated by him. They had complete faith in the efficacy of guerilla struggle, a line which was strongly supported by Lin Piao. According to their analysis there was no reason to doubt the existence at a 'national upsurge' and the previous failure of the CPI (ML) resulted mainly from the party's neglect in regard to the formation of a Red Army.

In West Bengal the main leaders of this group were Mahadeb Mukherjee, Bhowani Roy Choudari, Sanjay Bhattacharya[19] and the cadre comprised the youths who had been released from jail on account of the Supreme Court ruling on MISA, those who had broken out of jails and others who were out to avenge the death of their friends and relatives during the 1971-72 police offensive. In November-December 1973 the Lin Piao group held the Second Congress of the CPI (ML) in Kamalapur village of Burdwan district. On that occasion they released a document which reiterated "complete faith in revolutionary authority of our respected leader (Charu) and the correct thesis of Lin-Piao".[20] Calling themselves the only revolutionary party they refused to have any truck with other maoist groups. The group was quite active during 1974 in Burdwan, Nadia, 24 Parganas and Howrah district of Calcutta. In the main, their activities, in consonance with their stated objective of building a Red Army, consisted of snatching guns and collecting ammunition and between December 1973 and August 1974 they killed 19 persons and snatched 30 guns.[21] Because of their direct and frontal approach they often fought pitched battles with the police.

While for short periods their highly aggressive and unsystematic attacks kept the police guessing, the group was practically wiped out within a year. This was mainly due to their total alienation from the masses because of which "no shelter was available even to women with babies in arms. total isolation stared at us, cadre were left like a boat without sail".[22] By November 1974 when a meeting of the group was called at Debganga in 24 Paragnas serious doubts began to be raised about the party's tactics. Mahadeb Mukherjee found himself totally isolated and before anything came out of all this the police swooped down on the group and arrested 18 top leaders including Mahadeb Mukherjee[23]. With this, the police claimed to have crushed the movement for "those free do not include anyone capable of substituting even for Mukherjee. Charu Majumdar politics have at least been buried".[24]

In Andhra Pradesh the activities of the Pro-Lin group followed more or less the same pattern as in West Bengal. Since 1973 Mahadeb Mukherjee had been trying to organise his party in this State. That year, he met Kondapalli Seetharamaiah at Bilaspur in Madhya Pradesh. Inspite of his generally extremist leanings Seetharamaiah, refused to accept many of Mukherjee's formulations and instead opted to join Suniti Ghosh and the COC group.[25] However, Mukherjee found staunch supporters in Intha Ramana Reddy (who was awaiting in Visakhapatnam jail the execution of the death sentence on him) and Rawoof a lifer in Visakhapatnam jail.

With their help several youngsters who had earlier been involved in the 'Naxalite cases' in Rayalaseema and Circar districts, but had been acquitted or left out on bail because of their relatively minor status and insignificant roles, were organised as the nucleus of a new maoist party on the lines of Lin-Piao strategy. This group led by Intha Krishna Reddy (brother of Intha Ramana Reddy), B. Jaya Rao and others planned large scale activities in the mid-Pennar region consisting of Guntur, Ongole, Krishna, Kurnool and Nellore districts.[26] They committed a series of dacoities but none of these involved any killing. Subsequently they went in for more spectacular and eye catching activities with a view to gain publicity. They raided the Cherukupalli police station in Guntur district, axed to death the sentry and decamped with some arms and ammunition.[27] The action proved to be somewhat premature because following this incident the police unleashed a massive combing operation involving more than 1000 policemen and the maoists were in no position to defend themselves.[28] There were several encounters and many were caught or killed. However, this did not seem to have subdued them totally. They conducted several more raids during 1975 and in early 1976. The most publicised of these raids was conducted on the ashram of Jillellamudi Amma, among whose disciples were several Cabinet Ministers of the State and Centre. During the raid the telephone wires were cut, the car of a devotee destroyed and eighty tolas of gold as well as 150 tolas of silver was looted. Most of the cadres were however rounded in the ensuing police raids.

The Central Organising Committee :

After the Second Congress of CPI (ML) at Calcutta (1970) and before Charu's death (1972 August) the party broke into many splinters. Charu's death almost shattered what was left of it. There was hardly any contact left among the various State units, and the organisational methods which ruled CPI (ML) during 1970-75 i.e. large scale autonomy at the operational level combined with total centralisation at policy formulation level, had destroyed the party organisation making it depend on spontaneity. Charu's death meant destruction of party's last symbol and semblance of unity. With his death the necessity of new organisational forms was severely felt by all his followers. Previously his word was law but now it needed an interpreting agency.

In this situation Charu's followers got together to build a new organisation. However, they suffered a serious initial set back as they themselves were split into two. The group of Mahadeb Mukherjee which commanded a majority in West Bengal and Bihar insisted on following Charu's line exactly as it was in 1971. They swore by Charu's *authority* and praised Lin Piao. The others led by Suniti Ghosh were not willing to toe such a line. Though they commended Charu's contribution to Indian revolution, they were unwilling to accept his infallibility, and while supporting Charu's line on Bangladesh and on guerilla struggle they refused to go so far as to call guerilla struggle as the only form of struggle. They also refused Mukherjee's assessment that revolution would come in India by 1975 and this refusal meant moderation in tactical line, which was to be based on the understanding of "protracted war" and not "immediate victory". These and other differences led to parting of ways and while Mukherjee group declared themselves as CPI (ML) and held the Third Congress in November 1973, the others met in the same month and formed the Central Organising Committee (COC). Though the COC was initiated by Suniti Ghosh and Soumya in November 1973, it was fully constituted only in February 1974 by which time contacts were made with several State Committees.[30]

The organisational principles on which the COC members were united were two. One was the acceptance that CPI (ML) as it was constituted under the leadership of Charu until his death was the one and the only CPI (ML). They thus denied the claims of other groups for eg. that led by Satyanarayan Singh to be the representative of CPI (ML).[31] The task of COC in this context was seen to be to unite all those who at the time of Charu's death were in the party.

The strongest group to join the COC was that of Kondapalli Seetharmaiah of Andhra Pradesh. Kondapalli Seetharamaiah held sway over five active squads and several district committees besides having a powerful hold on several mass organisations. The Kashmir (ML) group led by R.P Saraf agreed to join but only on the condition that initially at least the new organisation would function on the basis of a co-ordination committee, so that the decisions would not be compulsive and binding on all members. The U.P. Committee laid down a further condition that the new organisation must be open to all maoists in India. The COC refused to meet the demands of these committees, and they opted to stay out of it.[32]

There was no clear theoretical agreement on many issues among COC members when they initially came together. What brought them together was their similar views on organisation and a vague theoretical position which did not lean either towards Mahadeb Mukherjee's formulation or Satyanarayana Singh's programme. They were not willing to accept Charu's line as it stood in 1972, nor were they willing to go as far towards mass organisations, united front, economic struggles, forest base areas, and abandonment of annihilation tactic as Satyanarayana Singh was doing. While their antipathies were clear their exact position was not. In this situation they got together and issued a document which skipped over most of the controversial areas. This document which was to be the basis of future action contained besides the usual description of revolutionary situation in country, only three other definite formulations. On the question of revolutionary alliance it recommended the unity of working class, poor peasant, landless labourers, petty bourgeoisie and national bourgeoise. Thus the concept of national bourgeoisie was brought in resulting in a retreat from the 1970 programme which maintained that the bourgeoisie in India was comprador and ruled out alliance of any sort with them. Secondly on the question of contradiction, it stated that the main contradiction was between, "feudalism and vast masses", thus restoring the need and significance of work in urban areas which was denied by the 1970 formulation which had maintained that the main contradiction was between "landlords and peasants". Thirdly, on the question of forms of struggle it averred that, "Armed Struggle is the main form of struggle".

This was a correction of the 1970 statement that guerilla struggle was the only form of struggle.[33]

The vagueness of the document was soon supplemented by explanatory writings by various COC leaders. In fact two divergent interpretations were made of the document almost leading to the breaking of the fragile unity of COC. Kondapalli Seetharamaiah issued an interpretation in which he made two points. The first was that the document had at no place categorically rejected "annihilation." The document, it was stated, was not a comprehensive one and it only laid down certain basic guidelines. Thus while several tactical prescriptions like "annihilation" and "snatching of arms" were not specifically mentioned, it did not mean that they were altogether rejected.[34] Secondly, though he accepted the need to lead and organise mass movements he qualified this by saying that "in practice these would turn into revolutionary, committees".[35] Thus he did not make the clear cut division between mass organisations and party organisations, which S.N., T.N., C.P. and others did. For him mass organisations were instruments for mobilising people for struggles on their own issues, and through these struggles develop their revolutionary consciousness and prepare them for revolutionary struggle. Similarly on the issue of partial struggles based on economic demands Kondapalli's understanding was different from those of C.P., S.N., and T.N. He was willing to use these struggles for propagating armed struggle. To him economic struggles were not a prelude to the coming armed struggle but a supplement to an already existing one. In his view armed struggle was the main form of struggle and by rejecting the formulation of it being the only one, he had only accepted the use of other forms of struggle but by no means had he accepted postponing of armed struggle or of the formulation made in certain quarters that it would come only at a certain stage of development of mass movements or economic struggles.

The Andhra group of COC was fully supported by the *Mass line* group in Kerala who while accepting the need for a protracted armed struggle, said that the basic problem of the Indian revolutionaries was that they did not have an army to start with like the Chinese revolutionaries had in 1927. Besides this, unlike in the thirties the, Indian Government was strong and unified. The methods of overcoming this problem was to have a "comparatively long phase of guerilla actions by scattered guerillas throughout the vast areas of the country, only by indirect control under the leadership of party can these guerillas units be organised into peoples liberation army".[36] Thus the guerilla was "raised to the level of strategy. Unlike China where it was often relegated to the status of subsidiary of regular warfare, it will remain as basic form of struggle till the end while all other forms of struggle (economic or mass movements etc.) will remain subsidiary".[37] It was only when annihilations were conducted without class struggle (meaning-by party cadre without local participation) that the movement suffered. The views of Andhra and Kerala groups thus were quite similar to the Lin Piao groups views except in that the former advocated some amount of use of the mass organisations and economic struggles.

The Bengal and Punjab groups rejected annihilation outright and stressed the need to participate in mass struggle build mass organisations and also conduct struggles on economic demands. They declared their line to be one of "establishing the leadership of party over mass organisations with a view to organise armed struggles of the peasants... building up the peoples-armed forces and rural base areas... is fundamentally different from the method propagated and practiced at a certain phase that ended with the death of Charu. While the method of COC depends for its success on the masses of the people led by the party the earlier method relied mainly on the vanguard".[38]

These differences of opinion in COC were welcomed by the CPI (ML) of Satyanarayan Singh and C.P. They said 'COC was born in an' opportunists. compromise on principle and was bound to die ... Factionalism and subjective prejudices led Suniti Ghosh and the mass liners to join the Charuities ... we wish the mass liners victory. We want unity with them, without further delay".[39]

However, the CPI (ML) (S.N. Group) plea fell on deaf ears as there were still several areas like "rich peasants" "base areas in forest regions" etc. upon which differences existed between them and the Suniti Ghosh faction, and the matter was not helped at all by the fact that there was little love lost between the leaders of the two factions who had on several occasions slandered each other in public.

The COC in Andhra Pradesh:

In the end the COC in Andhra represented an amalgam of various type of activities. On the one hand they continued to have roving squads which would conduct raids and carry out annihilations, while on the other they tried to arouse people in selected areas against local landlords and moneylenders. They also took to organising students and literary associations which would conduct agitations and carry out propaganda.

The squad actions of COC continued with several ups and downs between 1971 and 1976. On the whole they were limited to the Telangana region, as in the Andhra region the followers of Charu Majumdar went over to the Lin Piao group. In 1971 under the leadership of K.G. Satyamurty and Kondapalli Seetharamaiah three squads were organised. These were the Barla Yadagiri Raju squad which was to function in Warangal district, the Inguva Mallikarjuna Sharma squad which was to function in Nalgonda district and Linga Vijaya Kumar squad which was to function in Khammam district. All three leaders were students in their early twenties.[40] They chalked out a programme consisting of (a) killing police personnel and seizing their arms, (b) killing police informers, (c) attacks on class enemies, their annihilation and confiscation of their property, (d) recruiting youth for armed struggle and (e) organising the Red Army.[41] In pursuance of this programme six annihilations, twenty dacoities and four attacks on police were made. Besides these six other offences were reported during 1971-1973.[42] Following leakage of information from the maoist circles the police arrested K.G. Satyamurty in November 1973. This was followed by a spate of arrests leading to the disorganisation of COC squads. The final blow was dealt on January 17, 1974, when the entire squad of Linga Vijaya Kumar was arrested following their abortive attempt at a day light dacoity on the State Bank of Hyderabad branch at Nadigudem.[43] The squad actions of COC were subsequently revived during 1974-76. Kotagiri Venkati an unemployed student organised a squad which created terror in Medak district. This squad committed nearly thirty dacoities during 1974 and a similar number in 1975.[44] However, the squad's activities came to an end after June 25, 1976 when Kotagiri Venkati was shot dead in an encounter at Mupparam in Warangal.

Besides the activity of these roving squads the COC also made efforts to work up support in selected areas. They made repeated efforts to organise revolt of the tribals of Godavari forest region.[47] Their activity was confined to quick propaganda and exhortation but no efforts were made to draw the tribal. They had no units of organisation and depended on spontaneous support and action from the tribals, and this was not forthcoming. COC also organised struggles of peasants for proprietorship of common lands in Dharmavaram taluq of Anantapur district. Nearly 1000 acres was occupied but the movement came to an end with the murder by landlords of soom peasants including their top leader Sriramulu.[48] Besides this the COC organised strikes of agricultural labour in Ankusapuram area of Hyderabad district,[49] in Ongole[50] and Nalgonda districts[51] and in the Kandukur area of Nellore district.[52] However, all of them ended after gaining limited concessions from local landlords. It was also claimed by magazines sympathetic to COC that strikes conducted in Nizamabad Cement Factory, Usha Engineering and several other places were under COC's influence.[53]

However, what really brought the COC in Andhra into lime light during 1974-75 was the support it received from intellectuals—particularly writers and poets. The tribal struggle in Srikakulam captured the imagination of many young poets like Varavara Rao and the *Digambara*[54] group of writers. They set up the Revolutionary Writers Association (RWA) which attracted a good deal of support not only from the younger poets but also among the established ones. Sri Sri often regarded as the father of modern Telugu poetry became its President, Rachakonda Viswanatha Shastry its Vice-

President and Kodavaganti Kutumba Rao a leading short story writer and literary critique, its General Secretary. The RWA soon set up its branches throughout the State.[55] Though in the initial years (1969-72) RWA restricted itself to literary activity, in the later years (1972-75) its members undertook open political activity, probably because of the fact that while a general atmosphere of unrest was prevailing within the country with strong agitations being carried out in Bihar and Gujarat hardly any of the top maoist cadre in Andhra was out side. The RWA members started touring the state holding public meetings and since most of them were powerful and attractive speakers they always managed to get large audiences wherever they went. Such activities were supplemented by the *Jana Natya Mandali* (Peoples Cultural Association) which arranged troupes of singers and folk artists to tour the state giving performances meant to popularise the maoist policies and views. In these circumstances the Government cracked down on the poets and arrested most of the mas accused in *The Secunderabad Conspiracy case.* Only Sri Sri was left out because of his stature and age. The charge sheet of the case alleged that most of the poets were writing seditious and inflammatory material besides directly aiding and abetting the COC squads. Su bsequently the RWA was further weakened by desertion of a small group of poets led Jwalamukhi (owing allegiance to T.N. group) who held that the poets, field did not include practice but only propaganda.

Revolt of the Rural Leaders:

The policies of Charu and his followers lead to an increasing dependence on their part on new, and more youthful cadre. This served only to alienate those leaders who had throughout relied on rural masses for support and one by one they began setting up their own organisations. Each of them left at a different time, for the pressures of circumstances and the issues of contention with Cha ru Majumdar which they had to confront were many and varied. Unity among these factions was a tortuous process completed only under the hammer blow dealt by the Indian Governments' Declaration of Emergency on June 26 of 1975.

The banner of revolt was originally raised by Satyanarayan Singh who had led the maoist peasant movements in Bihar. He was later on followed in chronological order, by Shiv Kumar Mishra, the architect of peasant revolt in Lakshmipur Kheri of U.P., Ashim Chatterjee the organiser of Debrah Gopiballabhpur peasant struggle in Bengal, Sushital Roy Chowdhury who as Chief Editor of party's ma azines had been closely connected with the rural line, Pyla Vasudeva Rao, the only surviving leader of Srikakulam tribal revolt; and finally Kanu Sanyal the leader of Naxalbari peasants struggle. All of them denounced Charu Majumdar for 'adventurism' and set out with their own ideas on how to set right the situation.

Satyanarayan Singh as noted earlier had been in a discontended mood even on the eve of the Second Congress of CPI (ML). If he did not break away then, it was only because he was unsure about the support he would receive. He said that anybody opposing Charu was being branded as revisionist and that his arguments were brushed aside rather than answered. He opposed the party being converted into what he called the "Action Party", by reorganising the committees to include only those who "had dipped their hands in class enemy's blood". He objected to the sacrifices of many young party cadre in meaningless actions, on the spurious pretext of "steeling" them. He also pointed out various exaggerations and overestimations in which the party papers were indulging, and said that they could only bring about harmful results.[57]

Revolt by Srikakulam Unit:

Their staggering losses had been forcing many of the Srikakulam leaders to rethink about the efficacy of the line adopted by them. The first to give an open expression to the doubts about dependence solely on guerilla actions was Tejeswara Rao who was at that time Secretary of CPI (ML's) Andhra Unit, as well as a member of the Party's Central Committee. He was promptly denounced as revisionist and soon removed from all party posts. However, the demoralisation that set in with Vempatapu's death made the other Srikakulam leaders also question the party line. They included among others Nagabhushan Patnaik and Appala Suri—the only surviving Andhra members in CPI (ML)'s higher committee. However, this did not last long and before something concrete could be done they were arrested.[58]

In the meantime, the Srikakulam maoists conducted a regional plenum of all its members under the leadership of Pyla Vasudeva Rao. They reviewed their movement and came to the conclusion that the losses incurred were owing to an essentially adventurist and sectarian political line. They felt that they had w ongly characterised Srikakulam as Yenan of India and had compounded the mistake by neglecting the organisation and propaganda and by concentrating only on 'actions'. "We thought action first and organisation next, we thought that only by actions we can mobilise." They stated that they had wrongly thought "wherever there is a revolutionary he must kill class enemies...and all landlords are killers. Their presence is invitation to our death." The result of such an analysis they felt had resulted in indiscriminate killings. By "fighting with everyone and compromising with none", they had become isolated. They had recognised only those as revolutionaries who "entered armed struggle, took to arms and left their homes". Thus by taking all their supporters into the field they had snapped all their contacts in towns and villages. Besides these main reasons, neglect of propaganda activities in tribal areas during the struggle, lack of modern weapons, badly organised dens; inefficient couriers; unrealiable contacts and so on, had caused losses.[59] In sum, while the Srikakulam plenums review was essentially pragmatic and tactical, it did not raise any serious theoretical questions or evolve clear plans for future. This was inevitable given the fact that the leadership left in the area was by and large inexperienced in the field of theoretical formulations. Therefore providing a theoretical framework for their new thinking was not broached. On the question of annihilation their review was vague. Though it condemned killing of all and sundry, it advocated annihilations preceded by propaganda and with "peoples approval" (note—not participation). However, the influence of Satyanarayana Singh seems to have slowly brought the Srikakulam maoists around accepting the general programmatic and tactical views expressed in S.N.'s documents.

Polarisation:

Thus between April 1970 when the Second Congress of CPI (ML) took place and the middle of 1972 by which time the effects of Mrs. Gandhi's sweep over elections was clearly felt in all political circles, the maoists in India were split into innumerable small groups. Their sense of isolation was heightened by the twin factors of lack of response to their policies from the people and persistent repression that was in operation throughout this period. At the same time the changes at the national political level between 1972-74, the violent agitations in Gujarat and Bihar, the separatist agitations in Andhra and the general mood of unrest and discontent symbolised by the J.P. movement, brought home to the maoist leaders the pressing need for regrouping themselves so as to be in a position to take advantage of the volatile but contradictory situation. As a consequence, between 1972-75 many efforts were made to unite. While they did not succeed in bringing about any unity they could achieve some kind of polarisation which ultimately resulted in three distinct sets of moaist groups emerging. The best organised among these was the S.N. faction which called itself CPI (ML). The relatively more moderate groups rallied around T.N. and his CPI (R) while the extremist groups like Pro-Lin, Anti-Lin, ATZ factions remained quite uneffected. Another group, the COC on the other hand vacillated between alliance with S.N. and separate existence.

Satyanarayana Singh was the first leader to make efforts towards unity among maoist groups. After having freed himself from contradictory pressures of both Ashim Chatterjee and U.P. groups. S.N. issued the *Self Critical Report* in 1973. This document for the first time unequivocally condemned annihilation and recognised the crucial importance of land occupation struggles—the latter was to be organised as a precondition to armed struggle and be based on peoples' own demands. The form of struggle to achieve the demands were to be appropriate to the existing level of peoples' consciousness. The need for building mass organisations of all kinds was also emphasised. He tried to base his moves on this general policy. His biggest success was in Andhra Pradesh where both the C.P. group as well as Pyla Vasudeva Rao in Srikakulam joined him. This merger carried with it the much needed financial and organisational strength. In a common statement with the Andhra leaders he issued an appeal calling for the termination of antagonistic relations among maoist groups, mutual exchange of documents and the starting of earnest efforts to form an all-India co-ordination committee.[61] Following this appeal the Maharashtra Committee of CPI (ML) passed a resolution expressing broad agreement with S.N. and C.P. and also expressed its willingness to merge with CPI (ML).[62] The S.N. group also succeeded in setting up branches in U.P., Bengal and Punjab besides initiating talks to gain some amount of co-operation with the COC groups. S.N. even established a steering committee for co-operation with Ashim Chatterjee group in Bengal.[63]

Having organisationally strengthened itself the CPI (ML) reiterated its theoretical position of dependence on mass organisations and mass struggles. In several documents the leaders stressed the importance of land occupation movements and also of the need to work in towns and among workers.[64] Further in the context of J.P.'s movement there were several theoretical innovations during 1974-75. The situation was seen as one in which the "ruling classes were split with a section which had lost dominance in Government launching *peoples movements* to overthrow the present regime.[65] CPI (ML) further went on to say that it "makes a distinction between the section of ruling class entrenched in governmental power and the pro-American section which has lost dominance"[66]. So the CPI (ML) gave a call to establish the "regime of patriotic and democratic unity". The purpose of this call was to enable the unity of CPI (ML) with all anti-establishment forces irrespective of their social ideologies.[67]

The S.N. group openly extended its support to the J.P. led movement.[68] But this support was not unequivocal. Their slogan was "March separately, strive unitedly". This meant that while J.P.'s demands and agitations were to be supported, the CPI (ML) was to keep its organisation separate and to choose independent forms of action.[69] The party also openly and repeatedly expressed many of its reservations about J.P. movement. For instance it asserted that every precaution must be taken to see that "American Imperialism (JP) does not replace Soviet Imperialism (Indira) for it makes no difference whether one dies of cholera or typhoid".[70] And, again while the party supported J.P. in his fight against "corruption, inflation, unemployment, useless education system and land concentration",[71] it also condemned his "failure to formulate socioeconomic programme, failure to formulate independent foreign policy and denial of working class its proper role in revolution".[72]

The CPI (ML) in A.P.—The activities of the C.P. group :

In Andhra, where the J.P. movement did not catch on, the CPI (ML) support to it remained only on paper. However, in keeping with the general policy of participating in all mass movements the C.P. group had earlier extended its support to the separate Andhra agitation which had taken shape during 1972-73.[73]

After 1972 the biggest achievement of CPI (ML) was in the field of student organisations. The forest movement of the C.P. group in Telangana region had always evoked some sympathy among students of the Osmania University which covers the Telangana region. The pro-maoist students had been active in the University since 1969 but their activities were limited to recruiting cadre for peasant struggles and were not directed at mobilising students as a body to fight for their own demands. It was in 1972 under the leadership of George Reddy—a student of Science college, Osmania University, that pro-maoist students started organising themselves into a distinct group. The subsequent murder of George by students belonging to RSS acted only as a temporary set back. Conventions were held in various parts of the State to enrol members and formally establish the organisation. These climaxed in the First State Conference of Progressive Democratic Students Union (PDSU) in October 1974.

Apart from organising work through front organisations the CPI (ML) continued its activity in forests and rural areas. Even in Srikakulam where the movement had received crushing blows during 1969-70, there were some signs of renewed activity during 1974-75. As late as in May 30, 1976, Chelluri Simhachalam, a leading approver in the Naxalbari conspiracy case was killed by maoist squad near Rajam at Srikakulam. In fact, Nukalavu Lakshmandas, a State Cabinet Minister was constrained to note that "Naxalite activity is on the increase in Srikakulam"[74]. Pyla Vasudeva Rao on whose head a Rs. 50,000/- prize had been declared by Government had led a squad which conducted not less than six annihilations during 1975.[75] On June 20, 1975 an incident was reported in which about 100 tribals under the influence of maoists had attacked a police party causing injuries to seven constables[76].

The failure of CPI (ML)'s Unity moves:

Despite all efforts the moderate maoist groups refused to have any truck with the CPI (ML). These groups rallied around T.N. who initially formed the "All India Preparatory Committee of Communist Unity Centre", which received support from the Prithvi Singh group in Bihar, Promilla group in Delhi, a strong section of Punjab maoists, Santimoy Roy group in Bengal, Moniguha Parimal Sen Gupta group in Bengal and the Aryan Achyutan group in Kerala. T.N rejected the appeals of S.N. and C.P. to unite with them. The reasons his group gave were mainly organisational. For instance they claimed that there had been no proper self criticism, no adequate attempts at rectification by S.N , who had himself been a follower of Charu Majumdar's left adventurist line until recently, was being made and that the S.N.—C.P. group were continuing to launch public and scurrilous attacks on the T.N. group. They claimed further that S.N., C.P. etc. were trying to create unity within ones own narrow periphery from established centres. This is "a great obstacle on the party to unite"[87]. Even otherwise, both on long term and short term issues the two groups never really saw eye-to-eye. T.N. and C.P. had in fact, earlier split on the basis of their complete divergence of views in respect of the tactics and strategies to be deployed during the course of the movement. While S.N. was supporting J.P. and his movement, T.N. held that J.P. had "no direct class programme or even a national programme"[78] and that his slogan of total revolution was a total deception. All this resulted in T.N. continuing in his efforts to set up an all India body for such of those maoists who broadly agreed with him.[79]

The relatively more extremist groups which still swore by Charu Majumdar also did not respond favourably to the unity calls of S.N. While groups like the Anti-Lin & Pro-Lin remained aloof the COC group showed some vaccillation. They were willing to co-operate but there existed several issues which impeded the progress towards unity or full alliance with S.N. led CPI (ML). By and large these stemmed from the fact that the COC group continued to support Charu's line on issues like annihilation which they refused to condemn outright and from their general unwillingness to accept the efficacy of mass struggles and mass organisations without reservations. Towards J.P. too the COC group was somewhat unfavourable and it held that he was "a senile old man without the understanding of the social forces at work... it will be a suicidal step on the part of the revolutionary forces if they form a coalition with any section of the ruling class".[80]

Thus when emergency was declared the maoists were far from achieving any sort of unity and in A.P. as in most other states almost every group had its bunch of supporters some large and some small. The declaration of emergency by the Indian Government led to a reassessment of the present national situation and a rethinking and revision of the tactics and organisational methods in conformity with their assessment by the various maoist groups.

The CPI (ML) and the declaration of emergency:

The CPI (ML) led by S.N. and C.P. analysed the prevailing national situation and formulated its tactics accordingly. It characterised the situation as one in which there was a weakening of ruling class due to mass upsurge and as a manifest reaction to the growing contradictions and rift within the ruling classes. This had, according to them, resulted in the Indira Gandhi group, gaining an upper hand, and thus antagonising many other sections within the ruling class and other parties. The CPI (ML) therefore envisaged united actions with these dissatisfied and disgruntled elements, so as to isolate the ruling class in the government culminating in the overthrowing of the government and the creation of a regime of "patriotic and democratic unity". In the process of these struggles, the party was to strengthen itself and lead independently armed agrarian and working class movements.

The CPI (ML) felt that the government was forced to declare emergency because the country was in the grip of an economic and political crisis. The Government, they felt, was confronted with a number of mass struggles led by revolutionary and other parties, and some led by the opposition sections within the ruling class. These struggles had crossed the legal boundaries, and threatened the ruling class supporting the Government. At the same time the internal contradictions within the ruling class itself was deepening, and the rivalry between the group supported by U.S. imperialism and that supported by Soviet social imperialism was leading to "an open confrontation and a dog fight for power" between them. In such a situation, Indira Gandhi with the backing of the soviet Social imperialism had gained an upperhand and had created "the fascist dictatorship".

The declaration of emergency according to the CPI (ML) thus implied that the Soviet social imperialism had become "the main and immediate enemy of the people", and that it was "no longer possible for ruling clique to govern the people by normal methods" and it had been forced to resort to curbing fundamental rights, the censorship of the press, arrests of many people—including lawyers, judges, ex-judges, army generals, government officials, and attack all other parties including the opposition section of the ruling class. The party felt that "this fascist dictatorship would continue till it was completely overthrown by the people".

Under the circumstances the party sought to take best advantage of the situation created by the declaration of the emergency and utilise the contradictions within the ruling class to build up a monolithic party and overthrow the Government. The course of action proposed that firstly the party was "to isolate and strike at the main enemy" by releasing "a vigorous, powerful, broad-based political campaign among the people, explain the fascist nature of Indira Gandhi's dictatorship, its subservient role with regard to Soviet social imperialism". Secondly, it was proposed to build a "United Council of Action" with other parties. Since the Government had attacked and antagonised many parties, the CPI (ML) felt that, taking advantage of the common ground it had with these parties it could unite with them so as to isolate the ruling class in power. If some of the leaders disagreed with this proposal then the CPI (ML) was to directly appeal to the masses behind them, that in the present circumstances "no single party can overthrow the fascist dictatorship of Indira Gandhi". The cadres of the CPI (M) and the followers of J.P. and other socialist parties were to be given priority. At the same time while aligning with the CPI (M) it would continue to be their task to expose the bankruptcy of their leadership and their line. The CPI (ML) thus shifted from its earlier position that it would have no truck with the revisionists, or any other party which was not revolutionary.

After forming the "United Council for Action" the plan was to initiate united struggles on issues where a common ground existed as for example against the repressive measures of the Government. These were to be later developed into united struggles on various demands relating to the lives of workers, peasants, agricultural labourers, middle classes and so on. While these struggles were on, depending upon the consciousness and preparedness of the people, volunteer squads, were to be organised and a secret people's committees both in rural and urban areas formed, "to effectively counter the attacks of the Government and goondas".

The nature of the alliance with the other parties was seen as one of "unity and struggle i.e. while uniting with them to carry out struggles, the party's task was to expose their class nature, their links with U.S. imperialism" and so on. However, this was not to be carried to such an extent as would impair united action. At the same time it would avoid the impression that the party was aligning itself with the other parties. In fact, in as much as the purpose for such an united action was to strengthen the party, the party was to "maintain independence of its armed squads and volunteer corps and make energetic efforts to mobilise masses under its banner".

In the process of an united struggle with the other parties, the CPI (ML) proposed to build an united front of workers, students, peasants and of all "patriotic and democratic classes". Under the United Front through a protracted armed struggle the Government would be overthrown and a regime of "Patriotic and Democratic Unity" established. This regime may or may not be under the control of the working class and peasant leadership. With the building up of an armed agrarian revolution, and a strong working class movement, under the leadership of the party these classes would develop into the core of the United Front. They would ensure that the regime fully implemented the minimum programme of achieving complete independence and sovereignty.

It should be noted however that the CPI (ML) envisaged an alliance with the other parties, only on certain issues, and that too for a limited period of time. Secondly the main purpose of uniting with these parties was to strengthen its own position. Therefore, while carrying out united struggles towards creation of a 'Patriotic and Democratic Regime' the party was to build up armed agrarian revolution in the rural areas, mobilise the working class, students, and other sections of people towards fulfilling the tasks of revolution. In the process it was to organise its own secret village committees, volunteer squads, armed squads at all levels. In its programme of carrying out anti-feudal struggle against all landlords, it made a distinction between those who supported the Government and the rest and declared that with regard to forcible seizure of land or property the former was to be the target of attack. This would enable the CPI (ML) to weaken the ruling class. With regard to the working class, the CPI (ML) saw that its function was to concentrate more seriously on the Trade Union front and take over the leadership, as they were bound to rise into militant struggles due to freezing of wages, slashing of bonuses, banning of strikes etc. and other measures after the declaration of emergency.[81]

The reaction of the COC:

The COC also viewed the declaration of emergency as a result of the economic and political crisis developing within the country and the sharpening of the contradiction between the ruling class and the people (as reflected by the upsurge in Bihar, Gujarat etc.) shaking the ruling class. They too felt that the contradiction had intensified within the ruling class, where the mass movements backed by U.S. imperialism threatened the existence of Indira government backed by Soviet imperialism. and it was to overcome this situation that emergency had been declared with the full support of Soviet imperialism and the "Dange clique".

To the COC emergency implied an increase in tensions and contradiction between the "ruling clique" and the people. It also indicated the isolation of the ruling class from the people due to the former's policies of retrenchments, suspensions and exposed the reformistic nature of the programme of the Government.

The COC too saw the need to build a revolutionary front of all classes, parties, groups and individuals. At the same time, however, it was also thought necessary to build a net work of underground organisations consisting of working class, peasantry, urban petti-bourgeoisie under the party banner so as to put "once again the gun on the agenda" for it was felt that "it is only with guns that people can fight and silence the guns in a handful of oppressors and build a new India".[82]

Thus, in general, the declaration of emergency implied for the maoists three things. Firstly, it could no longer build up mass support through open and legal mass organisations. Secondly it was visualised as providing them with an opportunity to win over those sections, parties and groups, who were either vaccillating, or were apathetic and could no longer function in the open, and thus isolate the "enemy". Thirdly, the maoist groups CPI (ML) of S.N. and C.P. and COC, the Unity Committee CPI (ML) and UCCRI (ML) realised that in the present situation it was imperative that they strengthen themselves organisationally in order to meet the government offensive against them. And it was to this end that an "All India Joint Committee of Communist Revolutionaries" consisting of the above mentioned maoist organisations was set up "to co-ordinate mass movements, and to take steps to build the United Front".[83]

NOTES & REFERENCES

1. Satyanarayan Singh (S.N.'s) *Self-Critical Report* of CC of CPI (ML) 1973, p. 30.
2. *Ibid.*
3. *Ibid.*
4. *Rendu pandhala madhya poratam*, CPI (ML) 1974 (printed), p. 25.
5. *Ibid.*
6. *Ibid.*
7. Charu Majumdar, "One Year After Party Congress", *Indian Left Review*, September 1971, p. 81.
8. *Rendu pandhala...etc. op. cit.* p. 32.
9. *Ibid.*, p. 34.
10. Charge Sheet of NCC, *op. cit.*, p. 13.
11. C. Bhaskara Rao, *op. cit.*, p. 34.
12. Achanta Laxman Rao and Pujari Balaraju—both had been peripherally connected with communist movement for a long time and had contested the 1967 general elections to the Assembly and Parliament and lost very narrowly. The maoists blamed their association with

these unreliable local leaders and open kind of activity taken up on their advice as the cause for their losses and failures.

13. For example, see Cr. Nos. 47/69 and 48/69 of P.S. Repalle and Cr. No. 30/69, 31/69 of P.S. Firangipur. In these cases the maoists killed and looted landlords and moneylenders to finance operations in Srikakulam. In one of the most famous of such cases the maoists of Vijayawada allegedly aided a faction of Congressmen by killing their opponent Valloori Purnachandra Rao—the President of Panchayati Samiti in return for cash and ammunition. See confessional statements of Tippani Venkatarathna and Kalyani Krishna in the NCC.

14. See FIR of 11.9.1970 of Cr. No. 39/70 P.S. Veldurti, FIR of 12.6.1970 of Cr. No. 37/70 of P.S. Bandar and Cr. No. 161/69 of PS Narasaraopet.

15. FIR of Cr. No. 6/70 Kavali, FIR of Kodavaluru conspiracy case and judgement of Kodavaluru conspiracy case.

16. Though both had been close to the CPI (M) for a number of years they had not been full time activists. Only after the emergence of maoist politics did they leave their jobs to take up full time work. Incidentally both were in early fifties and were immigrants to Telangana from Andhra region.

17. For example see Cr. Nos. 33 to 102/70 of P.S. Mahabubabad.

18. For details of activities of these squads see Judgement of 26.3.1971. Prosecution witness statements and exhibits in Adilabad sessions case No. 9/71 and also Cr. No. 14 and 15/69, P.S. Nalevitla and Cr. No. 39/70, P.S. Husnabad as also *Errajanda*, CPI (ML) A.P. Committee, January 1972, pp. 72-76.

19. Mahadeb Mukherjee was a veteran trade unionist of Calcutta. Bhovani Roy Choudari *alias* Bibudida a former correspondent of the *Statesman* who resigned in 1971 to

join the maoist and Sanjay Bhattacharya *alias Subroto*, a former student leader from Dum Dum, jailed in July 1972, see *Current*, August 3, 1974.

20. Document of CPI (ML), *Frontier*, February 23, 1974.
21. *New Wave*, February 16, 1973.
22. *Current, op. cit.*
23. *Statesman*, May 31, 1975.
24. *Ibid.*
25. Kondapalli Seetaramaiah at this time was the only top pro-Charu leader still at large. *Current op. cit.*
26. "Naxalism is not dead in Andhra" *Free Press Journal*, June 15, 1975 and also *Deccan Chronicle*, May 28, 1975.
27. *Deccan Chronicle*, May 22, 1975.
28. *Ibid*, May 28, 1975 and September 17, 1975.
29. See the *Hindu*, April 10, 1976, the *Hindu* May 8, 1975, *Deccan Chronicle*, November 26, 1975, *Indian Express*, January 1, 1976.
30. D. Satya Prasad, "CPI (ML) Kendra Committee Punaniramanam" *Pilupu* June 1, 1975. Four major groups joined together to form the COC *viz*; (i) Suniti Ghosh in Bengal; (ii) the *Mass Line* group in Kerala; (iii) Sohail Singh of Punjab; (iv) Kondapalli Sitaramaiah of Andhra Pradesh.
31. "CPI (ML) Kendra Committee Prakatana", *Pilupu*, April 16, 1974, p. 2.
32. D. Satya Prasad *op. cit.*
33. *passim* "CPI (ML) Kendra Committee Prakatana" *op. cit.*
34. COC, *CPI (ML) Prakatana Pi Kendra Committee Sabhyuni Vivarana*, mimeograph (probably end of 1974)
35. *Ibid.*
36. Gopal "Role of Guerilla War", *Mass Line*, June 1975, p. 28.

37. *Ibid.* p. 32.
38. Suniti Ghosh, *Frontier*, August 3, 1974.
39. "COC and inner Struggle in it", *Liberation*, February-March 1975.
40. Charge Sheet of Secunderabad Conspiracy Case p. 10.
41. *Ibid*, p. 3.
42. *Ibid*, p. 35.
43. Cr. No. 2/74, P.S. Munagala.
44. *Daily News*, April 8, 1975.
45. For example, squad members including a young woman were killed in an encounter of Mahbubabad forest on January 10, 1975, see the *Hindu*, 11.1.1975.
46. *Indian Herald*, June 25, 1976.
47. See the charge sheets of Isuka Nadugu Conspiracy Case, Kondamodalu Conspiracy case, and Gangamma Chilaka Naxalite case all of which were tried by Sessions Judge at Kakinada.
48. K.V.R. "A Little known agrarian struggle", *Mass Line*. July 1975.
49. *Srujana*, July 1974.
50. *Ibid.*
51. *Srujana*, November 1974.
52. *Srujana*, October 1974.
53. *Pilupu* October 1, and October 15, 1974.
54. This group consisted of five poets—Jwala Mukhi, Nagnamuni, Cherabanda Raju etc. They called themselves *Digambara* (naked) because they were exposing society in its reality not sparing any words of expressions in the name of propriety.
55. See charge sheet of Secunderabad Conspiracy Case. *op. cit.* for names and details of magazines.

56. An exception must be made here of anti-Lin group which proclaimed its loyalty to Charu Majumdar and was quite strong among rural poor in Bhojpur. However their popularity was mainly due to their exploiting the cast factor along with peasant problems.

57. See Sushital Roy Choudary *Vama Paksha Avakasha Vidhanani Pratighatinchandi* (printed) 1972, and also Saroj Dutta in *Deshabrati* quoted in this book.

58. *Indian Express*, July 22, 1970.

59. *Passim Self critical Report*, Srikakulam Regional plenum, CPI (ML), August 1973.

60. *Ibid.*

61. "*Cammunist Revolutionaries of India-Unite*, April 1973. (mimeo)

62. "Resolution of Maharashtra Committee of CPI (ML)" *Liberation* April – May 1975, pp. 11-12.

63. *The Hindu*, August 11, 1975.

64. See "Carry forward Revolution by pursuing Mass Line" *Liberation* January-April 1974, commemorating the Third Anniversary of CPI (ML).

66. *Ibid.*

67. *Ibid.*

68. *Amrit Bazar Patrika*, November 30, 1974, and *Times of India*, November 30, 1974.

69. Pamphlet "Lokanayak—J.P.".

70. "Call to People", *op, cit.*

71. "Bihar Andolan our Kranti Karik Kartavya' *Janyudh* Jan-Feb. 1975.

72. "T otal Revolution or Total Delusion", *Liberation* Feb-March, 1975.

73. *On Andhra Agitation*, April 1973, Mimeo.

74. 'Naxalism is not dead in Andhra", *Free Press Journal.* June 15, 1975.

75. *Ibid.*

76. *Skyline* June 20, 1975 and *Deccan Chronicle* June 20, 1975.

77. Letter to Communist Revolutionaries, *Proletarian Path*, May-June 1975, p. 21.

78. *Ibid.*

79. the *Hindu*, April 4, 1979, *Times of India*, May 18, 1974 and *Deccan Chronicle*, May 18, 1974.

80. Gopan "J.P.'s Manoeuvres" *Mass Line*, May 1975, p. 3.

81. *Passim*, "*Unite to overthrow Fascist Dictatorship of Indira Gandhi*, CC of CPI (ML) S.N. group (typescript) 1976.

82. *Passim*, *Road to Revolution* COC 1975 (typescript).

83. *Joint Communique of CC of CPI* (ML) etc. (typescript) January 2, 1976.

CHAPTER 9

Post Emergency Developments

Post Emergency Developments

While the immediate per-emergency period was marked by fragmentation and hasty alliance of maoist groups the post emergency situation in Andhra Pradesh saw the emergence of comparatively stable groups. It also saw a tremendous diversification in terms of area of operation as well as in terms of issues taken up with the activity spreading to the plains areas also. Students, teachers, youth, unemployed, the agricultural labour, the small farmer, tribals and so on were all sought to be mobilised resulting in the emergence of a totally new situation. The post-emergency developments, in Andhra Pradesh coincided with the growth of one particular maoist group, the Communist Party of India (Marxist Leninist-People's War Group), popularly know as the Peopl's War Group (PWG), led by Kondapalli Seetaramaiah (K.S.) whose approach to a large extent epitomises the "new line" that was formulated in this period. In this chapter an effort is made to piece together the various trends and developments that emerged in the post-emergency period in Andhra Pradesh. In doing this we shall also discuss in detail the strategy and the policies of the dominant group, CPI (ML) People's War Group.

Maoist activity in the post emergency period in Andhra Pradesh was dominated by the two major groups the CC, CPI (ML), CP group and the CPI (ML) People's War Group led by Kondapalli Seetaramaiah. While the former operated mainly in its traditional strongholds in the forest areas of Khammam and Mulug and to a certain extent in the forests of East Godavari the latter established itself in Warangal town and its surrounding villages and in Adilabad and Karimnagar. The Telangana area thus continued to be the hunting ground for the maoists. Each one of the groups evolved its own party line and while there were several common features between the two, these were overshadowed by certain fundamental differences. It is on these aspects of maoist activity in Andhra Pradesh during the post emergency period that we shall concentrate in this chapter.

The Impact of Emergency

The imposition of emergency had led to a set back in the maoist movement. This set back occured despite the fact that the party had always operated under severe restrictions imposed by the Disturbed Areas Act in most of the areas. The main reason for this was that whereas the Disturbed Areas Act was a specific measure applied to specified regions that too mainly in the rural areas, emergency affected the entire country. To the maoists this meant firstly that all lines of communication were cut off and second that, with repression being stepped up everywhere even those sympathisers in the urban areas who were earlier willing to provide shelter to the maoists no longer did so now. Again, the increased usage of Preventive Detention under MISA to detain persons without option of bail also put a lot of activists out of action. Added to all this was the fact that the government's twenty point programmewhich had as its target group the same strata of the society which the party aimed at mobilising, was vigorously publicised during this period. *Harijan Sanghams* were formed by the government in certain areas, as in Karimnagar and even according to the maoists, "peoples aspirations and expectations regarding the programme were so widely prevalent that even the activists who went underground had to join these *Sanghams* and expressed their demands in the language of the *Sangham*".[1] As a consequence of this squad actions almost came to a standstill in this period. The only places where the CC, CPI

(ML) CP Group could still continue were in the Godavari valley of Yellavaram and Rampachodavaram and in the case of the COC,in Adilabad and Karimnagar district.

With the lifting of the emergency, there was a revival of the movement. The oppressive measures adopted during emergency had been the main platform on which the Congress lost to the Janata Party in the crucial 1977 elections. Following this was the severe indictment of the bureaucracy and police during the emergency by the Shah Commission [2] and a host of other bodies which put the government heavily on the defensive and made it easier for the maoists to operate. The manner in which they did so however revealed some changes. The main change related to the fact that by the time emergency was revoked the schisms within the CPI (ML) as a whole had crystallised. In the long period of forced isolation during the emergency it had become clear to the various groups that while achieving some sort of unity was desirable the large divergences in their understanding of the situation as it existed made this a very difficult task. It thus became essential for each group to develop its own line and some of these developments were immediately apparent in Andhra Pradesh.

Changes in the C.P. Group's Policies

As soon as elections were called for the State Assembly in 1978 the C.P. group announced that it would participate in them. This was a sharp deviation from the strong anti-election stance they had adopted earlier. It would be remembered that in 1969 the strongest opposition to T.N. continuing as an M.L.A. came from this very group. The group quoted two main reasons for its participation. One was to take advantage of the anti-Indira and anti-Congress atmosphere prevailing in the country and the second was to get enough representation to force the unconditional release of all political prisoners, an issue which had already received wide publicity in view of the fact that a number of opposition party members had been imprisoned during emergency.[3] To this extent they "tried to form a left block with other communist revolutionary groups and independent democrats...".[4] On the whole they contested twelve seats and won one at Yellandu in Khammam. The extent to which the group moderated its stand in regard to elections and electoral politics is indicated by the fact that they even supported "certain select Janata candidates who sincerely stood on the side of the people".[5] Participation in elections during the period were on the avowed basis of fighting for demands like release not just of its cadre but all those political prisoners who were still in custody of jails. This stand on elections continued and when the mid-term elections to the Lok Sabha were announced in 1980 it was felt that the policy of boycott had been based on the "wrong assessment" that there was an "intense hatred towards the policy of parliamentarianism so far pursued by revisionism".[6] In actual fact, it was felt, that many people still had "parliamentary illusions and are participating in elections and are not yet prepared for higher forms of struggle. In such circumstances boycott of elections meant nothing but leaving the political field free for ruling class parties, the revisionists, the neo-revisionists to deceive the people with deceptive slogans".[7] This being the case, it was argued that it was essential "to intervene, utilise the opportunity to propagate revolutionary politics, prepare people for protracted peoples war and expose the class character of the State".[8] The issue of electoral participation brought in its wake the question of alliance with other parties. On this issue, it was decided that all alliances should be avoided as this would increase "illusions", dilute party activities and ultimately force them to enter into many kinds of compromises.[9] When finally the group announced its manifesto, it included among other slogans, land to the tiller, widespread irrigation system, remunerative price to peasants for agricultural produce, withdrawal of the Industrial Bill, deletion of Preventive Detention and the release of all political prisoners.[10]

With this attitude towards elections, the C.P. group began participating in the elections even at the village Panchayat level. In fact it viewed these as even more important than those to the Lok Sabha. In these elections it often made compromises on the issue of alliances as for instance in Mulug where they supported a Congress candidate.[11] While they were particularly successful in Sudimella Samiti in Yellandu, the group claimed that in more than 100 villages in Khammam their candidates had become *Sarpanches* and it was because of this that they could conduct struggles such as the one against high arrack prices in 1983 so effectively.[12]

In countering the criticism to this trend of participation in election the C.P. group pointed out that it was only an extension of their policy to adopt all legal and illegal methods to mobilise the people. However, they denied that their stand on election was the same as that of CPI (M) on the ground that they were pursuing it as a tactic to expose the illusory nature of the parliamentary party and not as an alternative strategy to armed struggle.[13]

The other modification of the group's stance in the post emergency period related to "armed struggle". On scrutinizing the party documents one finds that the words "armed struggle" no longer find any place. Instead usage of words like "armed resistance" and "peasant struggles" are common. For instance while the January 1980 PCC resolution clearly stated that "in our country protracted peoples' war has to be conducted mainly in the form of Armed Agrarian Revolution"[14] their November 1982 resolution stated that the "Peoples' war based on Agrarian Revolution is the only national alternative to the path of Parliamentarianism......"[15] From this it appears that the party had extended the time frame work within which the protracted struggle was to be conducted and that it felt that it was too premature to apply the term 'armed struggle', which referred to a higher stage of the struggle, to anything taking place at the present juncture.

Civil Liberties Organisations

A significant development which took place in the post-emergency period was the increase in the activities of the civil liberties organisations. As early as in 1970 a united civil liberties association had been set up by all the maoist groups comprising the UCCRI (ML), CPI (ML), COC, and the APRCP. In 1973 however, differences cropped up and the UCCRI (ML) separated out and set up the Organisation for Protection of Democratic Rights (OPDR) which soon developed ed into a very active civil liberties organisation. It held its first State Convention in Hyderabad in May 1970. Like many other civil liberties organisations the OPDR served to agitate against the repressive laws of the Government, protest against 'fascist acts' and the 'despotic rule' of the establishment and to collect information in regard to cases of repression and harassment of poor citizens.[16] They also provided legal aid to the undertrial maoists and even agitated for the commutation of the death sentences awarded to political prisoners Bhoomiah and Kista Gowd.

The CPI (ML)/COC had felt the need to set up a civil liberties organisation to deal exclusively with their cases and hence in February 1974 they formed the Andhra Pradesh Civil Liberties Committee (APCLC). On the whole the APCLC functioned along the same lines as the OPDR but its effectiveness was restricted by the fact that although, like the OPDR, it was a legal body performing perfectly legal functions, most of its active members were persons who were closely associated with the underground activities of the party and hence unable to function openly. Because of this, even in the immediate post emergency period when the conditions were favourable for the functioning of civil liberties organisation, especially in the wake of the Shah Commission findings, it was the OPDR which was most active and which when the Bhargava Commission[17] sat to enquire into 'encounter deaths' collected material to substantiate the maoists' claims.

The CPI (ML) and COC realised this and in subsequent years the APCLC drew into its fold a number of people who had little to do with the core of the party organisation. This enabled the APCLC to function more effectively and at the same time broaden its base of support. In fact it even overshadowed the OPDR which was earlier the most active civil liberties organisation. By and large the members of the APCLC comprised the urban intelligentsia and were drawn from among lawyers, teachers, journalists and doctors. Very often they were former C.P. group activists who dropped out of the movement and who were looking for an outlet for expressing their sympathies with the movement, without at the same time indulging in full time party work.

The civil liberties organisations not only provided legal protection but also served a much bigger political function. By involving a number of non-party members it made sure that the issues dealt with were not treated merely as a party issue but as one of much wider significance affecting the society as a whole. Such associations of non-party members also invested the activities of the civil liberties organisations with a greater element of legitimacy.

To the party cadre the visit of a Civil Liberties committee group to their field of operation and the publicity that ensued served as a morale booster. Often Civil Liberty Groups were called upon by the party to indirectly activate an otherwise demoralised cadre and promote the cause of the party organisation.

The Split in the C.P. Group

By the end of the seventies there was a general stalemate in the movement in the forest belt of the Godavari valley where the C.P. group had been active.[18] At this juncture there was considerable rethinking among a section of the maoists as to how to raise the pitch of the movement and to end the stalemate. One line of thought that emerged was that their activities in the past had been alienating them from the people and therefore there was a need for change in the organisational structure which would enable them to work more openly and establish rapport with the people. It was felt that as a first step struggles should be started on issues within the framework of legality. These included grant of *pattas* to cultivators, stricter implemention of ceiling laws and many others. At the same time, it was felt that strengthening of the mass organisations should take precedence over reliance on armed squads which in other words meant giving preference to the mass line.[19]

C.P. who was without doubt the most dominant member of the CC and whose views by and large formed the accepted line of the party was not unaware of these developments. In 1980 he published his review of the progress of the movement in the preceding thirteen years. However, as an analysis it proved to be less than satisfactory to those questioning squad activists for it included no self criticism and contained little beyond a reiteration of his earlier policies along with certain justifications for deviations therefrom. In fact the main complaint against the review was that C.P. had failed to adequately stress the importance of the 'mass line' which he had accepted when the endorsed the *Immediate Programme* and that he had not stressed the fact that the "Pagideru incidents"[20] made a departure from the *Immediate Programme*.

Eventually, the above discussions led to a clear delineation of two groups within the CC, CPI (ML) one which supported the mass line and the other the existing one. Region-wise, the former which was in a majority, comprised the members of the Provincial Committees of Khammam and East Godavari, while the latter headed by C.P. drew support from the Warangal Karimnagar and Hyderabad areas. This division sharpend further when the dissenting squad activists launched an attack on C.P. himself accusing him of behaving in an authoritarian manner and of neglecting the observance of basic principles of democratic centralism. Specifically he was accused of encouraging lower committees to pass resolutions against higher ones, attempting to isolate his opponents and even of making parallel contacts in the organisation so as to carry on propaganda against his opponents.[21] By the end of 1981 all the elements of a split were discernible within the party and accusations and counter accusations began to be made indiscriminately. The pro-CP group charged the opposing group of becoming increasingly moderate, and of instilling among people illusions regarding electoral politics by proposing that electoral struggles were the highest form of legal struggles. It also criticised them in general for having supported CPI and CPI (M) candidates during elections and the Nizambad Zilla Committees and in particular for having participated in the 1983 general elections under the banner of Democratic Front without consulting the Provincial Committee. On matters of organisation it asserted that giving in to the arguments of the opposing group would amount to giving up of squad actions altogether and taking recourse to legal actions only.[22] Whereas the anti-C.P. group comprising mainly the

Khammam area committee (whose prominent members were Pyla Vasudeva Rao and Bose) kept quoting their losses in elections as examples indicative of their alienation from the masses, the C P. group felt that these losses were more due to the severe repression by the police than to any defects in the organisation. They went on to state that by utilising only legal methods they would be exposing their cadre more and this would make it all the more easy for the police to tackle them.[23]

A parting of ways of the two groups was thus very much in evidence. However, when the split actually occured in 1984 the reason given that there had been a disagreement over the functioning of the India-China friendship society. The C.P. group felt that this society was more of an association for promoting trade relations between the two countries than to support revolutionary struggles. They therefore advised all members of the CC, CPI (ML) to withdraw from the organisation. This view was contested by the other faction and ultimately it was to this difference of opinion that the split was attributed.[24]

The People's War Group

As mentioned earlier the other active maoist group in Telangana in the post emergency period was the CPI (ML), People's War Group (PWG), led by K.S. In the confusion that followed the death of Charu, Kondapalli Seetaramaiah had aligned himself with the COC group but at the same time struck an independent line especially in regard to the annihilation theory and the rise of mass movements. In general his views were more radical than those of C.P. Though he had not joined the movement at Srikakulam he is reported to have adopted the Charu line in Adilabad and Karimnagar where he had operated during the late sixties. This had made him more popular with the younger generation and he attracted them to his organisation in large numbers. With the increase in cadre strength K.S. began to develop on his earlier theoretical formulations and soon arrived at a line of his own. The formation of the CPI (ML) People's War Group in 1980 January was a part of this process.

The main thrust of People's War Group theory is revealed in its assessment of the existing socio-political situation. While accepting the fact that people's consciousness was uneven owing to the unevenness in the development of the national economy it still asserted that a country wide revolutionary situation did exist and quoted the "large scale struggles of the people of Andhra, Gujarat, Mysore, Bombay and Bihar started after the set back in revolutionary struggle"[25] as positive proof of this. Any view expressed to the contrary was seen by the People's War Group as being reactionary. Closely linked to this assessment was the PWG's view on armed struggle. According to this group whenever people violated the existing law and took up whatever arms they could and resorted to fighting it was nothing but armed struggle. If the struggle was confined to small pockets it only indicated the elementary state of the armed struggles'. Similarly the group felt that the different forms of struggle occuring due to the unevenness of people's political consciousness ultimately served the purpose of armed struggle and it could not be said that these struggles could not be developed into an armed struggle. In fact, according to the pWG's analysis, given a proletariat leadership all struggles inevitably served the cause of a protracted armed struggle.[26]

Thus while the C.P. group viewed armed struggle as a form of struggle yet to be adopted, something which was as yet distant, the PWG was of the opinion that the people were already fully prepared for armed struggle. The group went on to state that one need not wait for large areas to be liberated before starting the armed struggle as some others had claimed. According to them to postpone or avoid armed struggle on the plea that sufficient area was not available even when people were prepared was tantamount to a revisionist manifestation.

The Peoples War Group drew a distinction between the path of armed struggle and the armed form of struggle. Thus while "the path of armed struggle is the only correct path of the people's democratic revolution as opposed to parliamentary path, the armed form of struggle is not the only form of struggle"[27]. It felt that depending on the level of the political consciousness and preparedness of the people different forms of struggle would arise and all these struggles must be nurtured and led by the party because only then can the people be made to realise through their own experience the inevitability of armed struggle. Unless this was done it would neither be possible to wipe out bourgeois, petty-bourgeois and revisionist influence over the masses nor to establish proletarian hegemony over them, the latter being initially necessary to carry on the armed struggle successfully. The PWG stressed the fact that if on any plea the propagation of the politics of seizure of power was sought either to be undermined or avoided during the course of these other forms of struggles, or if these were sought to be confined to the bonds of legal limitations then "however many such struggles we may conduct all of them would certainly end up in economism and will never reach the stage of starting armed struggles".[28]

On the issue of annihilation the PWG differed considerably from CC, CPI (ML) C.P. group. The C.P. group saw no worth in annihilation and stated that it would carry "on irreconcilable ideological and political struggles against all theories of class collaboration and individual terrorism or annihilation of individuals by certain elements in the name of "annihilation of class enemies".[29] The PWG on the other hand asserted that people had been hasty in condemning annihilation. It was of the view that the mistake committed earlier was not so much the fact that annihilation of class enemy was accepted but that it was treated as a form of struggle capable of solving all the problems relating to armed peasant struggle. This, the group felt, had in turn led to the rejection of all other forms of struggle and organisation which was not a correct development as "no form of struggle can be of universal validity".[30] Every form of struggle including annihilation would ultimately transform into a higher form as the struggle intensified. Till such time as this actually happens annihilation would continue as one of the forms of struggle.[31]

The PWG differed very little from CPI (ML) CP group on the issue of United Front and agreed with the latter in general that "the alliance of working class and peasantry will form the basis of the United Front which would include "the urban petty bourgeoisie and the middle and small bourgeoisie i.e. the national bourgeoisie and rich peasantry"[32]. While the PWG accepted the fact that the latter would be a vacillating and unstable ally of the proletariat and may desert to the counter revolution it stated that whenever there is any contradiction between the components of the United Front, the party of the proletariat must necessarily stand on the side of the exploited classes and never play the role of a mediator. It was also, reiterated by the group that, as with all other forms of struggle, to convert the United Front to a powerful means for making the democratic revolution it had to be built under the hegemony of the proletariat.[33]

The People's War Group had very elaborate views on the various forms of organisation that were required to be utilised. According to it in the long period of protracted struggle people have to be organised in different forms according to the variations in their political consciousness slevels, because this variation required different forms of struggle. The over all view was that since ultimately "armed revolution" or "war" was to be the form of struggle, armed squads or army would have to be the form of organisation. Likewise, for all forms of struggle, auxillary to armed struggle, corresponding forms of organisation would have to be formed. Thus in the cities where the movement was as yet weak workers were to be mobilised through the tactic of penetrating the existing trade unions while the students were to be organised into Marxist-Leninist organisations. In the village, village committees were to be set up which would convert themselves into revolutionary councils once the armed struggle began and efforts were to be made to see that caste conflicts were channelised along class lines and that the leadership of the proletariat was established. The ultimate purpose of all this was to build an United Front of the village people under the hegemony of the proletariat against feudalism and to develop them as the fighting organ in order to make the Democratic Revolution successful.[34]

In consonance with these principles the party developed several front organisations. At the village level the main organisation was the Ryothu Coolie Sangham while among the students and youth they had the Radical Students Union (RSU) and Radical Youth League (RYL) respectively. Finally, along with the C.P. group they also participated in the activities of the APCLC. The main theme running through the activities of each one of these organisations was to link the respective struggles at each level to the Party's overall basic task of mobilisation and organisation of workers and peasants for the peoples' democratic revolution. To this extent the party maintained that there should be no difference between the slogans of any of the mass organisations and those of the party.[35] At the same time the group also warned its cadre that in doing this work care must be taken not to be bogged down by legalism for at every step one should know how to combine legal work with illegal work and the work of mass organisations with that of underground work.[36]

The Radical Students' Union

In the case of the People's War Group the objective of mixing legal and illegal work was closely applied by its Radical Students' Union (RSU) student organisation. The RSU was formed as a breakaway unit from the Progressive Democratic Students Union (PDSU) in 1975, after a disagreement over the issue of whether the armed struggle programme should be included in the Union's manifesto. The group which wanted this item to be included formed itself into the Andhra Pradesh Radical Students Union (APRSU) under the direction of K.S. who was at that time the Secretary of the A.P. Unit of CPI (ML) COC. The split itself was not a sudden development and reflected a parting of ways of two sets of student activists one from Hyderabad and the other from Warangal town and nearby areas.

The participation of Warangal students in maoist activities began as early as 1966-67, with K.G., K.S. serving as the ideologues. Study circles were set up by them in the Regional Engineering College, Warangal and the Kakatiya Medical College in a very systematic fashion. Ultimately when K.G. and K.S. chose to follow Charu's line they took with them most of the militant students from this area, into CPI (ML).

However, at this stage, in consonance with the Charu line any form of mass organisations was looked upon as being revisionist and bureaucratic and thus instead of organising themselves into student organisations the students took part in the movement as members of the squads in Adilabad, Jangaon, Karimnagar and Khammam. Meanwhile the PDSU which had developed into a fairly well organised Students Union began to gain popularity even in Warangal. This disadvantage of having neglected to form their own organisation forced the Warangal group of students to align themselves with the PDSU. However, within the span of a year, they began to assert themselves and in the first state conference of the PDSU in October 1974 they raised the demand that "armed struggle" should form a part of the manifesto and when this was rejected they broke away to form the RSU.[37] This 'split' was further exacerbated by the moves of C.P. and PWG groups who were looking for divergent methods for keeping the movement alive, while at the same time emphatically propagating their respective lines.

During the period just prior to and after the declaration of emergency a number of students belonging both to PDSU and RSU went underground to become full time party activists. Going by police reports the active members of RSU were by far more militant during this period than that of PDSU.[38] Along with the stabilisation and spread of the various activities of the People's War Group in the post emergency period the RSU too developed into an active students organisation. Like the PDSU it concerned itself not with problems concerning the student community alone but also with those concerning the society as a whole. The cornerstone of the RSU's programme was its campaign called "Go to villages campaign" the primary objective of which was to integrate the student activists with the rural masses and to "rouse consciousness in broad masses of peasantry and teach them the necessity of participation in People's Democratic Revolution to prepare them for agrarian revolution; to collect statistics of existing land distribution in villages and with the help of these concrete statistics prove the inevitable necessity of redistribution of land according to the principle of 'land to the tiller'; to mobilise the youth of the village and to organise youth league and educate them; to teach revolutionary songs so that they may echo the grand spirit of revolution".[39]

The campaign was strictly in consonance with the party's line that all organisations must ultimately serve the party's task of ushering in the Democratic Revolution. It consisted of firstly training the activists for four to five days where political theory was discussed, and secondly of learning to sing revolutionary songs and also to perform in street dramas and plays. In the second phase the group was split into batches of five and sent to the rural areas where each batch concentrated on a group of a minimum of ten villages spending at least of there days in each village. In these villages groups of youth were mobilised by singing and teaching revolutionary songs and attempts to educate them on the policies of seizure of power through armed struggle, as also on the need for an agrarian revolution were made.[40] The youth were also helped to form Radical Youth League (RYL) in these villages. Throughout the period the students stayed in the village, often in the *harijan bastees* and learnt the full details of the peasants' life. At no stage was the local party unit involved. In fact no effort was to be made even to find out who the party members in the village were. Between January 1978 and June 1980, the PWG claimed that four such campaigns were conducted in which in all about 800 to 900 students and youth received training.

The RSU was strongly influenced by the politics in and around Warangal town. This was because it drew heavily from the large number of educational institutions in Warangal. Being a smaller city than Hyderabad, Warangal attracted a number of rural youth and as a consequence the RSU with its "go to the villages campaign" flourished. This also meant that the village level politics got reflected in the student politics to a greater extent. The RSU's popularity in Warangal town as opposed to PDSU also arose from the fact that as maoists K.G. and K.S. had always been held in high esteem there. In Khammam which was a C.P.'s stronghold it was the PDSU which was dominant.

By and large the RSU and PDSU worked in collaboration. For instance in 1983-84 they fought the elections to the various students unions jointly. They even held joint processions and so on. On theoretical questions too there was very little difference between the two. However, there was a distinct difference in their respective styles of functioning. Unlike the RSU the PDSU concentrated more on issues directly concerning the students, for instance on the student demands like fees, hostel conditions, scholarships, exams, behaviour of the authorities, syllabii and so on. According to PDSU's own report it "brought over two lakh pamphlets throughout the state and over 2000 students actively moved into various colleges and schools, class to class campaign, hostel meetings, wall posters, cultural programmes were held all highlighting the revolutionary politics and the necessity of the students participating in the New Democratic Revolution in order to achieve scientific education system".[42] The link between PDSU activity and that of the party was also very remote. While the People's War Group maintained this link by organising campaigns like 'go to the village's and by forming Radical Youth Leagues the C.P. group had no such programme and in general the activities of the PDSU had very little practical connection with what the other wings of the organisation of the party did. Again while the aim of RSU was "to try its best to introduce politics to those students who are scared of politics" and not to "depoliticise the students already having politics, just to attract the general student to its fold,"[43] the PDSU indulged in raising only such slogans as would be supported by the students in general. However, it must be noted that despite all these differences the PWG claimed that since the aim of both the students union was to establish a Peoples' Democratic Society "there is material evidence for the RSU to unite with the PDSU to form a single organisation".[44]

The Radical Youth League

The Radical Youth League was an organisation specific to the People's War Group. Basically it sought to utilise the large section of non-student urban and rural youth who happened to be outside the educational system and was established to serve two main purposes. One was to act as an intermediary organisation between the RSU and Ryotu Coolie Sangham and the other to serve as a rallying point for the youth from where they could directly participate in the party activities. The Radical Youth League was often set up and organised by the members of the RSU during their 'go to the villages' campaign and this provided an opportunity for the former to establish links with the youth in the rural areas thus integrating the movement as a whole.

In the urban areas, the mainstay of the Radical Youth League were the unemployed youth. The People's War Group openly expressed the need for mobilising this section by quoting the of mentioned justification by Mao, "There is yet another noticeably large group of lumpen proletariat. They come from the classes of landless poor peasants and unemployed, displaced artisans. They live a life much worse than all the other classes. They have formed secret organisations. How do we deal with those who belong to this class. This is one of the question China is facing. They have the character to fight bravely. At the same time they can become victims to disruptive forces. Given proper guidance they would become a revolutionary force".[45]

The People's War Group argued that to ignore this group would only mean that they would be utilised by the anti-progressive forces as had happened in Hitler's Germany or in Chiang Kai Shek's China. According to them already in most of cities they were utilised by the ruling classes to its own advantage. To draw them into the fold of the People's War Group was thus seen as a necessary task and while the party did not underestimate the difficulties involved it felt that the advantage to be gained by channelising the activities of this group was worth the effort.[46]

Ryotu Coolie Sangham

The Ryotu Coolie Sangham was the village level organisation of the People's War Group. In fact even the CPI (ML) (CP) called its village level organisation also the Ryotu Coolie Sangham and in both cases the basic objective was the same *viz.* to mobilise the rural masses consistingly mainly of agricultural labourers and poor peasants, and organise them to carry out struggles at the village level. For the CPI (ML) CP group the task of forming Ryotu Coolie Sangham proceeded by stages. First of all the politics in the village where the Ryotu Collie Sangham was to be formed was to be studied and the issues on which struggles were to be conducted identified. All militants in the village who responded to the party programme continuously were made members of the *sangham* and given guidance on how the programme was to be carried forward. Once this was done the Ryotu Coolie Sangham in that village would be allowed to carry out an independent programme drawn up on its own initiative.

The manner in which the People's War Group proceeded to Ryotu Coolie Sangham set up was also the same. However, since it had an active Radical Youth League and Radical Students Union sometimes even before the regular *sanghams* were actually formed, situations arose where programmes had to be initiated immediately. In these circumstances the People's War Group did not wait to form the *sanghams* but went ahead with implementing the programme of struggle.[47]

The People's War Group also felt that while "there can be levels of consciousness among persons who join the Ryotu Coolie Sangham the aim is to see that all develop the same level of consciousness, to motivate them to get socialist consciousness and to not demoralise those who already are close to socialist consciousness".[48] Thus while as large a number as possible were to be mobilised, care was to be taken not to dilute the political content merely to attract large numbers.

Party Organisation

The People's War Group felt that in the past the importance of party organisation had been neglected and that this mistake should be rectified within the party. The group also saw the need for encouraging debate and to conduct inner party struggle with "patience" and by adopting "democratic methods rather than bureaucratic ones,".[49] In order to do this the People's War Group felt that "the best form of organisation would be the one embodying the principles of democratic centralism so that neither the initiatve of individual members nor discipline is sacrificed".[50] The People's War Group has been the only group that has referred to the development of "bureaucratic tendencies in the party organisation".[51] At the some time it once again reiterated its stand that there had been an over reaction to the mistakes committed earlier by the party and that in doing so certain groups instead of adopting democratic centralism to combat opportunism and careerism had embraced bureaucratic methods. This according to the PWG had only led to further chaos.[52] The People's War Group also makes special mention of the need to induct part-time party workers which it felt was essential for making the party a full fledged proletariat organisation.[43]

Despite all the stress placed on developing the organisation the People's War Group never viewed this as a pre-condition to starting armed struggle. In their opinion if there arose a situation wherein condition for an armed struggle developed before the organisation process was complete then the former should take precedence over the latter which should be allowed to develop along with the struggle.[54]

Methods of Operation

It would be recalled that in the Telangana region there had always been an intense debate on issues like whether or not squad action should be permitted and if so whether they should be armed and so on. In fact it was primarily because the C.P. group at that time had side stepped the APRCC's *Immediate Programme* and instead of following the mass line had resorted to squad action that the APR CC finally split. There is no evidence of discussion on this in the People's War Group. However, it is quite clear that they decided to simply adopt the tactic most suitable to the occasion. Thus it was not a question of mass line *or* squad action but of mass line *and* squad action. During the 1960's and early 1970's the People's War Group more or less followed the same line as the CPI (ML). The accent was on annihilation, and mass action was rarely if at all resorted to. After Charu's death when the CPI (ML) broke up there was considerable self criticism by the maoist leaders and K.S. was no exception. It was then that the tactics of the group were altered and the view that annihilation through squads action as the only method for carrying on the struggle was abandoned and it was decided that depending on the form of struggle and the region of operation the tactics should also change. Squad action for instance was to be confined to the forest and nearby areas which afforded some sort of protection from the police. In the plains areas where squads were particularly susceptible to police attacks two types of tactics were used. In respect of land occupation programmes and other partial struggles mass action was resorted to. On the other hand annihilation which continued to be a form of struggle, at least as far as the People's War Group was concerned, was carried out in these areas by a "modified" form of squad action. In this the squad was not a fixed one and members from different places collected at a point just prior to the action to carry out the attack. Thus there was no fixed squad group and as soon as the action was completed the squad dispersed. With this form of operation the element of secrecy was very high and it was difficult for the police to isolate the entire squad at one time. In fact tracing the identity of the members of the squad itself became a difficult proposition and therefore it was generally not necessary for the participants to go underground and to this extent the party's responsibility towards their maintenance was reduced.

The activities of the People's War Group were initially restricted to the plains areas. With its spread to the forest areas even this group formed several permanent squads. The main advantage of operating in squads was that given proper training a compact group could operate and sustain itself in the forest areas very efficiently. At the same time working as a group the squad members were in a better position to defend themselves against police attacks. The squads were given extensive training both in methods of offence and defence.[55]

Relationship between the People's War Group and the C.P. Group

By and large upto 1983 the relationship between the K.S. and C.P. groups were non-antagonistic. In fact for a short period in mid 1981 in Karimnagar they even entered into an agreement not to carry out any propaganda against each other or interfere in each other's activities.[56] Subsequently, however, the relationship between the two was subject to some tensions. This was so because in a number of areas, especially in Warangal and Karimnagar the People's War Group proved to be the more popular group of the two. So much so that this group began operating even in areas which had been the traditional strongholds of the C.P. group as for instance in the forest areas of Warangal, in Mulug and in parts of Karimnagar, in the industrial belt of Khammam and even in the forests of East Godavari. The popularity of the People's War Group in these areas was mainly the outcome of the more militant policy adopted by them which attracted a lot of youth especially from the rural areas and also due to their tight linking of the activities of the various organisations of the party *viz.* the Radical Students Union, Radical Youth League, Ryotu Coolie Sangham which brought about a greater identification of the party with the rural masses.

Stung by this "encroachment" on their strongholds the C.P. group came out strongly against the K.S. group and accused them of adopting a 'right deviationist theoretical line' and a 'left adventurist plan of action'. This development was not very surprising because even theoretically the two groups had always represented two different lines of thought. The K.S. group had always identified itself broadly with the Charu tradition which it had endorsed in 1968 and had attempted to maintain a certain continuity. While certain modifications such as acceptance of the need for a protracted armed struggle; utilisation of annihilation as just one of the forms of struggle and not as the only form; the supporting of certain types of partial struggles; the emphasising of the importance of the organisation were made, it remained a fact that the Peoples' War Group took pride in stating that "it is our party which could set up a glorious tradition of sacrifice under the leadership of Comrade Charu Majumnar".[57] In fact K.S. viewed the People's War Group as essentially being a logical development of the party which Charu had dominated in the late sixties.

The C.P. group on the other hand basing on its own experience with the AICCCR felt that in the late 60's the true nature of CPI (ML) had been blurred by the fact that Charu and his supporters had dominated it and had adopted the "left opportunist" line of individual annihilation and the sectarain line in organisation. It felt that it was only after the 10th Congress of the CPC in 1973 when the Charu line was exposed that the party was brought to adopt the correct line, which the CP group supported. Thus unlike the People's. War Group, the CC, CPI (ML), C.P. group saw its party as a development of the corrected CPI (ML) than of the one Charu dominated.[58]

With this background in view it is not surprising that the CC CPI (ML) CP group accused the People's. War Group of adopting left adventurist tactics. They disagreed with the latter's line of preparing for armed struggle and setting up guerilla zones, "How can they start an Armed Struggle or set up guerilla zones? What is the level of people's consciousness? How prepared are they? What economic and political struggles have they carried out? What are the United Front tactics to be adopted? What is the level of the peoples' movement obtaining which will enable a guerilla struggle to be started? What are these "glorious struggles" which the party claims to have started?"[59] These are some of the questions which the CC CPI (ML) asked of the People's War Group. They claimed that apart from the Nagas and Mizos no one had been able to mobilise people into armed struggle and that while people were dissatisfied the movement had not reached the level where an armed struggle could be conducted.[60] Thus to treat the struggles of the people for their immediate demands, whatever their level of spontaneity, as indication of their preparedness for armed struggle was according to them, nothing but left adventurism. In their view "it is necessary to carry on economic and political struggles to draw people towards armed struggle and to talk of guerilla warfare until this is done is nothing but stupidity".[61]

Continuing in this vein the CC, CPI (ML) claimed that the People's War Group was wrong in not combining the mass line with the resistance movement and because of this they had given an irresponsible call for guerilla zone. "What is peoples' war ? War where people participate."[62] The C.P. group stated and went on to condemn People's. War Group for claiming that they had spread to new areas and established guerilla zones as mere adventurism. "Such adventurism we could not recognise in 1969 and suffered losses".[63]

The CC, CPI (ML) as also attacked the People's War Group on grounds similar to those used against Charu. The C.P. group did not give much credence to the fact that the People's War Group have in their documents indicated that changes in Charu line were necessary and to this extent had altered their stance. This change they felt was only superficial. Thus when this group accused the People's War Group of not considering annihilation of class enemies as the highest stage, they did not attach any significance to the fact that the People's War Group had stated that while annihilation would not be abandoned it would be viewed only as one of the forms of struggle. Similarly the People's War Group was also accused of excluding national bourgeosie and rich peasants from the United Front, while in their documents as we have already noted, they had assigned a role for both national bourgeoisie and rich peasants in the United Front. The C.P. group's claim of left adventurism thus was based not so much on the theoretical line put forth by the People's War Group in their documents which indicated several deviations from the Charu line but on their analysis of how it was actually being implemented by that party in practice.

The CC, CPI (ML) had also differed with the PWG on their analysis of the international scene. They claimed that the People's War Group had not been forthright in condemning US imperialism and that they had in fact formed an United Front with Pro-US groups to tackle Soviet Social imperialism. At the same time the CC, CPI (ML) also condemned the People's War Group for having given a wrong interpretation of the international situation when they stated that "the clouds of world war is looming large". By overestimating the danger of world war, the C.P. group claimed, that the People's War

Group was only drawing closer to US imperialism. According to the C.P. group there could be no war situation unless and until the United States and Soviet Union prepared themselves, politically, economically and militarily, which they had not yet done. Thus what was required right now was not the raising of alarmist calls but to expose the cloak of peace work by the two super powers and to see that a war situation did not develop.[64]

The CC, CPI (ML) linked the entire issue of the People's War Group analysis of the international situation with their assessment of the national situation. They claimed that by overstating the imminence of a Third World War, the People's War Group only wanted to justify their stand that a revolutionary situation favourable to an armed struggle existed in the country and that once this lie was nailed the entire analysid of the PWG collapses.

The Peoples' War Group and Charu

When the CPI (ML) broke up totally after the death of Charu Majumdar, most leaders who had actively supported him during his life time did considerable rethinking on the line of action advocated by him since 1968. In the process each one incorporated such changes as were felt necessary by him, in order to arrive at a more 'correct' line which would enable them to avoid the mistakes that had been committed in the past. Several trends emerged in this process. One trend was to view the line followed all along as being essentially correct and that no changes were required and the other was that a completely new line would have to be evolved and methods used in the past done away with. The line which the Peoples' War Group adopted represented a mixture of these two trends. However, since they felt that magnifying the mistakes of the past was a far more dangerous tendency than refusing to admit mistaks, they tended to adhere more closely with the Charu line. On the whole People's War Group concentrated on avoiding the strait jacketed approach adopted by CPI (ML) under Charu's leadership. Thus while the existence of revolutionary consciousness, (the word "upsurge" is not used) is reasserted the People's War Group also accepted the fact that people's consciousness varied from region to region. Again although the People's War Group stressed the need for an immediate armed struggle it operated in a larger framework of time and believed in the inevitability of a protracted armed struggle. As a direct consequence of this the People's War Group relied on a greater range of tactics to mobilise the masses than the one track line of "annihilation of class enemies". Thus, mass struggles partial, struggles on economic issues and so on were all included in the PWG agenda. However, these struggles were not accepted simply as a means to raise the movement to the stage of armed struggle but as a part of the armed struggle. On this issue the PWG was quite clear and any form of struggle was acceptable if and only if it served the cause of armed struggle.

Certain categories of people were mentioned for the first time in Peoples' War Group literature as those who should be mobilised, as for instance *harijans*[65] and 'lumpens'. While the first category were normally included in the peasant class earlier and did not have a distinct identity of their own, mention of the latter groups had been altogether neglected.

On the issue of organisation too, the PWG deviated considerably from the Charu line which according to them advocated that "armed action sets right everything, without the necessity to bestow enough attention on mobilisation and organisation of the people and on the consolidation of Party Organisation."[66] In contrast to this the PWG laid a lot of stress on strengthening both mass and party organisations which it felt would stand it in good stead during times of crisis.

As one goes through the development of the People's War Group's line it is apparent that a conscious and deliberate attempt has been made to 'rectify' at least on paper the mistakes it felt were committed by the party under the leadership of Charu. At the same time there has been an effort by the group to see that in their anxiety to correct these mistakes they do not bend backwards and see mistakes where actually none have been committed. To this extent the group's line in fact represents a cautious deviation from the Charu line rather than a complete break from it.

NOTES & REFERENCES

1. "Peasant Struggle of Sircilla—Vemulavada", *Economic* and *Political Weekly*, November 27, 1982, reprinted in March, *Liberation*, Jan-Feb. 1983.
2. The Shah Commission of Enquiry was set up by the Janata Party when in office at the Centre in 1977 "to look into all complaints, excesses, malpractices, abuse of authority during Emergency and all matters related thereto". For a detailed study see John Dayal and Arun Bose, *The Shah Commission Begins*, Oiient Longman, 1978.
3. "Masses on the Move" in *For a dnewemocracy*, October/ November, 1978, Provisional Central Committee, CPI (ML), p. 50.
4. *Ibid* p. 52.
5. Here they cite the instance of their support to Kaloji Narayana Rao against Vengal Rao, erstwhile Chief Minister of Andhra Pradesh and who as a Home Minister in Andhra Pradesh put down effectively the movement.
6. "Agrarian Revolution and Electi ons", *New Democracy* CC, CPI (ML) *Theoretical Bulletin*, May 1980, p. 44.
7. *Ibid.*
8. *Ibid* and also "Mid-term Poll, The Height of the Ruling Class Parties and Groups", Resolution of PCC of CPI (ML), *For a New Democracy*, September-October, 1979.
9. "Passing Agrarian Revolution and Elections", *New Democracy* May, 1980, CC CPI (ML)'s Theoretical Bulletin, Hyderabad, pp. 44-48.
10. "Seventh Lok Sabha Elections—Call to the People" *For a New Democracy*, September-October, 1979,
11. Based on interviews. The CPI (ML) here contested against the candidate who had the support of all other left parties in the region.

12. "Advancing peoples struggles of Khammam, Warangal. Forest Area", *Road to Liberation,* October, 1981, pp. 36-37.

13. Despite this the fact remains that a lot of importance is given to the results of elections participated in and one finds assertions of popularity being made on the basis of these election results. Thus for instance the fact that their candidate had secured more votes than the UCCRI (ML) candidate in a particular election contest in which both lost their deposits was used as an indication of their parties greater popularity, *Road to Liberation.* May/June, 1983. p. 22.

14. Quoted in "Agrarian Revolution and Elections" *op. cit.,* p. 41.

15. "Intensify Peoples' Struggles", *Road to Liberation* November, 1982, p. 23. Some explanation of the change is found in "Peoples War" Party Mitavada Peda Dhorani Ativada Porata Ethugadalu" *Vimochana,* Hyderabad, 1983 pp. 11-12 which state "Armed Struggle is only goal towards which one must work in the country now, yes, people are dissatisfied with the government. People are participating in struggles on their demands—sometimes spontaneous. But to say that peoples movement has reached the level of armed struggle is not true".

16. Statement Filed by the Inspector General of Police on behalf of the Police Department of Andhra Pradesh, 1976, pp. 54-55.

17. Bhargava Commission was established in 1977 by the Government of Andhra Pradesh to enquire into "(1) The situation created in the State by the activities of the Naxalites, the steps taken and the instruction given by the government to deal with them and the results, (2) the facts and circumstances in regard to each of the encounters between the police and Naxalites from 1968 to 1977, (3) the allegations of murder, torture and brutal treatment of Naxalite prisoners, and (4) the administrative

measures which are required to deal with this problem in the future". At that time the Congress was in power in Andhra Pradesh while Janata Party was heading the Government at the Centre. In actual fact the hardening of the stand on alliances was brought about by the groups while working with the Janata Party and CPI (M) at the Bhargava Commission sittings.

18. According to the Party Review between 1969-77, they claim to have occupied 3 lakh acres of land, conducted struggles against illegal exactions by forest officials, *patels patvaris* and police and struggles for raise in wages in forest coups. See *Resist anarchist methods and factional activities defend Party unity,* Letter of CPI (ML) State Committee to all its Party Units (mimeo) December 1983, also *Road to Liberation* May/June, 1981, October 1981, *Foar a New Democracy,* "Letter from Andhra", September/October, 1979.

19. See *Resist anarchist op. cit.* The report on the meeting held of all squad members operating in the forest of Godavari valley, reflects this mood made in "Masses on the Move", *For a New Democracy,* October, 1978, p. 55.

20. For details on 'Pagideru Incidents, see chapter seven.

21. *Resist anarchist* op. cit., *Passim,* pp. 26-33.

22. *See Andhra Rashtra Committee lo manduku vacchina party vyatirekata pandhanu tiraskarinchandi* (*mimeo*) CP's reply 1984.

23. *Resist Anarchist op. cit.*

24. Press Statement on the split issued by CC CPI (ML) during this time.

25. *Summing up the Past let us advance victoriously along the path of struggle,* (cyclostyled) CPI (ML), Peoples, War Group, p. 75.

26. *Ibid, Passim.*

27. *Ibid* pp. 5)-51.

28. '*People's War' Party Mitavada Pedadhorani* : *op. cit.*

29. *Summing up the Past, op. cit.*, p. 47.

30. *Ibid* p. 45.

31. *Ibid.*

32. *Ibid*, p. 53.

33. *Ibid* p. 51.

34. "In the name of united Mass Organisation do not give up politics in Mass Organisations", *Peoples' War* Organ of CC of CPI (ML), October, 1981.

35. *Ibid.*

36. *Summing up the past, op. cit.*, pp. 92-94.

37. *Statement filed by the Police, op. eit.*, p. 38.

38. *Ibid.* A look at the list of names of the important members of two groups indicates the preponderance of Hyderabad based students in PDSU while RSU contained mainly students from Warangal and Karimnagar.

39. *Peoples' War*, October, 1981, p. 27.

40. One of the most popular and creative singers has been *Ghaddar*.

41. *Peoples War*, July, 1980, p. 108.

42. *New Democracy* January, 1981, p. 80.

43. *People's War*, October, 1981, *op. cit*

44. *Ibid.*

45. "*Vimochana*" *Party nayakatvapu mitavada avakashavada daga ‡ koru raaajakiyalanu odinchandi, CPI (ML)* (People's War) Andhra Pradesh Rashtra Committee, 1983, p. 95, quoted from Mao's Selected Works, Peking Edition, Volume 1, p. 97.

46. *Ibid*, see pp. 100-102.

47. Based on interviews with students and activists.

48. *Summing up the past* etc. *op. cit.*, p. 42.

49. *Ibid*, p. 93.

50. *Ibid.* However, how this is to be practised is not stated.

51. *Ibid.*

52. *Ibid.* p. 60.

53. *Our Tactical Line* CPI (M) Peoples' War Group (cyclostyled). p. 16.

54. *Ibid.*

55. Mention has been made earlier that the People's War Groups' view was that if it was peoples' war that was sought to be conducted the form of organisatiou mus be based on military lines. There is evidence to show that this view has in fact been attempted at in a practical form. The police claim to have captured documents which deal with camps held in the forests where training on military lines was imparted for over one thousand members. The weaponry used has also gained a certain amount of sophistication and it was suspected that some one with an army background is involved. See *Eenadu* 30 April, 1984. A detailed inventory is also maintained and each weapon numbered serially with an account of who possesses which weapon.

56. *Karimnagar zilla lo praja udyamam nirmanam perita varga shatruvulato chetulu kaluputunna 'Peoples War' group viplava vyatireka charyalanu khandichandi* CPI (ML), 25 July, 1981.

57. See *Our Tactical Line, op. cit.* and also *Summing up the Past*, op. cit., p. 5. The People's War Group feels that people have been unduly hasty in condemning the Charu line just because there had been some temporary set backs to the movement. In its opinion a wrong trend of magnifying the mistakes of the past and minimising the achievements could only serve to lead the party into a

"more of revisionism and to create insurmountable hurdles in practice in the path of armed struggle". Thus while left adventurist trends can and have to be combated one should not panic and see mistakes where there are none, *Ibid.* p. 6.

58. Baldev Singh, "Some serious deviations and New Democratic Revolution in India", *Road to Liberation* November/December, 1981. p. 24.

59. "*People's War Party*", *op. cit.* p. 11.

60. *Ibid.*

61. *Ibid.*

62. *Ibid.*

63. *Ibid.*

64. *Passim. Ibid.*

65. The stress on *harijans* to be taken into account as a caste was a characteristic of People's War Group while organising their *sangham*. No other maoist in the state mentioned caste as a feature to be kept in mind while mobilising the masses.

66. Summing *op. cit.* p. 32.

CHAPTER 10

Summing Up

Summing Up

In the foregoing chapters we have described the manner in which the maoist movement has progressed over a period of time in Andhra Pradesh. One thing that emerges clearly is that far from being static in character the movement has been in a continuous state of evolution. As the maoists drew lessons from their experiences they began to modify their attitudes towards most issues and this was reflected by a corresponding change in the character of the movement. In this chapter we shall endeavour to arrive at an understanding of the reasons behind these modifications and the trends which they initiated.

The concept which is most fundamental to the maoists is that of "armed struggle". While all the maoist groups accept unequivocally the need for an armed struggle, the interpretation and more so the scope given to the term itself have varied considerably. The CPI (ML) of Charu, for instance, treated it as the most urgent and immediate task on the agenda. Having assessed the national situation as being one in which there was revolutionary mass upsurge everywhere the party felt that immediate armed struggle for the seizure of power was the only logical programme to follow. In fact the task of conducting an immediate armed struggle was viewed not only as being a top priority item but also an essential prerequisite for the progress of the movement.

The group led T.N. and C.P. on the other hand viewed the armed struggle more as an ultimate stage in the movement, something of a grand finale, which was to be carried out only after the people had all been sufficiently motivated and their level of political consciousness raised. Linking this to its analysis that there existed as yet only a low level of political consciousness among the people the group felt that the necessary conditions for staging an immediate armed struggle did not exist and that such a struggle could take place only in the distant future.

On closer look one finds that both groups had essentially the same understanding of the concept of armed struggle in the sense that they both agreed that given a situation of revolutionary upsurge everywhere, armed struggle was the only line to follow. Where they differed was on the issue of the existence of this revolutionary upsurge. The group led by C.P. and T.N. contested the Charu group's assessment that the revolutionary upsurge already existed everywhere and felt that this was in fact a condition the creation of which had to be worked for. In other words this group felt that revolutionary political consciousness had to be first of all built up and only then armed struggle carried out. It was towards this end that they formulated their programme of protracted armed struggle.

Subsequent events showed how grossly over optimistic Charu's estimates of the existence of revolutionary upsurge really were. As the party programme of immediate armed struggle was carried out the people failed to respond as expected and instead of urging them towards greater and greater levels of mass militancy the programme only served to fuel the repressive machinery of the state and the movement floundered after a promising start. The programme of the group led by C.P. and T.N. involving as it did the concept of protracted armed struggle proceeded at a much lower pitch. Its strength lay in that it took the realities of the situation into account especially in regard to the non-uniformity in the development of revolutionary consciousness among the people. But what it gained by this it lost in terms of 'glamour'. The element of daring and romance that the programme of immediate armed struggle involved attracted a large number of youth towards Charu's CPI (ML) and this was an important and significant aspect because youth were the most active members in the maoist cadre. In fact for this very reason one finds that despite the fact the movement in Telangana had proved to be more versatile and resilient, the Srikakulam movement represents the quintessence of the maoist movement in Andhra Pradesh.

The People's War Group led by K.S. fully conscious of these developments took them into account while formulating its own policies. It thus talks of protracted armed struggle and the need for raising the level of people's political consciousness and in the same breath argues for the need for immediate armed struggle because of the existence of revolutionary upsurge. This it has managed to do by drawing a distinction between armed struggle and armed form of struggle obviously implying that even a form of struggle which is not an armed one can also be taken to be a part of armed struggle. Thus while the group led by T.N. and C.P. clearly viewed what the People's War Group calls armed form of struggle as the only form in which an armed struggle could be conducted the People's War Group felt that there is no reason to assume that other forms of struggle cannot equally well serve the cause of armed struggle. In fact as we have already seen, the group felt that any struggle which is established under the leadership of the rural proletariat will serve the cause of armed struggle. By indulging in this somewhat contrived logic the People's War Group managed to keep armed struggle on the party agenda and at the same time advocate mass struggles and other less militant forms of struggles. In adopting this "not-only-but-also" approach the group has not only gained the advantage of being able to project themselves as having a programme of high revolutionary content but have also put themselves in a position where they can utilise forms of struggle other than armed forms without appearing to be compromising on their revolutionary stance. As a consequence the group developed a reputation for being far more militant than other maoist the groups in Andhra Pradesh while at the same time projecting an image of being more pragmatic in its outlook than Charu's CPI (ML) had been.

When the maoists began their activities in 1967-68 they gave little thought to the issue of how State repression was to be countered. While the CPI (ML), at that time led by Charu, felt that the people would themselves rise and protect the movement, the *Immediate Programme* of T.N. and C.P. left the problem largely unanswered in any effective form. Serious thinking on these lines began only subsequently when the first series of activities brought in its wake severe repraisal attacks from the police. The Charu group's response was to adopt more and more militant forms of action until they finally began resorting to what they referred to as the highest stage—annihilation of class enemies. While to the group, operating as it was within a time framework which was very short, this seemed a logical move, in the end it proved to be no solution to the problem for it only succeeded in inviting further repression.

The group led by T.N. and C.P. had serious internal rifts on this issue which ultimately led to the breaking up of this group. T.N. believed in operating on the 'prevention is better than cure' lines. He felt that until a mass base was built up which could sustain a counter repression the activists would have to maintain a low profile if they did not want to get isolated from the people. To this end he strongly opposed the use of fire arms and tactics of offence against the police until this task had been completed. C.P. on the other hand, supported the view that unless at least the core of the active members of the party were given permission to use arms against the police they would not be able to proceed even with the initial task of raising the peoples consciousness without being ruthlessly suppressed. As a consequence following the "Pagideru incident" the members, who had organised themselves into squads, were allowed to acquire arms. However, despite this development the accent was on defence rather than offence. This guarded approach appears to have paid off in as much as the squads continued to survive. But this survival has had much to do with the terrain in which the squads have operated. The C.P. group has from the beginning, operated in the forest areas of Khammam and Warangal where there is abundant cover for the squads. Taking full advantage of this the squads managed to exert considerable dominance in these areas without involving themselves in much direct confrontation with the police.

The shelter which the forest provides is obviously not forthcoming in the plains areas where this aspect has to be looked after by the party organisation itself. Thus for the People's War Group, whose areas of operation at least initially, lay in the plains areas the major problem was one of providing cover for members who had gone underground and who unlike the members of the C.P. group cannot be 'accommodated' in the forest areas. In order to counter this problem this group has attempted to reduce to the minimum the number of underground party members. This they have done by taking full advantage of the cover provided by the front organisations which are for most parts made up of members indulging in perfectly legal work and with no outward links whatsoever with the party. In each one of the organisations there exist members of the party whose identity is a highly guarded secret and who do full time party work. Very often it is these persons who are utilised in carrying out what have earlier been referred to as "modified squad action". Thus unlike the squads of the forest areas, which consists of members who have already gone underground and whose identity is well known to the police the members of the 'modified squads' of the People's War Group operating in the plains areas are those who have not yet been identified and who have therefore not gone underground. The shelter which the forest gives to the squads there is thus now provided in the plains areas by the cloak of annonymity under which the squad members function. As long as none of the members of the "plains area" squads is caught the members can function in the open and thus save the party the task of maintaining them.

Within the forest areas the dalams or squads have come to stay. Their compact and self sufficient nature makes them ideal for the condition and terrain in which they have to operate, something which is amply illustrated by the fact that all maoist groups use this form of organisation in the forest areas. There were times when in certain areas, especially in Srikakulam, the squads used to consist of one or two party members while the rest consisted of volunteers from the village where an action was to be carried out or from other local sympathisers. Subsequently the squads became more a part of the party organisation itself rather than a separate entity, wherein the leader was usually a member of the area committee or the Provincial Commi ttee, or, in rare cases, even the Central Committee while the others were full time party workers if not committee members. The formation of squads as a part of the party organisation has been one manifestation of this development for at present in the forest areas it is these squads which are maintaining the movement. This development has much to do with the response that the movement has received from the people. Wherever, the people as a whole have risen in protest occasionally against their oppressors the squad consisted of local volunteers. However in recent times the more normal situation has been one of limited response from the masses and thus the task of sustaining the movement has devolved mainly on the party organisation itself.

Other changes in the nature of party organisation have also occured over the years. In the initial years for instance there was a tendency to go in for a more centralised leadership which in the case of Charu's CPI (ML) took the extreme form when an attempt was made to designate Churu as the Authority. Much of this tendency had to do with the charisma and stature of the maoist leaders who had initiated the breaking away from the Communist Party. In the case of the Charu group however it was also reinforced by the deep suspicion which the group had for any form or organisation whatsoever which resulted in their setting up only committees below the level of the Central Committee which were not invested with much powers.

The attitude of the government towards the activities of the maoist groups has been somewhat ambiguous. At an individual level one finds that the officers of the various departments and even ministers often admit that in many cases the oppressive conditions of the workers and peasants sought to be highlighted by the maoists do obtain, in both rural and urban areas. Often such an admission is even tinged with a certain amount of grudging respect for the maoists. As officials or as members of the cabinet however the same persons view the same maoists as trouble makers at best and at worst as thieves and murderers.* Such a dichotomy is inevitable because whatever their intention by the very nature of their philosophy which is strongly anti-establishment the maoists cannot be viewed by the government, as being anything but anti-government and anti-State. As such the activities of the maoists are by and large dealt with by the government machinery as law and order problems created by some "misguided elements".

While the manner in which the leaders of any maoist activity are dealt with never changes and is always one of repression the manner in which the supporting masses are attempted to be neutralised varies with the demands made. In certain cases the demands involve certain concessions from the State which may not prove to be as costly as would the consequences arising out of not granting them. In these cases the State does concede to the demands though the extent to which it actually does varies from situation to situation. Thus for instance we see that this carrot and stick policy was followed in Srikakulam where once the leaders of the movement were all eliminated, laws were enacted granting certain economic benefits to the tribals. and the government was able to draw away a bulk of them from the movement. This was despite the fact that several of the legislations, especially those involving agrarian issues, must have hit the landlords who were the traditional supporters of the ruling party in the State. Such concessions however cannot always be made and we find that in the post emergency period when demands were raised by youth activists and their supporters in several parts of Telangana on issues relating to unemployment and land redistribution the

---

*A classic instance of this is the manner in which NTR while he was campaigning during the elections in 1983 referred to naxalites, (as maoists are known in A.P.) as "true patriots", but once he became Chief Minister, he followed a policy no different from that of his predecessors as far as the maoists were concerned. In fact police repression actually increased after the NTR Government took over the administration.

State has resorted to an uniform policy of repression, setting up police camps and even requisitioning the CRPF. Repression, at least as far as the masses are concerned, seems therefore to be linked with the ability of the government to satisfy the demands raised and is resorted to increasingly whenever the cannot be met.

The fact that the police have been sustaining such a long standing operation against the maoists has also meant that over the years they have learnt to appreciate some of their own limitations, both in terms of personnel deployed and the policies adopted. For instance, the point has often been made that while the party is able to regularly recruit fresh cadre the police is forced to rely on the same staff for years. Thus while the party gets the benefit of younger, fitter men the police is compelled to continue to rely on their older and less mobile staff. Again, there has been the recognition on the part of the police that methods other than the utilisation of sheer brute force have to be adopted by them in dealing with the masses to prevent their total alienation from the latter. This is reflected in the calls given by the police department to the government, as early as in 1972, to route welfare programmes through them, a call which has since been repeated several times. The police department feels that it is particularly vulnerable in this regard because while they have to depend on the willing cooperation of the people for their effective functioning they not only have no methods of endearing themselves to the public but also have to adopt repressive measures against them each time the people support a radical movement however justified it may be. Because of this situation very often one finds that in the remote villages the police, especially the lower ranks have a tacit understanding with the local extremists leaders that as long as neither group resorts to any action, there should be no interference in each others activities. In fact it is quite common to find both policemen and extremists in the same village with the former disclaiming any knowledge of the existence in the latter.

Apart from realising some of their own limitations the police has also understood certain specific strengths of the maoists and have attempted to learn from them. As mentioned earlier the movement has attracted into its fold a large number of writers, poets and singers who have combined to set up the *Jana Natya Mandali.* In most cases the first exposure which a cadre member has to the activities of maoists is through the songs, writings and plays generated by the artists of the *Jana Natya Mandali.* In an effort to counter this they police have not only prevented the *Jana Natya Mandali* from performing anywhere but also have put plays of their own which attempt at popularising government policies.

All this is not to say that it is only the police who are drawing lessons from their dealings with the maoists. Even the latter have learnt to alter their methods of operation. One instance is the manner in which they have, with the help of Civil Liberties organisations, managed to make use of courts and the long winded court procedure. The police on their part blame their inexperienced staff for not being able to frame tighter cases, the maoists for intimidating the witnesses preventing them from giving evidence and the courts for delaying the entire process thus giving the accused a chance to intimidate the witness. Because they are unable to tackle all these issues the police in the past have been clamouring for strict bail laws. At the same time many of the maoists have been arrested under the National Security Act which provides for longer periods of detention without bail option.

Another way of looking at this use by the maoist of an institution like the courts which is so much a part of the establishment is that they are being slowly absorbed into the system as has happened in the case of the C.P. group which has even taken to participation in elections in a limited way.

Similar is the case of the routine annual money transactions between the forest contractors and the maoist cadre in the forest areas which has begun to be looked upon by both the contractors and the police as being nothing more than a minor nuisance. The contractor treats it more or less like any other bribe that has to be paid to keep his business going while the police tends to view it as an issue to be settled between the contractor and maoist since the contractor's commitment to the government is made once he has bid in the auction. In fact, the police feel that they have a greater problem on their hands when the contractors are not able to pay off the maoists. A good illustration of this point is the issue of arrack prices. In 1983-84 when the CPI (ML) People's War Group launched a struggle in Warangal and Karimnagar against the high sale price of arrack the contractors were quite unprepared because there had been no indication of any trouble at the time of auction and they had not made any allowance for this. At this stage the police had to intervene to help the contractors keep the arrack shops running In 1984-85, however, the contractors now fully wise after the event, reached an 'understanding' with the maoists in the area and as a consequence despite the fact that there was no lowering of arrack prices no incidents occured.

That there has been some amount of absorption into the system and, as a consequence, dilution of the revolutionary credentials of the existing maoist groups has been noted by the maoist groups. The CPI (ML) People's War Group of K.S. for instance has gone out of the way to condemn any sort of participation in elections. It has also indulged in several attacks on the forest contractor's properties in the forest areas of Kondamodalu in an effort to prove that as a revolutionary group its credentials are superior to that of the C.P. group whose traditional areas of operation lie in the forests.

As a final question it is only natural that one asks as to what extent the movement has has been able to achieve what it set out to do in the first place. In many ways this is a difficult question to answer in absolute terms. To the extent that all the maoist groups despite their differences have had as their ultimate goal the siezure of political power through an armed struggle, the movement is an abject failure. However, this is only half the story for the true contribution of the movement lies in the manner in which it has induced various developments as it progressed from one stage to another. What the movement has undeniably done is that it has made the masses more aware of the social, economic and political factors which shape their lives and which, despite their oppressive nature, have been all along taken for granted. In doing so the movement has on the one hand focussed attention on the tensions and frustrations of the masses and on the other hlighighted the incapacity and inadequacy of the government in dealing with them.

In many places the first direct contact which the people have had with the state machinery has been through the maoist movement and the State's reaction to it. The policeman, the administrator, and even the local MLA or MP who, to those in the remote areas where the movement first took root were mythical characters, almost became part and parcel of their daily life. With this came the further realisation that the people they had all along identified as their oppressors were mere cogs in the wheel of a system whose immensity they had been totally unaware of. In other words, the people for the first time realised that their standard of living depended not, as they had sofar believed on the local landlord or moneylender but a much large and infinitely more powerful entity—the State By far the most important outcome of the movement thus has been the greater awareness that it has created among the people of the true nature of the forces they are up against and the exposure it has given them to the larger framework in which they were operating.

Conversely the movement has also made the government more susceptible to local pressures and this is reflected in the attention paid to the "affected" areas by the latter. Thus the increased budgetary allocations, the creation of new welfare institutions, the passing of radical reforms and laws and so on are all to be linked to the anxiety of the government to project a better image of itself in these area.

These then are some of the broad changes that seventeen years of the maoist activity has brought about. The movement has neither been mammoth in proportion, nor startling in effect. Nevertbeless it has been an event which was grand in conception and heroic in effort. The question remains—what does the future porten ?

Over the years s we have noticed the movement has had a high turnover of sympathisers and this has been one of the factors which has given it strength. As different varieties of people are drawn into the movement there is a corresponding change in its character. The issues raised, the tactics deployed and so on all have had to adapt themselves to the changing support base and this has infused the movement with the much needed dynamism. The other trend has been that, as it has progressed, the movement has tried to adapt itself more and more to the local conditions. This has resulted in greater improvisation based on indigenous considerations. One can already see the impact of this on the theoretical framework adopted by the maoists. There are far fewer references to China and the Chinese experience than in the past. The emphasis is more on evolving a more relevant brand of 'maoism' than merely relying on the readymade formulations of the Chinese Communist Party. It is this that gives hope to the movement.

Index